SEEING THE FIRST AUSTRALIANS

EDITED BY
Ian Donaldson & Tamsin Donaldson

SEEING THE FIRST AUSTRALIANS

EDITED BY
Ian Donaldson & Tamsin Donaldson

GEORGE ALLEN & UNWIN
Sydney London Boston

First published in 1985 by
George Allen & Unwin Australia Pty Ltd
8 Napier Street, North Sydney, NSW 2060 Australia

George Allen & Unwin (Publishers) Ltd
Park Lane, Hemel Hempstead, Herts HP2 4TE, England

Allen & Unwin Inc.
9 Winchester Terrace, Winchester, Mass 01890 USA

National Library of Australia
Cataloguing-in-Publication entry:

Seeing the First Australians.

Includes index.
ISBN 0 86861 689 3.
ISBN 0 86861 697 4(pbk.).

[1]. Aborigines, Australian — Public opinion — History. 2. Europeans —
Australia — Attitudes — History. I. Donaldson, Ian, 1935- . II. Donaldson,
Tamsin, 1939-

994′.0049915

Endpapers: Dumont d'urville, Baie Jervis (Nouvelle Hollande)
Les marins de l'Astrolabe partagent leur pêche avec les Naturels.
Reproduced with permission of the National Library of Australia.

Library of Congress Catalog Card Number: 84-70762
Typeset by Setrite Typesetters, Hong Kong.
Printed in Hong Kong

CONTENTS

PLATES AND FIGURES

FIGURES

ACKNOWLEDGEMENTS

The editors thank J. C. Eade, Terry Smith and Virginia Spate for help and advice in preparing this book for publication.

Copyright illustrations are reproduced by kind permission of the owning institutions and individuals listed with the plates and figures, with whom copyright remains. See also additional acknowledgements at the ends of chapters. Every endeavour has been made to find copyright owners. Information relating to any who have not been contacted will be gratefully received by the publishers. The cover is taken from Louis Auguste de Sainson's coloured lithograph *Vue du Pont du Roi Georges, Nouvelle Hollande*, Plate 16 in Dumont d'Urville, *Voyage de la corvette l'Astrolabe ...*, Paris: Atlas, 1833. The endpapers come from another Sainson coloured lithograph, *Les marins de l'Astrolabe partagent leur pêche avec les Naturels*, Plate 34 of the same volume. The *Astrolabe* visited King George Sound in October, 1826, and Jervis Bay, where the crew shared their catch with the local people, in November of the same year. Both lithographs are reproduced by kind permission of the Rex Nan Kivell Collection, Australian National Library.

CONTRIBUTORS

IAN DONALDSON, Director of the Humanities Research Centre at the Australian National University, Canberra, convened the Centre's 1981 conference on 'Australia and the European Imagination' for which most of the papers in this collection were originally written.

TAMSIN DONALDSON is a linguist attached to the Australian Institute of Aboriginal Studies, Canberra, and author of *Ngiyambaa The Language of the Wangaaybuwan* (1980).

RHYS JONES is Senior Fellow in Prehistory in the Research School of Pacific Studies at the Australian National University. He has worked mainly in Arnhem Land and on archaeological sites in Tasmania.

ISABEL McBRYDE is Reader in Prehistory in the Faculty of Arts at the Australian National University, and Reviews Editor of *Aboriginal History*. She encountered Thomas Dick's Aboriginal studies while working on an archaeological survey of the New England region of New South Wales.

MARGARET MAYNARD is Lecturer in Fine Arts at Queensland University. She has particular interests in nineteenth-century Australian art and the history of dress.

D. J. MULVANEY, Professor of Prehistory in the Faculty of Arts, Australian National University, has written extensively on Australian Aboriginal topics, and is author of a forthcoming biography of Baldwin Spencer.

NICOLAS PETERSON is Senior Lecturer in Anthropology in the Faculty of Arts, Australian National University. He has worked principally in Arnhem Land and Central Australia, and is particularly interested in territorial organisation and ethnographic film-making.

BERNARD SMITH, Emeritus Professor of Contemporary Art and former Director of the Power Institute of Fine Arts at the University of Sydney, is currently preparing with Rüdiger Joppien *The Art of Captain Cook's Voyages*, in three volumes. His earlier books include *European Vision and the South Pacific*.

CONTRIBUTORS

HELEN TOPLISS has taught at Monash University and held Visiting Fellowships at the Australian National University's Humanities Research Centre. Her *catalogue raisonné* of Tom Roberts is to be published by Oxford University Press.

JAMES URRY is Lecturer in Anthropology at Victoria University, Wellington, and a former co-editor of *Aboriginal History*.

GLYNDWR WILLIAMS is Professor of History at Queen Mary College, University of London. He has written extensively on Pacific and North American trade and exploration.

ONE

FIRST
SIGHT

Ian Donaldson & Tamsin Donaldson

THE KINDS OF *seeing* which this book documents are those of white European explorers, settlers, missionaries, scientists, artists, and photographers; and of the contributors themselves (none of whom is Aboriginal). The European view of the Australian Aborigines has never been innocent, nor has it ever been neutral. Relative newcomers to the country, we have seen—or failed to see—its original inhabitants in relation to our social, cultural and political preoccupations, and our own taxonomies of knowledge. Ways of seeing may often reflect relationships of power, whether real or desired, as John Berger has pointed out in another context in relation to the visual arts (1972). The cruder manifestations of such power do not form the main subject of this book, though their reality is its necessary background. To shoot or poison the local people and appropriate their land is to exercise one kind of power. To measure their heads, cover their loins, record their tongues, sketch their faces, or film their ceremonies is to exercise quite another kind of power, milder, subtler, often benign in its intentions, yet possessed none the less of its own significance, implying a relationship of subject to object, observer to observed, and implying also a need for Europeans to work energetically in the cause of Aboriginal salvage or salvation. This book reflects upon and attempts to interpret that kind of power, those ways of seeing. Yet it cannot wholly escape being a part of the very process it describes. In tracing a small part of the complex story of European contact with the Australian Aborigines, the contributors recognise that, wittingly or unwittingly, they are the heirs of many of the European assumptions, positions and dilemmas they describe.

The book explores and extends the intellectual territory mapped by Bernard Smith over twenty years ago in his pioneering study *European Vision and the South Pacific 1768-1850*. For the sake of coherence, the present volume also focuses on European vision, and does not examine the equally interesting and relatively neglected question of the ways in which non-Europeans—early 'Macassan' navigators, Pacific islanders brought to Australia as indentured labourers, Chinese gold-diggers—have regarded the Australian Aborigines. (Relevant to this question is a recent issue of *Aboriginal History* on Aboriginal-Asian contact: 1981: 5, 1-2.) Nor is it primarily concerned with Aboriginal perceptions of the Europeans, with the view from what Henry Reynolds has called, in an important recent study (1981), 'the other side of the frontier'; though in the final essay of the volume Rhys Jones examines some of the differences between European and Aboriginal modes of vision.

'European' is an unsatisfactory word to describe those who have come from Europe to settle in Australia, or whose forebears came here many generations ago. Most of the early European explorers and settlers in Australia would probably not have thought of themselves primarily as 'Europeans', but as French or Portuguese or German or British (or English or Scottish or Welsh or Irish), as the case may have been. Significantly, the standard Arnhem Land term today for whites or Europeans is 'balanda', from 'Hollander' (Walker & Zorc, 1981). European settlers new or old, whatever their cultural background, however wavering their emotional loyalties, are now (moreover), in law or in fact, Australians. The Aborigines remain, however, *the first Australians*: first by right of settlement, the earliest Aboriginal people having lived in this country at least 40000 years before the arrival of Captain Arthur Phillip in 1788, and first, too, as it happens, by right of linguistic usage: the term 'Australian' having been applied to the Aborigines for many years before being used to refer to the non-Aboriginal residents. 'Australian' originally meant a native inhabitant of *Terra Australis*, the Great Southern Ocean including Australasia, Polynesia, and 'Magellanica'. The word enshrines a Eurocentric viewpoint just as surely as do 'Far East', 'Middle East', 'Near East', 'antipodes': terms which similarly attempt to locate a region in relation to an implied geographical centre. (Australians are southerners, living upside-down opposite the feet of Europeans: who might with equal justice be described as northerners, Borealians, living upside-down opposite the feet of Australians.) The concepts of aboriginality and of the *first* Australians come into being only with the arrival of the Europeans, people who have not been in the country *ab origine*, from the beginning, and who come in due course to be known as Australians too. 'Australian' and 'European' are thus ambiguous terms to use of the people whose vision forms the main subject of this book; and who are variously—but, it is hoped, unambiguously—referred to in the pages that follow.

The new invaders of the country examined the Aborigines with a gaze that was at once comparative and classificatory. Aboriginal society was commonly perceived or imagined to be more or less homogeneous. Diverse groups of people scattered across the length and breadth of the island-continent, often mutually hostile or mutually unknowing, separated by distance, by a sense of traditional territories, and by a plurality of languages (between 200 and 250 at the time of first contact), were seen as one people, as 'the Aborigines', their obvious differences from other major racial groups being naturally at first more remarkable than their less obvious differences from each other. Yet as Glyndwr Williams shows later in this volume, the early explorers of the eastern seaboard may well have compared (or conflated) the Australian Aborigines with other peoples whom they had recently seen or about whom they had read in primitivist and other writings of the period. Closer acquaintance with the Aborigines was to show that more careful discriminations had to be made. It was found, for example (as James Urry's essay reveals), that those who inhabited the inland regions, the 'woodsmen', lived in a rather different style from the coastal Aborigines, and that generalisations based upon an acquaintance only with the Port Jackson people might stand in need of qualification. Nor were the Aborigines quite like the Californian Indians or the inhabitants of Tierra del Fuego. John Mulvaney's essay describes the way in which anthropological interest was excited later in the nineteenth century by a sense of the uniqueness of the Aborigines, who were thought to be survivors of an early and 'primitive' stage in the evolution of mankind. This belief, premissed upon the assumption of European cultural and biological superiority, was to have a powerful impact upon subsequent scientific and political attitudes to the Aborigines.

European exploration and settlement were to facilitate certain kinds of contact between distant and often distinct Aboriginal groups. As James Urry and Tamsin Donaldson briefly indicate, words often passed via white speakers from one Australian Aboriginal language to another. Other words changed their range of reference in response to users' perceptions of the new social situations which arose. Aborigines sometimes suspected that the first Europeans whom they saw were not living people, but white-faced spirits of the dead, and referred to them accordingly (Curr, 1886-7: vol 1, 339; vol. 3, 50, 62, etc; Reynolds, 1981: 30), withholding the normal terms for 'person'. The latter were applied to black people as distinct from white, and could in consequence be translated simply as 'Aboriginal'. Some of these terms, such as *Koori* and *Nyungar*, came to be commonly used by the Aborigines of particular regions, when speaking English, in reference to themselves (Willmott, 1981: 16). Today English-speaking Aboriginal people from more and more places are using *Koori* self-descriptively in preference both to the European term 'Aboriginal' (and the less complimentary terms that whites tend to call blacks) and to the other words for 'person' that may be available to them from their own inherited languages.

While Aborigines were wondering whether Europeans were real people, the Europeans in turn entertained similar though less flattering doubts about the status of Aborigines. Only in recent years have Aborigines been admitted to full Australian citizenship. The question 'who is an Aboriginal?' and how Aboriginal population numbers should therefore be reckoned has been very perplexed; not until 1966 was a complete count of all people of Aboriginal descent even attempted (Lancaster Jones, 1970; Rowley, 1970: appendixes A and B; Smith, 1980). A systematic count, it was thought, would present insuperable practical problems, and be in any case of singularly little value, for the Aboriginal population appeared to be rapidly vanishing. 'Perhaps but little practical benefit would result from ascertaining in any year the number of these unfortunates, who seem destined to die out before advancing settlement', said the Queensland Registrar-General in 1881, adding that 'if only as a means of delaying for a little time the extinction of the race, or as a question of mere humanity, it seems desirable to know in what proportions they are melting away before the onward march of civilization' (Queensland Census Report, 1881, quoted in Smith, 1980: 17). The argument was circular, and the mythology self-reinforcing. People who were vanishing were scarcely worth counting; people who were imperfectly counted might be assumed to be vanishing. Questions of definition were crucial to the belief. Aboriginal Protection Acts passed in various colonies towards the end of the century tended to regard people of mixed descent as non-Aboriginal. The mythology was strengthened in other ways. Aborigines were not visible to the majority of the white population, having often been moved off their traditional lands or herded into out-of-town missions or settlements. The conditions in which they lived were generally very depressed.

The essays by Margaret Maynard, Helen Topliss, Nicolas Peterson, and Isabel McBryde in this collection reflect upon some of the ways in which this belief in the passing of the Aborigines affected photography and portraiture in the late nineteenth and early twentieth centuries, popular sociological views of the Aborigines being expressed in, and no doubt strengthened by, the pictorial views which photographers and artists created. John Mulvaney and Tamsin Donaldson show how the mythology of the dying race served as a spur and a licence to anthropological and philological interest in the Aborigines during roughly the same period. Mythology; but in many parts of the country Aborigines were indeed dying at a distressing rate from the catastrophic impact of white diseases, and also from white vendettas and official government policy. Part of this story was told a few years ago by

Tom Haydon and Rhys Jones in their film *The Last Tasmanian*. The controversy which that film aroused—'last' was regarded by the descendents of the original Tasmanians as constituting in itself an act of verbal genocide— showed how complex and how sensitive this general issue has remained.

In attacking Aboriginal society, Europeans have also paradoxically helped in some ways to unite it. The barbarities of white conduct have instilled in many present-day Aborigines a new and defiant sense of national identity and purpose: evidenced in the pitching of the umbrella (later tent) Aboriginal Embassy on the lawns of Parliament House, Canberra, on Australia Day, 1972, the creation of the Aboriginal flag and the move to establish a formal treaty of 'peace and friendship' between Aboriginal Australians and Torres Strait Islanders and the Commonwealth of Australia. The disparate Aboriginal societies that the Europeans assumed to be homogeneous are on their way towards becoming a new nation. (Many Aborigines are in fact sceptical about the proposed treaty on the grounds that it appears to disregard the fact that Aborigines are 'a nation in their own right, having never ceded sovereignty' (*Aboriginal Treaty News* no. 4, February 1982: 1).) This sense of national identity is strengthened by an awareness of the plight and progress of other indigenous people in countries overseas. To a degree unprecedented in their history, Australian Aborigines are seeing other people, and seeing themselves; and with such seeing comes a sense of knowledge and possible power.

Yet such 'power' is hedged about by many limitations and many ironies. One such irony is that the self-perception of Aborigines is sometimes necessarily derivative in part from the perception of Europeans—the traditional destroyers and (where they chose) the observers and selective preservers of their culture. Knowledge about the Aboriginal past is to be gained from the descendents of those people whose arrival in Australia helped to sever the natural continuity of past and present: from the writings, the archives and the institutions of white Europeans, not merely through the resilient and far-reaching oral traditions of the Aboriginal people themselves. Most self-perceptions are to some degree dependent upon the perceptions of others: in this general sense, the Aboriginal situation is not unique. Yet the legal, moral and human problems here are many and delicate. Who are the rightful owners of the Aboriginal artefacts imperiously and painstakingly collected in the past by Europeans, and now displayed in museums and galleries in Australia and overseas? How can white anthropologists, linguists and others continue their research into Aboriginal matters without paternalism and without pre-emption of the Aboriginal right to scrutinise, protect, recall, forget or exploit their own past in such manner as they themselves see fit? In what manifold and unknown ways will Aboriginal self-perception and self-esteem be affected by the ever-increasing numbers of tourists who come, see, photograph, purchase their chosen morsel of Aboriginal culture, and clamber wearily back into the waiting bus: by the new colonialism of the jet-age traveller?

The questions which this book explores are thus not merely historical. They have a continuing urgency and continuing importance for the way in which we choose to live in (or visit) this country, and—in the fullest and most humanly discerning sense of the phrase—see the first Australians.

Acknowledgements

This volume derives from a conference on 'Australia and the European Imagination' which was held at the Humanities Research Centre of the Australian National University, Canberra, from 5 to 10 May 1981. The conference was convened by Ian Donaldson and Alan Frost. Bernard Smith's paper has been specially commissioned for this volume. Margaret Maynard's paper was not delivered at the conference, but relates to a small exhibition of late nineteenth-century Aboriginal portraiture which she arranged in conjunction with it. Other papers from the conference, relating to early European notions of the antipodes, *Terra Australis*, and southern utopias, and the gradual European exploration and assumption of the 'fourth part of the world', have been published by the Humanities Research Centre. The entire conference proceedings were recorded by the National Library of Australia, and may be consulted in the National Film and Sound Archive.

Bibliography

Berger, J. (1972) *Ways of Seeing* Harmondsworth: BBC and Penguin

Curr, E. M. (1886-7) *The Australian Race* 3 vols, Melbourne: John Ferres, Government Printer; London: Trübner & Co.

Lancaster Jones, F. (1970) *The Structure and Growth of Australia's Aboriginal Population* Canberra: ANU Press

Reynolds, H. (1981) *The Other Side of the Frontier* Townsville: History Department, James Cook University

Rowley, C. D. (1970) *The Destruction of Aboriginal Society* Harmondsworth: Penguin

Smith, B. (1960) *European Vision and the South Pacific 1768-1850* Melbourne; Oxford University Press

Smith, L. R. (1980) *The Aboriginal Population of Australia* Canberra: ANU Press

Walker, A. and R. D. Zorc (1981) 'Austronesian Loanwords in Yolngu-Matha of Northeast Arnhem Land' *Aboriginal History* 5, 1-2, pp. 109-34

Willmott, Eric Paul (1981) 'The Culture of Literary' in W. Menary (ed.) *Aborigines and Schooling, Essays in Honour of Max Hart,* pp. 9-19. Adelaide: Adelaide College of the Arts and Education

TWO

THE FIRST
EUROPEAN DEPICTIONS

Bernard Smith

I

SYDNEY PARKINSON, JOSEPH BANKS' artist on Cook's first voyage to the Pacific (1768-71), made many drawings of Polynesians and Maoris, but his drawings of Australian Aborigines are few in number. There are only five sheets of drawings known which depict Aborigines; four are by Parkinson, and one by an unknown artist working in an untrained manner who may well have been Joseph Banks himself (Joppien & Smith, forthcoming). There is also a drawing made by John Frederick Miller in 1771 of Aboriginal artefacts collected on the *Endeavour*'s voyage.

The main reason for this paucity of visual material is that Cook and his company had difficulty in making contact with Aborigines of a kind stable and amicable enough to permit detailed drawings to be produced. There is only one drawing, and that is almost certainly a copy from a lost original by Parkinson, which would suggest that an Aboriginal had actually posed for his portrait.

Difficulty in establishing contact is clear from the accounts of both Cook and Banks. The latter writes:

That they are a very pusilanimous people we have reason to suppose from every part of their conduct in every place where we were except Sting Rays [Botany] bay, and there only the instance of the two people who opposd the Landing of our two boats full of men for near a quarter of an hour and were not to be drove away till several times wounded with small shot, which we were obligd to do so as at that time we suspected their Lances to be poisned from the quantity of gum which was about their points; but upon every other occasion both there and every where else they behavd alike, shunning us and giving up any part of the countrey which we landed upon at once . . . (Beaglehole, 1962: vol. 2, 134).

There is another less important but not insignificant reason for the paucity of visual material. Parkinson was employed by Banks as his natural history draughtsman, and his first duty was to draw plants—for botany was Banks' first interest. When his figure draughtsman, Alexander Buchan, died a few days after the *Endeavour* arrived at Tahiti, Banks employed his secretary, Hermann Spöring, to make drawings of peoples and places as best he could. But Spöring was not much good at this kind of drawing, even though he had an excellent eye for detail when depicting artefacts. He had not been trained in drawing either figures or landscapes. Nor for that matter had Alexander Buchan; which is surprising, considering the nature of his employment. The *Endeavour* lacked a skilled figure draughtsman. The best of the three was Parkinson, and even he had obviously not been trained at figure drawing. His professional skill lay in botanical draughtsmanship; but there is no firm evidence—despite Dr A. M. Lysaght's contention (1979) that he had been instructed by William de la Cour—of his having received training of any kind. Parkinson also acquired a facility for figure composition and picturesque landscape wash drawing.

It seems reasonably clear from the available evidence and from the behaviour of both Banks and Stanfield Parkinson (Sydney's brother) after the conclusion of the voyage that Sydney took the view that his obligation to Banks—who had promised to pay him £80 for the voyage—was to provide natural history drawings only. Other drawings were made in his spare time as part of his personal record of the voyage; like his *Journal*, these were to be regarded as his own property. Uncertainty concerning the delimitation of Parkinson's work and of his responsibility to Banks led to a complicated legal dispute after his death (Parkinson, 1784, with Stanfield's preface and John Fothergill's reply). There can be no doubt, however, that Parkinson's first duty was to draw sketches of plants collected on the voyage. In all he made 955 drawings of plants, 675 of which were sketches and 280 finished drawings, usually in colour (Stearn, 1969: 85). By the time the *Endeavour* left New Zealand in March 1770 the number of plants collected had become so great that Parkinson abandoned any attempt to provide finished drawings and concentrated instead upon sketches of the basic facts of structure and colour before the specimens withered and faded. In Australia the backlog of plants to be drawn increased dramatically. In these circumstances Parkinson would have had little time to make drawings of Aboriginal people. Spöring, so far as we know, made no attempt to do so. He too, as an assistant naturalist, was also most probably fully occupied in the collection and description of plants. On Cook's first voyage (1768-71) visual depiction for scientific purposes was, because of Banks' interests and the general condition of science at that time, directed largely towards botany. It is not until Cook's third voyage (1776-80) that the growing interest in ethnography is supported by an artist, in the person of John Webber, sufficiently skilled to meet its particular needs.

Plate 2.1   Sydney Parkinson (1770) *Two Australian Aborigines and other drawings*

II

Parkinson's field sketches of Australian Aborigines are contained in a guard book in the Department of Manuscripts, British Library (Add. MS. 9345). It binds together what were most probably two sketch-books of different size kept by Parkinson on the voyage. The smaller (152 × 190 mm) contains drawings only of subjects related to the Society Islands. The larger (185 × 236 mm) contains drawings related to both the earlier (Madeira, Rio) and later (New Zealand, Australia, Batavia) sections of the voyage.

The first sheet (f.14ᵛ) contains ten drawings (plate 2.1). Two are of Aboriginal men, four of a bark canoe in various positions with one depicting an Aboriginal paddling. There are also drawings of a bark hut, two of shields, and one of a paddle. These drawings were probably executed on or about 28 April 1770 when the *Endeavour* was at Botany Bay. Parkinson's sketches of the canoes and paddles accord closely with his *Journal* entry for that day:

Their canoes were made of one piece of bark, gathered at the two ends, and extended in the middle by two sticks. Their paddles were very small, two of which they used at one time (Parkinson, 1784: 135).

A more detailed drawing of a canoe and two views of a bark hut occur on a second sheet of drawings (f.20ᵛ) (plate 2.2). These seem to have been developed from the field sketches on f.14ᵛ (plate 2.1) and may have been completed after leaving the Endeavour River. Significantly the same sheet contains a drawing of a fan palm and a 'Javanese house', both probably drawn on Savu.

The figure at lower right (plate 2.1) of the man launching a lance from a throwing stick also suggests that f.14ᵛ was drawn at Botany Bay. In his *Journal* Parkinson recorded on 28 April: 'After we had landed, they threw two of their lances at us; one of which fell between my feet' (1784: 134); and he proceeded later to describe the body paint worn:

Plate 2.2 Sydney Parkinson (1770) *Sketches of different objects including a Javanese house*

... some ... were painted white, having a streak round their thighs, two below their knees, one like a sash over their shoulders, which ran diagonally downwards, and another across their foreheads (ibid).

All these features can be seen on the man except the second band below the knees. Parkinson also describes the shields used: 'of an oval figure, painted white in the middle, with two holes in it to see through' (ibid). This accords with the drawings he made of shields, except for the two holes. They are not there in the drawing, nor in Banks' description of Aboriginal shields, nor in the artefact drawn by Miller (plate 2.3). Nevertheless they are depicted in the engraving in Parkinson's *Journal* entitled *Two of the Natives of New Holland, Advancing to Combat* by Thomas Chambers (or Chambars) (plate 2.4).

The man at lower right in plate 2.1 is depicted using a throwing stick, the first such drawing made. Yet Parkinson does not describe it verbally in his *Journal*, though he speaks of lances and a wooden sword. Banks, however, immediately understood the use of the woomera when he first saw a man in action at Botany Bay with 'a short stick which he seemed to handle as if it

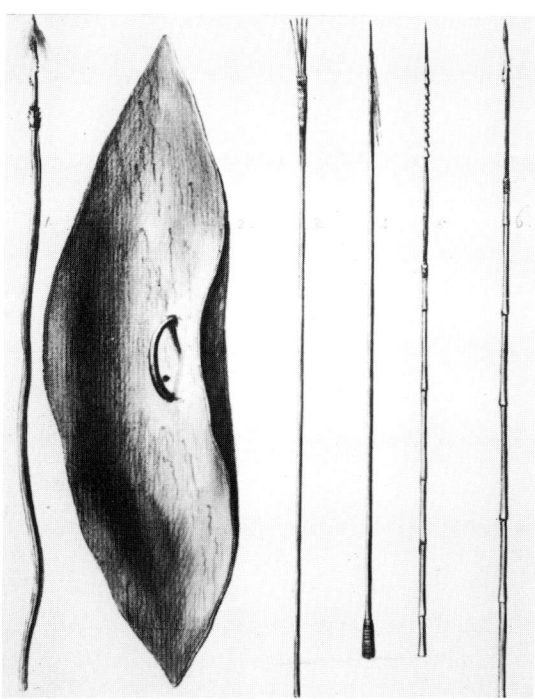

Plate 2.3 John Frederick Miller (1771) *Five spears and a shield from New Zealand, Australia and New Guinea*

Plate 2.4   Thomas Chambers (1773) *Two of the Natives of New Holland Advancing to Combat*

Plate 2.5   Charles Praval (1770) *Portrait of an Australian Aborigine on the Endeavour River***, from a lost drawing by Sydney Parkinson**

was a machine to throw the lance' (Beaglehole, 1962: vol. 2, 54). Later in his general description of Aboriginal weapons, etc., written after they had left the Endeavour River, Banks also wrote: 'these I beleive to be the things which many of our people were deceivd by imagining them to be wooden swords, Clubs etc. according to the direction in which they happned to see them' (Beaglehole, 1962: vol. 2, 133). Parkinson may have been one of the people so deceived, being able to draw it accurately enough but unable to put a name to it. As a result of his confusion Thomas Chambers, following Parkinson's text and without the field drawing at hand to correct him, drew the two famous defenders of New Holland advancing with dart and sword heroically but inaccurately (plate 2.4).

The drawing of the man at lower left in plate 2.1 possesses some strange features. What looks like a pair of spectacles is most probably intended to depict the facial paint which Banks mentions in his general description ('They lay it on in circles round their eyes'), and may be seen more clearly in Charles Praval's drawing (plate 2.5). Neither Banks nor Parkinson mentions having noticed such facial marking while at Botany Bay. So that if f.14^v was executed at Botany Bay, as seems likely, this is the earliest record we have of such markings. The drawing upon the chest of the same man, however, raises large questions. The designs on the man at lower right correspond with Parkinson's observations in his *Journal* (already noted) concerning the body paint worn on shoulder and breast by Aborigines at Botany Bay. On the man at lower left, however, Parkinson has drawn a crucifix figure as an integral part of the design across the man's chest. The simplest explanation is that the man's breast markings when first seen reminded him of a crucifix, and wishing to preserve the original perception, he drew them in that way. The fact that it was close to the Easter season while the *Endeavour* was at Botany Bay may also be relevant. The markings had reminded Banks of 'a soldiers cross belts' (Beaglehole, 1962: vol. 2, 53). These sketches, as we mentioned above, were personal notes, not scientific records for Banks. Nevertheless the drawing is quite exceptional in Parkinson's oeuvre. On no other occasion did he produce a work of this kind in which his imagination is allowed a free rein. It is true that we have several *verbal* accounts of preconceptions colouring vision on Cook's voyages. An amusing one is that of the seaman who at the Endeavour River saw what was presumably a flying fox, but informed Banks that whatever it was it was 'as black as the Devil and had 2 horns on its head' (Beaglehole, 1962: vol. 2, 84). On the second voyage J. R. Forster insisted that the colonial pines he saw on Norfolk Island were basaltic pillars similar to those on the Giant's Causeway:

... all the military Men think them to be Trees, whereas the Experimental-Men are of the Opinion that they are Stone-pillars erected by Nature. We go by Analogy and judge from what we have seen and read before, but they think it impossible that such Rocks could be formed naturally (Hoare, 1982: vol. 4, 660).

Whether Parkinson intended anything more than a visual metaphor with his crucifix figure must remain a matter of speculation. He was, however, the most devout of all the 'experimental men'—to use Forster's phrase—on the *Endeavour* and the one who of all the ship's company, as his brother Stanfield rightly insisted, developed the closest rapport with the native peoples of the Pacific:

engaging their attention by the powers of his pencil, disarming them of their native ferocity, and rendering them even serviceable to the great end of the voyage in chearfully furnishing him with the choicest productions of the soil and climate, which neither force nor strategem might otherwise have procured (Parkinson, 1784: vii).

It was Parkinson who developed not only the most sympathetic relationships with but also the greatest sympathy for the peoples of the Pacific. This happened almost immediately. Only two days after the arrival at Tahiti Parkinson recorded his disgust at the way Tahitians were treated in an affray which developed after one of them had seized a musket from a sentinel:

A boy, a midshipman, was the commanding officer, and giving orders to fire, they obeyed with the greatest glee imaginable, as if they had been shooting wild ducks, killed one stout man, and wounded many others. What a pity, that such brutality should be exercised by civilized people upon unarmed ignorant Indians (Parkinson, 1784: 15).

Such a ready and sympathetic identification with native peoples unjustly treated rather than with his own companions may have been due in part to Parkinson's Quaker upbringing. But it owed much also to the artist's vocation. In order to execute accurate visual records of Pacific peoples, Parkinson, like Hodges and Webber after him, had to cultivate cordial and amicable relationships before he could successfully begin his work. It was essential for artists on scientific voyages of exploration to cultivate such relationships in order to prosecute their work. The importance of these negotiations has never been fully appreciated. Although the act of drawing was itself a kind of assertion of European power, a pre-emptive acquisition of knowledge for the future, including future action, it could not be asserted, as other modes of power were, simply by the use of physical force. Drawings of the living not the dead were required, and these presupposed amicability and interaction. In this respect the so-called 'scientific' drawing of people differed fundamentally from the drawing of plants and animals, that were first cut, snared, trapped or shot. Yet the cordial relationships which the artist's vocation demanded depended upon the prior use of force. Just as Cook's friendly relationships with the Tahitians depended in no small measure upon Wallis' brutal use of force in the year preceding Cook's first visit, so Parkinson's capacity to utilise the social space created by friendship, so essential to the practice of drawing, depended considerably upon those raw assertions of power he found so distasteful. Art in this respect, like trade, followed the flag. Yet even though Parkinson in the practice of his art was conducting a kind of second order of power relationship, we must realise that a redemptive process was already at work. The friendships which were an aspect of his vocational practice were valued on both sides. It was a relationship not wholly of dominance and subordination. Transfers of loyalty could occur.

Such general considerations provide a context for Parkinson's drawing. The crucifix is implanted on the unknown Aboriginal like the stigmata upon St Francis of Assisi. Here, as in Tahiti, Parkinson seems to have felt for the local people as victims. But he does not view them as the simple children of nature, 'far more happier than we Europeans'—Cook's phrase (Beaglehole, 1955: 399); rather, they are 'ignorant Indians' for whom Parkinson's Christ died (Parkinson, 1784: 15). Parkinson's drawing reveals a different kind of sympathy, that sympathy for the lost souls of pagan brothers which generated the missionary enterprise that was yet to come to the Pacific.

If such thoughts and feelings do indeed lie behind Parkinson's little drawing, then the engraving by Thomas Chambers presents a problem (plate 2.4). None of the field drawings made by Parkinson bears any close relationship to the engravings published in his *Journal*, except the portrait of the Maori (plate XXI in the *Journal*). Yet some of these drawings may well have provided information upon which more finished drawings (now lost) were developed and came later into the possession of the engravers who executed the plates for the *Journal*. It is probable that more developed drawings were later made from the two figures in plate 2.1, and that Chambers' engraved plate derives from these. But if so, the transformation effected is considerable. None of Parkinson's surviving field drawings resort to the vocabulary of postures provided by classical statuary for presenting full-length figures. Which is not to say that Parkinson was wholly immune from neo-classical influences. There is some evidence to suggest that he had read Hogarth on composition. But he certainly lacked training in figure drawing.

It is likely therefore that the two figures depicted in the engraving owe their stance and posture to the engraver Thomas Chambers and not to Sydney Parkinson. Chambers was an Associate of the Royal Academy who exhibited with the Society of Artists between 1761 and 1773 and also at the Academy. He was exposed to the influences of classicism far more fully than was Parkinson. It may be noted that the other two full-length figures which he engraved for Parkinson's *Journal* also adopt classical attitudes: *The Tahitian Woman* (plate V in the *Journal*) adopts a modified Venus de Medici pose; *The New Zealand Warrior* (plate XV) a modified Apollo Belvedere pose. Engravings of this kind lent a certain elegance to the publication. They were essentially illustrations to words in the text rather than engravings developed from field sketches—even when such sketches played a part in the final result. This process of elevation was due in part to the high status of history painting, the currency of the grand style, the neo-classical taste of the engraver, and the conventions of fine-book illustration. What Chambers has done essentially is to draw an illustration expressive of true heroic courage based in part upon antique models, such as the Borghese Gladiator, the Tyrant Slayers and the Horse Tamers, and in part upon words chosen from Parkinson's text:

We attempted to frighten them by firing a gun loaded with small shot; but attempted it in vain. One of them repaired to a house immediately, and brought out a shield, of an oval figure, painted white in the middle, with two holes in it to see through, and also a wooden sword, and then they advanced boldly . . . (1784: 134).

For it was fundamental to the grand style that the general truths of action, not particularities of detail, should be seized upon in presenting historic events. Even so, ethnographic details such as nose ornaments and body paint could still be indicated with a tolerable accuracy. But it was the heroic character of the act that determined the category of the depiction.

III

The stay at Endeavour River was much longer than that at Botany Bay, and a greater degree of contact was established with the local Aborigines. This is the clue to the problem surrounding a puzzling drawing which has been usually described as representing a Melanesian native (British Library, Add. MS. 15508, f.13) (plate 2.5). It is drawn in ink and signed Ch. Praval. Without doubt this is Charles Praval, a seaman enlisted at Batavia and engaged to make copies of drawings by Parkinson and Spöring after the two artists died in January 1771. Cook required the copies to illustrate his Admiralty log (Joppien & Smith, forthcoming). There seems little doubt that plate 2.5 is a copy of a lost drawing by Parkinson executed at the Endeavour River. There is no good reason for describing the man as Melanesian, for the drawing certainly comes from the *Endeavour*'s voyage in which contact with New Guinea was brief, and such that no Melanesian could possibly have posed in this way for his portrait.

On the other hand, the drawing, despite its naivety, accords closely enough with descriptions of Aborigines seen at Endeavour River. They had, Parkinson informs us, 'flattish noses', the hair of some was 'curled and bushy'; 'Their noses had holes bored in them, through which they drew a piece of white bone about three or five inches long and two round'. 'Some of them had necklaces made of oval pieces of bright shells, which lay imbricated over one another, and linked together by two strings.' 'Their bones were so small, that I could more than span their ancles; and their arms too, above the elbow joint' (Parkinson, 1784: 146-7). From Banks we have a description of the armbands, 'bracelets wore round the upper part of their arms, consisting of strings lapd round with other strings as what we Call gymp in England' (Beaglehole, 1962: vol. 2, 93), and it was Banks also, as was mentioned earlier, who described the painted bands about the eyes. 'Their Beards', Cook informs us, 'which are generaly black they like wise crop short or singe off' (Beaglehole, 1955: 395). Their shields were usually ovate in form.

However, the Aborigines at Endeavour River (as elsewhere) went naked, and this man is clothed in some kind of garment and holds a small branch of a plant in his right hand. Can it be that the original drawing by Parkinson, now lost, depicted an Aboriginal whom Parkinson had prevailed upon to pose in a garment given to him, holding a green branch as an emblem of friendship? Parkinson, as he himself tells us, was one of a party of three who gave a shirt to some Aborigines; this was 'found afterwards torn into rags' (Parkinson, 1784: 153). It may be that he prevailed upon one of them to pose for his portrait, dressed in the manner depicted. There is an element of prudery in Parkinson's sketches of the men in plate 2.1—the genitals are never drawn clearly—and the over-all manner of composition in plate 2.5 suggests Parkinson's reluctance to show his subject in a state of total nudity. Here too one observes the beginning of a long tradition of Aboriginal acculturation in the ways of Europeans.

Another sketch (British Library, Add. MS. 9354, f.20) (plate 2.6) supports this view. It too was probably drawn on the Endeavour River. The

Plate 2.6   Sydney Parkinson (1770) *A figure in European clothes and other sketches*

other drawings on the sheet, the shields, the head of the lance, the throwing stick, the palm tree and fish were all probably drawn there. The figure beneath the palm tree is clothed in a shirt, a neckerchief, and what looks like a short skirt of some kind. He holds a stick or lance in his right hand and some kind of object, possibly a small shield, in his left. Although the figure looks more like a European than an Aboriginal, Parkinson is not known to have depicted members of the *Endeavour*'s company during the three years of the voyage. Nor, so far as we know, did Hodges on the Second, or Webber on the third voyage. To do so here would have been quite exceptional. Furthermore it may be noted that the hair of the standing man is somewhat similar to that of the man seated in the canoe in plate 2.2. If plate 2.5 is indeed, as seems likely, a drawing of an Aboriginal dressed up for the occasion at Endeavour River, then it may be a field sketch preliminary to the execution of the lost drawing from which Praval's drawing was copied. Drawings of Pacific peoples in European costume, though extremely rare, were made on other occasions on Cook's voyages. Thus, on the second voyage, William Hodges depicted a young Tongan woman clothed in a blanket which she had apparently acquired from some member of the *Resolution*'s company (wash drawing entitled *Tongatabu*, National Library of Australia). Such drawings remind us that the depiction of native peoples took place in an interactive situation.

Plate 2.7   Artist of the Chief Mourner (1770) *Australian Aborigines in bark canoes*

The last drawing to be noted here is by the 'Artist of the Chief Mourner' (British Library, Add. MS. 15508, f.9), who was probably Joseph Banks. It has not been previously identified as a drawing of Aborigines because it is headed 'Otaheite' in the portfolio in which it is preserved (British Library, Add. MS. 15508, f.10) (plate 2.7), but it is obviously a drawing of Aborigines paddling bark canoes. The man in the canoe at right is striking a fish with a four-pronged lance (or fish gig) in his right hand while holding a short paddle in his left. His nakedness and the cicatrices across his upper arm suggest he is an Australian Aboriginal. Though the details do not exactly tally, the drawing may well be a record of a fishing party which Banks observed at Botany Bay on 26 April 1770:

Under the South head . . . were four small canoes; in each of these was one man who held in his hand a long pole with which he struck fish (Beaglehole, 1962: vol. 2, 53).

Bibliography

Beaglehole, J. C. (ed.) (1955) *The Journals of Captain Cook on his Voyages of Discovery* vol. 1, *The Voyage of the Endeavour 1768-1771* Cambridge: Cambridge University Press for the Hakluyt Society

—— (ed.) (1962) *The Endeavour Journal of Joseph Banks 1768-1771* 2 vols, Sydney: Public Library of NSW with Angus & Robertson

Hoare, M. (1982) *The Resolution Journal of Johann Reinhold Forster* London: Hakluyt Society

Joppien, R. and B. Smith (forthcoming) *The Art of Cook's Voyages* 3 vols, Melbourne: Oxford University Press

Lysaght, A. M. (1979) 'Banks' Artists and his *Endeavour* Collections' *British Museum Yearbook 3, Captain Cook and the South Pacific* London

Parkinson, Sydney (1784) *A Journal of a Voyage to the South Seas* London: Stanfield Parkinson

Stearn, W. T. (1969) 'A Royal Society Appointment with Venus in 1769: The Voyage of Cook and Banks in the *Endeavour* in 1768-1771 and its Botanical Results' *Notes and Records of the Royal Society of London* 24, 1, June

THREE

REACTIONS ON
COOK'S VOYAGE

Glyndwr Williams

COOK'S FIRST PACIFIC voyage was remarkable in many ways: the revelation of a navigator supreme, the charting of New Zealand, the long stay in Tahiti, and not least the observations on the east coast of Australia and its Aboriginal inhabitants. In Cook's journal these observations reached an unexpected climax in his final words on the Aborigines:

From what I have said of the Natives of New-Holland they may appear to some to be the most wretched people upon Earth, but in reality they are far more happier than we Europeans; being wholly unacquainted not only with the superfluous but the necessary Conveniences so much sought after in Europe, they are happy in not knowing the use of them. They live in a Tranquillity which is not disturb'd by the Inequality of Condition: The Earth and sea of their own accord furnishes them with all things necessary for life, they covet not Magnificent Houses, Household-stuff etc., they live in a warm and fine Climate and enjoy a very wholesome Air, so that they have very little need of Clothing ... In short they seem'd to set no Value upon any thing we gave them, nor would they ever part with any thing of their own for any one article we could offer them... (Beaglehole, 1955: 399).

What are we to make of this? As always with Cook, we turn first to J. C. Beaglehole, though knowing in advance what we are likely to hear. It was Beaglehole after all who in his 1955 edition of Cook's journal of this voyage had dismissed Commerson's sentimental lucubrations on Tahiti with the forthright words, 'this preposterous sublimity, this nonsense on stilts'. Of Cook's passage on the Aborigines Beaglehole in this same edition records his 'double shock' that 'Cook, the genius of the matter-of-fact, writes nonsense about Australian society'. At the same point in time in his 1962 edition of Banks' journal, Beaglehole comments that 'Banks does not go very far; Cook (of all people) is far sillier'. Finally, in his 1974 *Life* of Cook Beaglehole returns to the charge:

Cook bursts into a panegyric that almost persuades me that he had spent the voyage reading Rousseau ... or ... has he been listening to some oration of Banks, while the ship lay at anchor in the night; or read through some piece of paper adorned with the Banks version of the fashionable intellectual indiscretions? (Beaglehole, 1955: cxcii, clxxiii; 1962: vol. 2, 44; 1974: 251).

When Beaglehole asks questions on Cook, even rhetorical questions, others tread warily and circumspectly. At this stage, the only claim advanced is that the whole matter of the observations made by Cook (and Banks) on the Aborigines in 1770 repays investigation. At the end, we may accept Beaglehole's indictment that Cook, uncharacteristically, was writing 'nonsense'; but conceivably we may learn something more about Cook's attitude towards the Aborigines, and the background of observation and perception which shaped that attitude.

Obviously, Cook and Banks did not come 'cold', so to speak, to the shores of eastern Australia. They had been to Tahiti, to New Zealand, and perhaps of most direct interest in this connection, they had touched near the beginning of the voyage at Tierra del Fuego. There they had made fleeting contact with a people whose condition in several respects paralleled that of the Aborigines. Banks' description of the Fuegans has a hint of things to follow on the coast of New Holland. They seemed to lack, he wrote, any form of government or religion; nor did they have much in the way of material possessions, or indeed the desire for such. He continued:

no thing bearing the name of a hut could possibly be built with less trouble . . . a few poles . . . a little grass . . . Furniture I may justly say they had none . . . In these few hutts and with this small share or rather none at all of what we call the nescessaries and conveniences of life livd about 50 men women and children . . . to all appearance contented with what they had nor wishing for any thing we could give them except beads (Beaglehole, 1962: vol. 1, 224).

Cook's description was briefer. On their contentment or otherwise he ventured no opinion. Their lack of shelter and possessions in so severe a climate was simply evidence to him that the Fuegans 'must be a very hardy race', and he finished with the brusque comment, 'in a Word they are perhaps as miserable a set of People as are this day upon Earth' (Beaglehole, 1955: 45). It was left to Hawkesworth to inflate and decorate these remarks, embroidering Banks rather than Cook in a passage of considerable pomposity to which we shall return.

Fifteen months later the *Endeavour* reached the south-east coast of Australia. In between there had been Tahiti and New Zealand, a host of experiences, much observation and much writing on strange customs and exotic societies. Nothing seen so far had quite prepared the discoverers for New Holland. The reactions of Cook and Banks were to be fused by Hawkesworth, but their individual journals reveal differences of approach which, though in some cases trivial, amount to a good deal in the end. Banks in particular was struck by the differences between the Aborigines they saw, and those on the north-west coast of Australia described by William Dampier in the late seventeenth century. Dampier's well-known remarks, after encounters in 1688 and 1699, were disparaging in the extreme:

the miserablest People in the World ... setting aside their Humane Shape, they differ but little from Brutes ... Their Eyelids are always half closed, to keep the Flies out of their Eyes ... They have great Bottle-Noses, pretty full Lips, and wide Mouths ... Their Hair is black, short, and curl'd, like that of the Negroes ... The Colour of their Skins, both of their Faces and the rest of their Body, is Coal-black ... They all of them have the most unpleasant Looks and the worst Features of any People that ever I saw, tho I have seen a great variety of Savages (Gray, 1937: 312-13; Williamson, 1939: 102-3).[1]

The preconceptions instilled in Banks after reading Dampier were strong, as he himself was ready to admit. The Australian coast was sighted on 19 April 1770, and three days later the first signs of life were seen ashore. Banks wrote:

we stood in with the land near enough to discern 5 people who appeard through our glasses to be enormously black: so far did the prejudices which we had built on Dampiers account influence us that we fancied we could see their Colour when we could scarce distinguish whether or not they were men (Beaglehole, 1962: vol. 2, 50).

Cook was more noncommital:

were so near the Shore as to distinguish several people upon the Sea beach. They appear'd to be of a very dark or black Colour but whether this was the real colour of their skins or the C[l]othes they might have on I know not (Beaglehole, 1955: 301).

A nearer glimpse a few days later left Banks again convinced that they were 'as well as we could judge at that distance exceedingly black' (Beaglehole, 1962: vol. 2, 52); Cook made no comment on their colour. The next day the boats put ashore, at the spot soon to become celebrated as Botany Bay, where the first contact was made with the Aborigines, two of whom armed with spears and throwing-sticks seemed determined to resist the landing, though vastly out-numbered. It took the firing of several muskets loaded with small shot before they made off, and Cook, Banks, Solander and Tupaia (the Raiatean *arii* and priest taken on board at Tahiti) were able to investigate the half-dozen or so bark huts, a huddle of frightened children, and a few canoes, 'the worst I think I ever saw', wrote Cook. Their 'lances' or 'darts' proved not to be smeared with poison, as Banks had suspected, and Cook thought that 'those we have seen seem to be intend[ed] more for striking fish than offensive weapons' (Beaglehole, 1955: 306).

The following days brought a number of further sightings of the Aborigines, and on occasion some approaches to within twenty yards or so. Some half-hearted spear throwing accompanied these encounters, but no serious violence. Banks' verdict was that the Aborigines were 'rank cowards'; Cook put rather a different interpretation on the timidity of the Aborigines and their distant gestures of defiance—'all they seem'd to want for us to be gone' (Beaglehole, 1962: vol. 2, 59; 1955: 306). As Banks and Cook summed up their first impressions, both clearly had Dampier's comments in mind. Banks carefully noted that

the people were blacker than any we have seen in the Voyage tho by no means negroes; their beards were thick and bushy and they seemed to have a redundancy of hair upon those parts of the body where it commonly grows; the hair of their heads was bushy and thick but by no means woolly like that of a Negro; they were of a common size, lean and seemed active and nimble; their voices were coarse and strong (Beaglehole, 1962: vol. 2, 55).

Cook wrote in similar terms:

those I saw were about as tall as Europeans, of a very dark brown colour but not black nor had they wooly frizled hair, but black and lank much like ours. No sort of cloathing or ornaments were ever seen by any of us upon any one of them ... (Beaglehole, 1962: 312).

Of the other logs kept on board, only Pickersgill's struck a personal— though hardly original—note, when he observed, 'The people have nothing to cover themselves, but go quite naked, men and women, and, in short, are the most wretched set I ever beheld or heard of' (*Historical Records*, 1893: 1, pt 1, 215).

Near the end of the stay a midshipman accidentally stumbled upon an old man and woman with some children, and they all remained in a state of mutual fright and incomprehension for a while; but as the *Endeavour* left the bay Cook was definite about the general lack of contact:

We could know but little of their customs as we never were able to form any connections with them, they had not so much as touch'd the things we had left in their hutts on purpose for them to take away (Beaglehole, 1955: 312).

Some modification of this assertion of a total lack of communication during the stay at Botany Bay may be necessary. A recent monograph prints three word-lists (vocabularies would be too elaborate a term to apply to them) collected by the surgeon William Monkhouse, the second lieutenant Zachary Hicks, and the midshipman Isaac Smith. Not only do they represent the South Kuri language of the locality, but two of the word-lists are dated 2 May 1770—about mid-point in the period spent at Botany Bay (Lanyon-Orgill, 1979: 33-5). (The authenticity of these word-lists, however, is dubious. There seem, for example, to be lists from areas where, according to the logs, no landings were made (Lanyon-Orgill, 1979: 4-6, 42-3)). The word-lists would seem to provide evidence of more contact between crew members and Aborigines than the journals of Cook and Banks reveal, and raise the wider question—though not one to be pursued here—of how representative of the entire range of crew activities were the relatively few journals kept (or at least extant) on a discovery voyage of this nature.

From Botany Bay the *Endeavour* sailed north to its fateful, almost fatal, encounter with the Great Barrier Reef. After its escape the vessel remained from 17 June to 3 August at the mouth of the Endeavour River undergoing repairs, and during this time contact with the Aboriginal population was closer and more frequent. At first the Aborigines proved as elusive as at Botany Bay, and Banks was soon writing with some irritation of 'their unaccountable timidity' (Beaglehole, 1962: vol. 2, 90). But on 10 July came the first real contact, with Tupaia acting as intermediary. Soon the 'Indians' were introducing themselves by name, visiting the ship, and as Banks put it 'became our very good friends'. Cook simply wrote that they 'came to us without shewing the least signs of fear' (Beaglehole, 1962: vol. 2, 95; 1955: 360). But the women were kept well away, and on 19 July a dramatic if more-or-less bloodless incident occurred which demonstrated the fragility of the relationship. A refusal to allow the Aborigines to take away turtle which were lying on the deck of the *Endeavour* led to a fine display of temper by the visitors. Banks wrote that they 'shewd great marks of Resentment; one who had askd me on my refusal stamping with his foot pushd me from him with a countenance full of disdain'. Cook noted, more laconically, that 'they grew a little troublesome and were for throwing every thing over board they could lay their hands upon'. Rebuffed, the Aborigines paddled ashore where they lit grass fires which threatened to engulf fishing nets, washing and a tent from the ship, and retreated only when Cook fired small shot at them. One man was hit, but after a while the rest returned, 'making signs as they came along that they would not set fire to the grass again and we distributing musket balls among them and by our signs explaining their effect' (Beaglehole, 1962: vol. 2, 96-7; 1955: 361-2).

Although relations seem to have been repaired after all the excitement, this was apparently the last occasion on which the Aborigines ventured near the ship. Occasional encounters away from the beach, fires in the hills at night, empty huts or canoes, became the only entries in the journals about the Aborigines, and these mostly by Banks, for Cook was busy getting the *Endeavour* ready for sea. Characteristic was the note of disillusionment in Banks' entry for 23 July: 'In Botanizing today on the other side of the river we accidentaly found the greatest part of the clothes which had been given to the Indians left all in a heap together, doubtless as lumber not worth carriage' (Beaglehole, 1962: vol. 2, 98-9). This lack of interest in their possessions and gifts was a matter of continuing bafflement to the journal-keepers. In a way it was a welcome relief from the pressing, never-ending demands elsewhere for iron, clothes, firearms, trinkets; on the other hand, to find their accoutrements treated with contemptuous disdain clearly produced feelings of unease and uncertainty among the crew.

As the *Endeavour* left the Australian coast both Cook and Banks composed their customary descriptive sections on the land, its products and its inhabitants, Cook's being only about half the length of Banks' (Beaglehole, 1955: 392-401; 1962: vol. 2, 111-37). This was to be expected: once at sea, where these general sections seem to have been written, Banks had time on his hands, Cook did not. There is only occasional evidence of copying between the two journals; indeed, there are differences which show that these were generally independent accounts. Thus, Cook writes that the Aborigines were of 'middle stature', Banks that they were 'remarkably short'; Cook that their voices were 'soft and tunable', Banks that they were 'shrill and effeminate'. A more fundamental difference appears when they turn to the disposition of the Aborigines. Cook insisted, 'I do not look upon them to be a warlike People, on the Contrary I think them a timorous and inoffensive race, no ways inclinable to cruelty . . .' Banks on the contrary speculated that one reason for their lack of numbers might be that 'their small tribes have frequent wars in which many are destroyed', and went on to describe their 'most cruel weapons', armed with barbs 'certain to make the wound ten times more difficult to cure than it otherwise would be'. The hurling of a single spear by a man hidden in a tree was adduced by Banks as proof 'that they use stratagems in war', though in general they were 'a very pusilanimous people'.

Of the other accounts, Parkinson's has most detail—in particular, a careful description of the physical appearance of the Aborigines, together with the fullest word-list collected. Unlike Banks, who grumbled that the bone worn through the nose 'compleatly stop'd up both nostrils so that they spoke in the nose in a manner one should think scarce intelligible', Parkinson maintained that 'they articulated their words very distinctly'. There are some details in Parkinson not found in the other journals, and an interesting account of the hesitant approach of the Aborigines and the first contacts at the Endeavour River:

They became at length, more free when only three of us were present, and made signs for us to take off some of our garments, which we did accordingly. They viewed them with surprize; but they seemed to have no idea of cloaths; nor did they express a desire for any; and a shirt, which we gave them, we found afterwards torn into rags (Parkinson, 1773: 147, 153).

The Aboriginal attitude to clothes, or rather to the lack of them, continued to fascinate the visitors. Although Cook and Banks had seen nudity, both total and part, often enough on the voyage, both mention the unabashed nakedness of the Aborigines repeatedly in their journals, and return to the subject in their final generalisations. It is clear that what intrigued, and bothered, them was that the Aborigines, regardless of age and sex, never seemed to wear clothing of any kind at any time. Nudity as uncompromising as this was more than a novelty, it was a challenge. Cook concluded, 'They go quite naked both Men and women without any manner of Cloathing whatever, even the Women do not so much as Cover their privities.' Banks was more elaborate: 'Of Cloths they had not the least part but naked as ever our general father was before his fall, they seemed no more conscious of their nakedness than if they had not been the children of Parents who eat the fruit of the tree of knowledge.' Their life style was as simple and primitive as their appearance, both Cook and Banks stressed. Cook wrote that although they had 'mean small hovels', not much bigger than an oven, they often slept in the open, and lived entirely by hunting and fishing. 'We never saw one Inch of Cultivated land in the whole Country.' Banks said much the same thing in different words, with his depiction of the Aborigines 'wandering like the Arabs from place to place . . . where sufficient supplys of food are to be met with, and as soon as these are exhausted remove to another'. He went on to describe how the Aborigines carried 'their worldly treasures' in a small bag, consisting of some fish hooks and lines, a lump of paint (pipe-clay), some resin and other odds-and-ends. This led Banks into some general reflections—'Thus live these I had almost said happy people, content with little nay almost nothing.' But the passage which follows soon abandons consideration of the Aborigines in favour of a general philosophical statement. It begins with some standard criticism of that form of European materialism which confuses luxuries with necessities, and ends with some convoluted prose aimed at showing that because the needs and living standards of the rich are higher than those of the poor all men in fact exist in a state of equal happiness.[2] Banks then added a few more pages of detailed observations, finishing the whole section with a short word-list.

Cook's equivalent passage of reflections on the Aborigines (quoted at the beginning of this paper) is differently placed. It comes after his vocabulary, and concludes his general section on New Holland except for some technical notes on currents and tides. In subject matter too the difference between Cook and Banks is sharp. Banks uses the condition of the Aborigines as a pretext for a disquisition on the nature of human contentment; Cook turns the whole of his remarks towards the Aborigines, and relates their life style to their environment—a benign climate and an adequate supply of food. Nowhere in Banks is there any parallel to Cook's direct thrust, 'in reality they are far more happier than we Europeans'. Nor can Cook's comments be dismissed as a passing whim. After his return he wrote to his old master, John Walker of Whitby, and repeated the gist of his remarks on the superior happiness of the Aborigines. From the similarity of language he was writing with his journal before him, but he ended even more emphatically with the additional comment that the Aborigines 'sleep as sound in a small hovel or even in the open as the King in His Pallace on a Bed of down' (Beaglehole, 1955: 509).[3]

Although Cook's sentiments are of a different nature from those of Banks, he seems to have taken the idea of using the life style of the Aborigines as the basis for some comparison of Aboriginal and European societies from Banks. As we have seen, Banks' general passage follows naturally from the detailed context of his descriptive remarks, whereas Cook's has more the appearance of a postscript, perhaps even an afterthought. Further evidence is provided by the similarity between the last lines of Cook's reflections and some comments made by Banks earlier:

These people seemd to have no Idea of traffick nor could we teach them; indeed it seemd that we had no one thing on which they set a value equal to induce them to part with the smallest trifle ... They readily receivd the things we gave them but never would understand our signs when we askd for returns (Beaglehole, 1962: vol. 2, 125).

The probability is that although Cook and Banks wrote independent accounts, at some stage Cook saw Banks' journal and was encouraged or—given the different nature of their general remarks—provoked to add some reflections on the lot of the Aborigines. Undoubtedly he had seen Banks' journal before writing his final version of his log entry of 16 August (one week before the long general section) which described in hair-raising detail how the *Endeavour* was swept towards the Great Barrier Reef. So, if we like, he had 'read through some piece of paper adorned with the Banks version of the fashionable intellectual indiscretions'. Here, one might agree with Beaglehole's inference—Banks is playing at being the philosopher. But the further inference of the great Cook scholar—that Cook's own remarks are somehow an aberration, not worthy of the explorer—is less acceptable.

In one sense of course Beaglehole is absolutely right in dismissing Cook's assertions, since the observations which supported them were slight in the extreme. The Aborigines had been seen only as timorous visitors to the ship; at no stage had they been viewed in their own domestic setting. No Aboriginal woman had been seen at close quarters—except, Cook added in an intriguing note, by one (unnamed) crew member—and no conversation had been possible. Banks in particular was emphatic on this last point. Although he had collected a few words used by the Aborigines,

Our aquaintance with them was of so short a duration that none of us attempted to use a single word of it to them, consequently the list of words I have given could be got no other manner than by signs enquiring of them what in their Language signified such a thing, a method obnoxious to many mistakes (Beaglehole, 1962: vol. 2, 136).

It is unlikely that the Cook of the second and third voyages would have committed himself to such large generalisations on the basis of so little knowledge. At Tonga, for example, in 1777, where Cook had Omai to act as interpreter, the difficulties of describing, let alone explaining, the culture of the Tongans hung heavily on him. Few were willing to take his questions seriously, and when they did misunderstanding resulted in 'a hundred mistakes'. Furthermore, the very presence of the ships halted the normal processes of living (Beaglehole, 1967: 114).

How then are we to explain Cook's remarks of August 1770? To find an answer, we have to understand something of Cook's developing outlook on the first voyage, and speculate—we can do no more—on how much he had assimilated of long-standing European attitudes towards primitivism. Something of the latter he might have gained from Banks' conversation and books, but since we have little firm knowledge of the naturalist's own opinions on this, to push too far in this direction would be to plunge into a quagmire of uncertainty (Carter, 1978). We can simply note that embedded in the Western European intellectual heritage was a sympathy and respect for primitivism which extended from the classical writers to the more recent accounts of the North American Indians. Examples of the latter abounded, in poetry and prose, in fact and fiction. It would be difficult for a literate person to avoid them totally. They deeply influenced a writer we know Banks had come across at some stage, Fénelon, whose utopian novel, *Aventures de Télémaque*, first published in 1699, went through repeated English editions, that of 1769 with a translation by Hawkesworth, editor-to-be of the journals of the voyage. The inhabitants of Fénelon's ideal commonwealth lived in skin tents or bark houses; they were healthy and long-lived; they abhorred all material possessions, which 'soften, intoxicate and torment the Possessors of them, and tempt those that are depriv'd of them to acquire them by Injustice and Violence' (Fénelon 1707: 2, 107-21).[4]

But we can get nearer to the Aborigines, and to Cook, than this. Among the books on the *Endeavour* was George Shelvocke's *Voyage Round the World* of 1726 (Beaglehole, 1962: vol. 2, 270). Its description of the Indians of southern California makes an interesting comparison with Cook on the Aborigines. The men, though not the women, went 'quite naked'; sheltered by the slightest of dwellings they lived mainly on raw fish; but their behaviour was 'endowed with all the humanity imaginable, and they make some nations (who would give these poor people the epithet of Savages or Barbarians) blush to think that they deserve that appellation more than they'. So, they lead a careless life, and have everything in common amongst them, and search for nothing except the necessary supports of life, viz., meat and drink, by which means they are free from the anxious troubles to which those nations are subject where luxury and pride have got any footing; a solid content seems to dwell in the midst of them, so that they covet (and have no reason for it), nothing belonging to one another . . . In a word they seem to pass their lives in the purest simplicity of the earliest ages of the world, before discord and contention were heard amongst men . . . In short, in every respect, they seem to enjoy a perfect tranquility . . . (Perrin, 1928:224).

Finally, another book which Cook would certainly have known, and had probably read, was the 1760 compilation put together under Thomas Jefferys's name, *The Natural and Civil History of the French Dominions in North and South America.*[5] The book's comments on the North American Indians so closely parallel those of Cook on the Aborigines that the two passages seem almost to be paraphrases of one another:

as they covet only the necessaries of life, with which nature has abundantly provided them, they scarce so much as think of its superfluities . . . the Indians are the happiest of all mortals . . . they neither know, nor desire to know, those false enjoyments which we purchase with so much pains, and with the loss of that which is solid and real. And their most admirable quality is that truly philosophical way of thinking, which makes them contemn all the parades of wealth and magnificence . . . (Jefferys, 1760: 96).

There is no need to labour the point further. One is not seeking to show Cook as a plagiarist, but to stress that he had to hand a well-established tradition of primitivism into which a people as lacking in material possessions and outward forms of social organisation as the Aborigines could be fitted. Nor is this to say that Cook was applying, uncritically, the received ideas of his day to the hard lot of the Aborigines. This would be to misinterpret the man. He had not fallen, for example, into the languorous trap of Tahiti, bastion now and for decades to come of the 'noble savagery' school of thought, even though he was appreciative enough of its climate and easy living to copy into his journal large chunks of Banks' enthusiastic description. On the east coast of Australia he was assessing an indigenous people against its own background, not against the standards of contemporary Europe. These he had discarded, for in parenthesis Cook's analysis of Aboriginal life, however superficial, was an indictment of the society from which he came and of its conventional views on property. Cook's statement on the Aborigines is not the only example of this; on the second voyage he was to lament the vanishing of the Maoris' 'happy tranquillity', and added with an indignant flash, 'If any one denies the truth of this assertion let him tell me what the Natives of the whole extent of America have gained by the commerce they have had with the Europeans' (Beaglehole, 1961: 175).

Clearly there are problems here: apathy might be mistaken for quiet contentment, mere survival in a harsh environment for a deliberate eschewing of material goods. But this is an important step in the making of Cook the explorer, for his greatness lay not simply in his superb navigational skills and the breadth of his geographical concepts, but also in his insistent curiosity about the peoples of the Pacific, and in his determination to view them in their own setting.

The matter is not altogether a simple one. I have argued elsewhere that Cook's voyages took place at a time of debate and controversy in Britain between two distinct interpretations of non-European societies: the fading school of primitivist thought, and the chillier assumptions of the 'four stages' theorists, who arranged societies in an order dependent upon their form of subsistence (Williams, 1979). These latter placed the Aborigines, together with the Fuegans, Hottentots and others, in the first and most rudimentary stage of human development as a nomadic, non-agricultural people, either backward or degenerate. That great natural scientist, Louis Leclerc, Comte de Buffon, described the Aborigines in his *Varietés dans l'espèce humaine* of 1749 as 'peut-être les gens du monde les plus misérables, et ceux de tous les humains qui approchent le plus des brutes . . .' They were bracketed by Buffon with others who lived in extreme, inhospitable climates such as the Eskimos. 'Ces hommes', it has been written, 'qui vivent à l'écart à l'extrême limite du monde habité, forment une humanité presque marginale' (on this, and much else, see Duchet, 1971: 252, 254). The assumptions of ethnocentrism are strong here. Cook himself was to be influenced by them, and still more by his own observations and experiences. He was never to return to the east coast of Australia, and so it is impossible to put the matter precisely to the test, but it is inconceivable that in his later years he would have written in similar terms to the entry of August 1770. When, in January 1777, he briefly encountered the Aborigines of Van Diemen's Land, though one or two of his officers' logs talk of happy innocents, Cook refrained from any but factual observations (Beaglehole, 1967: 52-6, esp. 54 nn. 2 and 4). He had seen and experienced much since the first voyage, and in the end disillusionment was not confined to European *mores*. But if we look again at Cook in 1770 at Botany Bay and the Endeavour River what is striking is the open-mindedness of the approach. There is none of Banks' impetuous initial judgements about negroid characteristics, poisoned weapons and treacherous behaviour. There is little prejudice as far as we can discern, and instead a readiness to view a strange and primitive life style on its own terms.

The events of the next half-century were to be a sad commentary on this. Cook's views were not contradicted or simply ignored—they were not known. His journal was not to be published in anything approaching its original form until the late nineteenth century, though there is no likelihood that even if it had appeared earlier it would have made one jot of difference to the treatment of the Aborigines by settlers and officials. When Cook's general observations on the Aborigines were finally printed in 1893, the editor, Captain Wharton, felt compelled to add a corrective footnote:

The native Australians may be happy in their condition, but they are without doubt among the lowest of mankind. Confirmed cannibals, they lose no opportunity of gratifying their love of human flesh. Mothers will kill and eat their own children ... Internecine war exists between the different tribes ... Their treachery, which is unsurpassed, is simply an outcome of their savage ideas (Wharton, 1893: 232n.).

When the journals of Cook and Banks were published, in mangled form, in 1773, the reflective observations of both men on the Aborigines were omitted. Instead, Hawkesworth concluded his account of them with an abrupt remark which he put into Cook's mouth: 'I have faithfully related facts, the reader must judge of the people for himself' (Hawkesworth, 1773: vol. 3, 241). Hawkesworth, of course, was not the man to overlook completely philosophical sentiments in his authors; as Bernard Smith spotted years ago, he coolly transferred the gist of Banks' comments on the life style of the Aborigines to the inhabitants of Tierra del Fuego. So we read that the Fuegans

suffered nothing from the want of the innumerable articles which we consider, not as the luxuries and conveniencies only, but the necessaries of life: as their desires are few, they probably enjoy them all, and how much they may be gainers by an exemption from the care, labour and solicitude, which arise from a perpetual and unsuccessful effort to gratify that infinite variety of desires which the refinements of artificial life have produced among us, is not very easy to determine ... (Hawkesworth, 1773: vol. 2, 59; Smith, 1960: 22).

In making this switch, Hawkesworth was guilty of more than unscholarly conduct; he was making arrant nonsense of the growing eighteenth-century conviction that climate was one of the main determinants of social organisation. The comments of Cook and Banks on the Aborigines related their life style specifically to physical environment, to their 'warm and fine Climate' as Cook put it. It was this misplaced passage in Hawkesworth which seems to have provoked Georg Forster into exclaiming in his account of Cook's second voyage, that

Till it can be proved, that a man in continual pain, from the rigours of climate, is happy, I shall not give credit to the eloquence of philosophers, who have either had no opportunity of contemplating human nature under all its modifications, or who have not felt what they have seen (Forster, 1968: 618).

The elder Forster, too, seized on the example of the Fuegans to launch into a long disquisition on the 'transitory and delusive ... happiness of the savage', unaware that the comments printed in Hawkesworth applied originally to the Aborigines. Nor could he know that when he insisted that the Fuegan would not exchange 'his wretched hut for a comfortable European house, nay, not even for the most magnificent palace', he was echoing Cook's words to John Walker on the Aborigines (Forster, 1778: 301).

Of the other accounts of the *Endeavour* voyage which appeared in print soon after the return little mention was made of the Aborigines: Tahiti dominated the narratives, with New Zealand running second, and New Holland a poor third. In one of the few newspaper reports which got that far we read that 'The savages were very troublesome upon New Holland, attacking us very often ... a warlike, stout people, ever jealous of our encroachments; nor would they suffer us to land without various attacks' (*London Evening Post*, 29 August 1771, printed in Beaglehole, 1955: 653). Similarly distorted and incoherent comments on the Aborigines appear in the more general works of the time. Quickest off the mark was William Robertson, who in his revised edition of Thomas Salmon's *New Geographical and Historical Grammar* of 1772 managed to squeeze in a hasty reference to Cook and his recent discoveries:

New Holland is an island at least as large as all Europe; and may, in the interior parts, have civilized nations, although the people on some of the coasts, which have been visited, appear to have little more of the human kind than the figure (Salmon, 1772: 515).

There is not much advance on Dampier here. In 1774 the first volume of Lord Monboddo's *Origin and Progress of Language* was published in which he used the example of the Aborigines to argue that a people 'living in the lowest stage of barbarity' existed in a state of 'brutish insensibility'. Two inhabitants of New Holland brought to Batavia by Gonzal in 1756 were described by Monboddo as being, in the judgement of an acquaintance who had seen them, 'perfectly stupid and idiotical'. Elsewhere Monboddo interrupted a description of the beaver to make the quite gratuitous point that their lodges were better built than the casual shelters of the Aborigines (Burnet, 1774: 188, 283n.).

By now, the general accounts and collections relied on Hawkesworth for their description of New Holland and its inhabitants, though often adding some cautionary comment. Thus, one compilation of 1779, after paraphrasing Hawkesworth, noted:

It is difficult to account for the small number of the human species dispersed in this extensive country. If the increase of the inhabitants is not prevented by some natural cause, perhaps it arises from the horrid appetite for devouring each other, which prevails in New Zealand. From the extreme ignorance of the natives, however, with respect to those arts that are generally found to be more or less cultivated by the most uncivilized people, there is reason to place them among the lowest of human kind (Carver, 1779: 665).

The editor of another collection put this allegation in the context of the 'four stages' theory when he explained that 'from their total ignorance of agriculture, commerce, and the means of procuring the comforts and conveniences of life, it is plain that they are amongst the most miserable of beings, that can be stiled human' (Bankes et al., *c.* 1787: 7). Of those who had been on the voyage it was Banks who was looked to for authoritative recollections of New Holland. But his memory of the Aborigines seems to blur with the years; the detail fades and the prejudices already evident in 1770 strengthen. In 1779 he described them to a Committee of the House of Commons as 'naked, treacherous, and armed with Lances, but extremely cowardly'. Although his evidence before the Beauchamp Committee in 1785 was more circumstantial, its main intent was to show that the Aborigines were a nomadic people, with no trace of political authority, social organisation or religious belief, and that the east coast of New Holland was, accordingly, *terra nullius*, open to European settlement and dominion (on Banks' evidence, see Frost, 1981; 1980: esp. chs 2, 9). The First Fleet, with all that followed, was now not far distant.[6]

Notes

1 These passages from Dampier were repeated in several of the collections of voyages published during the first half of the eighteeth century, for example in John Harris (1744-8: vol. 1, 84-130).

2 It is tempting to wonder whether Banks is arguing here against the view of David Hume, expressed in his essay 'Of Luxury', printed in his *Political Discourses* of 1752 (Rendall, 1978: 187). See Adam Ferguson and John Millar on 'luxury' (ibid.: 201-5).

3 It was this repetition by Cook, first in his journal, and then in this letter, which gave John Beaglehole the 'double shock' referred to earlier.

4 Professor Bernard Smith tells me that the manuscript catalogue (in the British Library) of Banks' books made by Sophia Banks shows that Banks left two copies of *Telemachus*.

5 The evidence for this is circumstantial, but to my mind persuasive. Cook's campaigning and surveying experience in North America at the time of the book's publication would give him an obvious interest in the latest book on the region, with its maps and plans of the St Lawrence, Louisbourg and Quebec. Moreover, Cook was beginning a professional relationship with Jefferys, one of Britain's leading cartographical engravers. It was Jefferys who after the fall of Quebec published in 1760 the splendid 'New Chart' of the St Lawrence made by Cook and his colleagues; later he was to publish Cook's surveys of the coasts of Newfoundland and Labrador.

6 This article is republished with permission (and with minor alterations) from *Historical Studies*, 19, 1981, 499-512.

Bibliography

Bankes, T. et al. (*c.* 1787) *A New Royal Authentic and Complete System of Universal Geography* London

Beaglehole, J. C. (ed.) (1955) *The Journals of Captain James Cook on his Voyages of Discovery* vol. 1, *The Voyage of the Endeavour 1768-1771* Cambridge: Cambridge University Press for the Hakluyt Society

———— (ed.) (1961) ibid. vol. 2, *The Voyage of the Resolution and Adventure 1772-1775* Cambridge: Cambridge University Press for the Hakluyt Society

———— (ed.) (1967) ibid. vol. 3, *The Voyage of the Resolution and Discovery 1776-1780* Cambridge: Cambridge University Press for the Hakluyt Society

———— (ed.) (1962) *The Endeavour Journal of Joseph Banks 1768-1771* 2 vols, Sydney: Public Library of NSW with Angus & Robertson

———— (1974) *The Life of Captain James Cook* London: Adam & Charles Black

Burnet, J. (Lord Monboddo) (1774) *Of the Origin and Progress of Language* vol. 1, Edinburgh: J. Balfour

Carter, H. B. (1978) 'Cook's Oxford Tutor: Sir Joseph Banks and European Expansion in the Pacific Region, 1767-1820', paper read at the Cook Conference, Simon Fraser University, April

Carver, J. (1779) *The New Universal Traveller* London: G. Robinson

Duchet, M. (1971) *Anthropologie et histoire au siècle des lumières* Paris: F. Maspero

Fénelon, F. de S. de la M. (1707) *The Adventures of Telemachus* 6th edn, London

Forster, G. (1968) A Voyage Round the World... London (1777), vol. 1 of *Georg Forsters Werke* Berlin: Akademie-Verlag

Forster, J. R. (1778) *Observations Made During a Voyage Round the World* London

Frost, A. (1980) *Convicts and Empire: A Naval Question 1776-1811* Melbourne: Oxford University Press

———— (1981) 'New South Wales as *terra nullius*: The British Denial of Aboriginal Land Rights' *Historical Studies* 19, 513-23

Gray, A. (ed.) (1937) *William Dampier, A New Voyage Round the World* (1697) London: Adam & Charles Black

Harris, J. (1744-8) *Navigantium atque Itinerantium Bibliotheca* London: J. Campbell

Hawkesworth, J. (1773) *An Account of the Voyages Undertaken... For Making Discoveries in the Southern Hemisphere*, London: W. Strahan, T. Cadell

Historical Records of New South Wales (1893) Sydney

Jefferys, T. (compiler) (1760) *The Natural and Civil History of the French Dominions in North and South America* London

Lanyon-Orgill, P. A. (ed.) (1979) *Captain Cook's South Sea Vocabularies* London: Lanyon-Orgill

Parkinson, Sydney (1773) *A Journal of a Voyage to the South Seas* London: Stanfield Parkinson

Perrin, W. G. (ed.) (1928) *George Shelvocke, A Voyage Round the World* London: Cassell & Co.

Salmon, T. (1772) *A New Geographical and Historical Grammar* 12th edn (rev. W. Robertson), London: C. Bathurst, W. Strahan, etc.

Smith, B. (1960) *European Vision and the South Pacific 1768-1850* London: Oxford University Press

Wharton, W. J. L. (ed.) (1893) *Captain Cook's Journal During His First Voyage* . . . London: Elliot Stock

Williams, G. (1979) 'Seamen and Philosophers in the South Seas in the Age of Captain Cook' *The Mariner's Mirror* 65, pp. 3-22

Williamson, J. A. (ed.) (1939) *William Dampier, a Voyage to New Holland* London: Argonaut Press

FOUR

'SAVAGE SPORTSMEN'

James Urry

W.E.H. STANNER, SUMMARISING changing European attitudes to Aborigines after 1788, wrote:

In the early years of settlement insensibility towards the Aborigines' human status hardened into contempt, derision and indifference. The romantic idealism, unable to stand the shock of experience drifted through dismay into pessimism about the natives' capacity for civilisation (1979:145).

My object in this paper is to examine one aspect of this process of change, of the hardening of attitudes and the continued 'shock of experience', in spite of well-intentioned efforts to comprehend and to explain Aboriginal life-styles. My focus will be extremely narrow both in time and subject: I will merely consider the very early years of settlement and European attitudes to how Aborigines subsisted in the topsy-turvy world of the Europeans' Antipodean exile. Finally I will say something about why Aborigines have had such little effect on European/Australian culture and identity. As Stanner (1977) indicated, indifference emerged at the very outset of contact between Europeans and Aborigines with frightening consequences for the shocking history of Aboriginal and white relations which was to follow in the nineteenth century.

I

All the early accounts of Aborigines in the Sydney area by officers of the First Fleet stress the maritime orientation of the Aborigines they encountered. The Aborigines, they noted, were 'utter strangers' to the cultivation of the soil and were dependent upon gathering wild fruits and roots and particularly on fishing (Tench, 1789:80-1). But European perception of the Australian environment in the early years of settlement was also coloured by a maritime orientation. Stranded as the Europeans were on the eastern seaboard, distant from other European settlements, the early colonists looked to the sea not only as a source of sustenance but also as their only means of communication and 'civilisation'. Though expeditions were mounted into the interior, the desolate environment encountered and the apparent lack of water always forced exploration parties back to the security of the coast.

It is not surprising that the early Europeans thought the inland either uninhabited or at best sparsely populated. Watkin Tench wrote of an early inland expedition:

To their great surprize, they observed indisputable tracks of the natives having been lately there, though in their whole route none of them were to be seen; nor any means to be traced, by which they could procure subsistence so far from the sea shore (1789:105-6).

Many authors over the next twenty years were to make a similar distinction between coastal-grounds and inland Aborigines in the Sydney area. John Hunter stated in 1793:

All the human race, which we have seen here, appear to live chiefly on what the sea affords, and consequently we find the sea-coast, more fully inhabited than the interior, or that part of the country which we have had an opportunity of visiting more remote from the sea (1968[1793]:44).

Hunter continued:

In the months of March and April, we found the natives to decrease in their numbers considerably; but we have no reason to suppose that they retire back into the interior parts of the country; for in all the excursions which have been made inland, very few have been seen. The sea-coast, we have every reason present to believe, is the only part of this country which is inhabited by the human race; the land seems to afford them but a very scanty subsistence (1968[1793]:45).

Governor Phillip, however, did note the presence of Aborigines inland from the coast in a number of his early reports. He believed most subsisted by the chase and thus could not lead such an easy life as Aborigines on the coast. The presence of fires in the mountains he interpreted as signs of Aboriginal habitation (*Historical Records of Australia* Sydney, series 1, vol. 1, 1914: 30-1, 161). Yet it is surprising how long the idea of a barren, uninhabited interior persisted among Europeans in the Sydney area. In spite of increasing penetration of the inland and meetings with Aborigines, the major focus of attention remained the coastal region. Indeed the close associations which had developed between the colonists and the coastal Aboriginal bands helped to sustain the Europeans' limited vision of the interior. When a group of inland Aborigines attacked and robbed a group of Europeans in the late 1790s Barrington wrote:

They instantly made off into the woods; ... They were of the hunter or woodman's tribe, who were seldom among us, and consequently very little known (1801:25).

If there were Aborigines in the interior the problem for the Europeans was: how did they live? To Europeans fishing on the coasts could afford some form of livelihood for the Aborigines, but the barren interior, where Aborigines cultivated neither 'herb or animal', could not have provided an adequate source of human sustenance. A writer to the *Sydney Gazette* in 1804 examined the condition of the Aborigines and concluded the letter with the following words:

Thus, then, even though the supply of their immediate wants by chance research constitutes their only *civil* occupation, still it is mysterious how the hordes of the interior, who have not the advantage of fishing, can possibly supply those wants throughout the year without indulging in all terrible excesses of refined barbarity (*Sydney Gazette*, 4 June, 2(69)).

Among the 'terrible excesses of refined barbarity' the author had in mind was cannibalism. The only answer he could provide as to how peoples of the interior could survive was that they consumed their fellow beings. This explanation had other advantages than just accounting for their subsistence patterns; these cannibalistic habits also helped explain the low number of Aborigines in the interior as well as their barbaric state of savagery.

Many Europeans who penetrated inland in the 1800s, however, began to form new opinions of the peoples they encountered. George Caley, who made extensive natural history collections for Joseph Banks, reported in 1809 that inland Aborigines were extremely useful to collectors like himself. Not only did they know the country and the wildlife but they were also 'in general ... excellent marksmen and quicker sighted than our people' (Caley, 1966:177). Caley continued:

It is the inland or Bush natives that I have been representing, for the water natives have different customs, and are more confined to one place of abode. They know nothing of climbing trees, no farther than in getting up for to strip off the bark, for to make canoes, which the inland natives do dexterously (1966:178).

Tench also makes similar comments on the relative abilities of coastal and inland groups to climb trees (1793:125). At the same period another correspondent of the *Sydney Gazette*, who went under the pseudonym 'A Woodman', wrote two letters to the paper detailing the customs of inland Aborigines. Pointing out that he had penetrated the interior 'to a considerable distance' with Aboriginal guides, he provided details of the subsistence habits of the 'woodland tribes' which previously had been a mystery. He pointed out how skilful the Aborigines were at finding food, but noted that the diet consisted of grubs, reptiles, honey and the sugary deposits of ants. After contemplating such food the correspondent wrote:

we must acknowledge that Nature has been bountiful to all her children ... although I could myself have submitted to a death of famine rather than have partaken of a repast which upon a short experience sickened me to look at, yet she has providentially moulded their appetites to such subjects as she had provided them ... (*Sydney Gazette* 18 September 1808, 6(246)).

The two letters from 'A Woodman' provoked another writer (*Sydney Gazette* 6 November 1808, 6(253)), to verse over the customs of the Aborigines:

> *Your sage Correspondent affects to describe,*
> *The Habits that grace Australia's Black tribe;*
> *But* Habits *means* Dress, *you'll permit me to call,*
> *The Dress of HER Natives, — No Habit at all.*

Other Europeans, however, noted that the hunting of animals such as kangaroos was common in the interior. Francis Barrallier, who in 1802 had penetrated deep into the foothills of the Blue Mountains, reported that the Aborigines he encountered were skilful hunters and he presented a new breed of inland Aborigines he called the 'Mountaineers' who had different weapons from those nearer the coast and skin cloaks to keep them warm (Barrallier, 1975). It is obvious that as Europeans became aware of the differences between the Aborigines around their settlement, differences apparent in their customs, languages and modes of subsistence, so also they began to rank them according to particular characteristics. David Collins had already begun this process in 1798:

The natives who live in the woods and on the margins of rivers are compelled to seek a different subsistence [from those on the coasts] and are driven to a harder exercise of their abilities to procure it (1975[1798]:462).

Barrington stated that those Aborigines who 'reside in the woods' had longer limbs than those who lived on the coasts, perhaps because they were more used to climbing trees to collect honey and capture possums (Barrington, 1810:9). Hunting was obviously more invigorating and manly than fishing, and this was clearly reflected in the human physique and perhaps in the intellect of men of the inland. 'A Woodman' in his letter made the point quite clearly:

... the natives of the interior exhibit much stronger proofs of ingenuity than the tribes on the sea coast have occasion to exhibit [,] as the latter depend more upon the dexterity of their women in their mode of fishing than upon any exertion of their own (*Sydney Gazette* 21 August 1808, 6(242)).

Why then was there this change of vision? I would suggest that part of the reason lies in European notions of hunting at this period, which made the chase a worthy, noble and manly occupation.

II

Hunting has long had an ambivalent place in English thought. Hunting to provide the necessities for daily sustenance was generally acceptable, but the killing of beasts for sport and pleasure was condemned by many humanists from medieval times (Uhlig, 1970:89-98). The rituals of hunting and the imagery of the chase and the kill were not only used to glorify sportsmen in sixteenth-, seventeenth-, and eighteenth-century literature, but also as political allegory to condemn people in high office (see Miller, 1979/80, on Pope's *Windsor-Forest*). But hunting was to become a political and social issue itself from the end of the seventeenth century onwards as the sport of gentlemen was maintained only at the expense of the genuine needs of common people. As fields and common lands were enclosed to the advantage of a rural gentry, the monopoly of the right to hunt became an expression of the gentry's right to property itself; hunting rights were protected by the imposition of harsh game laws (Thompson, 1975). Though such legislation had existed in England since the Middle Ages, the Game Act of 1671 set the tone for legislation in the eighteenth and nineteenth centuries (Munsche, 1977, 1981b); hunting gradually became the prerogative of a particular class at the expense of another. Even within the hunting community, however, social differences emerged associated with differences in hunting techniques.

Two major traditions of hunting developed in English society from the end of the seventeenth century onwards. The 'hunt', where mounted riders, dressed in bright finery accompanied by packs of hounds, pursued game across the countryside, was an élite sport of aristocrats and the wealthier gentry. Maintaining suitable mounts and hound packs was an expensive and occasionally full-time occupation of many country gentlemen. The other major form of hunting, less gregarious, less colourful and also less pre-stigious, consisted of the solitary hunter stalking his prey, combining skill, instinct and intelligence, gun and dog at the ready. This was more the preserve of the lesser gentry and the independent farmer. During the eighteenth century both modes of hunting were to undergo change. In the late nineteenth century Oscar Wilde described an English country gentle-man out foxhunting as 'the unspeakable in full pursuit of the uneatable', but the historical development of the hunt during the eighteenth century might better be described as a progress from the edible to the inedible. At the start of the century stags were hunted, later hares were chased until, by the end of the century, foxes became the ultimate quarry. But the solitary hunter continued to shoot both for food and sport, although the preservation of foxes for the hunt in the nineteenth century was to be an endless source of conflict between shooters and local hunts as game birds were cultivated for shooting and were taken by foxes preserved for the hunt (Itzkowitz, 1977; Munsche, 1981a:97-8). Such conflicts reflected deeper class differences between foxhunters and shooters which developed in the eighteenth century. Shooting gained in respectability, however, during the eighteenth century with developments in gun technology which minimised the risks of injury to the shooter from his weapon and increased the accuracy of the firearm. By the late eighteenth century hunters could shoot moving targets, animals running and birds in flight, whereas previously these had been shot at rest or on the ground. In fact it was no longer legitimate for 'real' sportsmen to shoot stationary prey; it was just plain ungentlemanly and unsporting to shoot a sitting duck (Longrigg, 1977)!

Hunting by the late eighteenth century had become entwined in a complex set of social conventions which reflected differences in wealth, class and occupation. The chase was seen as a legitimate sport of gentlemen, a means by which they could exhibit their prowess, skill and social bearing (Itzkowitz, 1977). Military officers were encouraged to join hunts as it was believed hunting improved their martial arts and skill at riding (Itzkowitz, 1977:21). Hunting had also acquired by the end of the century an etiquette of its own, as well as an extensive paraphernalia of special dress, finely made guns, well-bred horses and hounds and servants skilled in the maintenance of animals and equipment. The poor object who was the attention of all this effort, the prey, was thus just the end to a means.

Hunting for some gentlemen was not just sport, but a way of life. Indeed, country gentlemen not only devoted their lives but also their fortunes to its pursuit. This cultural tradition had its own rich and colourful vocabulary; some terms are well known, but others sound exotic, if not slightly quaint, to modern ears. It is not at all surprising therefore, that those European gentlemen and military officers who came to Australia at the end of the eighteenth century were forced to use such terms when discussing the subsistence activities of Aborigines, nor that at times that they should wax lyrical upon the subject. Aborigines were sportsmen, involved in the chase after game; even if they were naked and had peculiar customs, no one could deny them this sense of dignity.

Although the gentlemen and officers in the early years of settlement may have wished for an idle life and the pleasure of the chase, the early conditions in the colonies prevented them from enjoying much sport. Certainly hunting was carried out extensively from the first days of settlement, but hunting for food soon became an essential part of everyday life. Supplies in the colony were short and the position of the colonists precarious; kangaroos and birds of every description became important sources of food (Davey, Macpherson & Clements, 1948). It is interesting that special men were appointed for this hunting; Governor Phillip had his own gamekeeper to stock his table. In fact this gamekeeper, John MacIntyre (or MacIntire or M'Entire), appears to have been far from popular with the Aborigines for reasons which remain obscure; they killed him with one of their particularly vicious spears in December 1790. Tench (1793:55, 70, 89-91) provides details of MacIntyre's relations with Aborigines and an account of his death. The fact that the huntsmen were called 'game keepers' is significant as people of such a social status engaged in a mundane profession were not to be confused with sportsmen (see Munsche, 1981a, on the status of gamekeepers). Although few of the convicts transported to Australia were poachers (Robson, 1965:210), some of those appointed as gamekeepers may have been convicted for poaching; MacIntyre, however, came from Durham and had been transported for larceny (Cobley, 1970:175).

Such hunting as a necessity continued for a long time in the Sydney area as did hunting for the collection of natural history specimens. Kangaroo meat was often offered for sale, though it was not particularly favoured by officers and gentlemen. The commercial exploitation of kangaroos for their skins appears to have been a later innovation, certainly after seal skins had begun to be collected in large numbers in Bass Strait. 'Crispinius', in a letter to the *Sydney Gazette* in 1806, recommended kangaroo skins for tanning and shortly afterwards skins in quite large quantities were offered for sale in the local paper (*Sydney Gazette* 23 March 1806, 4(158); 11 January 1807, 4(200); 15 January 1809, 7(263); 18 June 1809, 7(285)).

But hunting for pleasure and profit could be combined in the Sydney area by the 1800s. High quality dogs, often referred to as greyhounds, were offered for sale or were reported as lost in the newspapers (*Sydney Gazette* 2 September 1804, 2(79)). It also appears that 'seasons' for hunting certain types of birds were recognised as early as 1805 (*Sydney Gazette* 3 February 1805, 2(101)). Hunting purely for pleasure also had become a possibility by this date; another report in the *Sydney Gazette* from 1807 contains an account of a hunting party north of Sydney:

A novel spectacle afforded much diversion to a pleasure party last week who had made an excursion to Newcastle—Provided with excellent dogs, the kangaroo afforded a pleasant and profitable sport—One of the creatures, closely pursued, coursed to the water side; and despairing of escape, at length plunged in. One of the dogs continued the chase, regardless of the change of element, and seized the victim, which by diving avoided the unmannerly grasp. She appeared again upon the surface, and as soon as overtaken once more avoided as before the sanguinary tusk of the pursuer. A third time she rose; again she dived—but never more appeared (*Sydney Gazette* 23 August 1807, 5(226)).

It is obvious, therefore, that a sporting atmosphere existed among Europeans in the Sydney area at the time when penetration of the interior located Aboriginal hunting groups. Even if in the European vision of hunting there was a connection between the sport of civilised man and the activities of Aborigines, it was one mixed with a sense of ambivalence. As the letters of 'A Woodman' indicate, the inlanders were considered more 'manly' than the coastal peoples, but the glory of chasing kangaroos across open plains could not easily be reconciled with the idea of a people who relished grubs and lizards as delicious fare.

If the officers and gentlemen of Sydney had reservations about always seeing Aborigines as noble sportsmen, the illustrator of a book published in London in 1813 with the title *Field Sports ... of the Native Inhabitants of New South Wales* (Clark, 1813), had no doubts as to how to portray them. The illustrator, John Heaviside Clark, who had undoubtedly never seen an Aboriginal at first hand in the Australian environment (Rienits & Rienits, 1963:197), portrayed Aborigines as noble and savage sportsmen. The illustrations cover a number of aspects of Aboriginal life: dancing (*The Dance*), domesticity (*Repose*), and the martial arts—*Warriors of New S. Wales* and *Trial*, the latter picturing a man undergoing trial by combat, a common theme in accounts of Aborigines in the Sydney area; in these,

Plate 4.1   John Heaviside Clark (1813) *Fishing*

Aborigines appear in striking poses. The major illustrations, however, depict scenes of subsistence activities: two show fishing (plate 4.1), two possum-hunting in trees (plate 4.2), and finally two pictures are of major significance to this paper, *Throwing the Spear* and *Hunting the Kangaroo* (see plates 4.3 and 4.4).

Plate 4.2   John Heaviside Clark (1813) *Climbing Trees*

The picture *Throwing the Spear* shows Aborigines spearing birds, which in terms of their beaks resemble parrots but in the form of wing and tail shape clearly reflect the stylised form of European game birds, such as pheasants, pictured in early nineteenth-century hunting prints (Coombs, 1978:162). The important point is that the birds are being speared on the wing, just as European sportsmen shot game birds in flight (Mann, 1811:46). The analogy is obviously with game shooting. In the picture of *Hunting the Kangaroo* the animals have been coursed to water by the hunters who are spearing them before they run to cover in the forest. The allusion is undoubtedly to fox hunting, and this view is strengthened by the drawings of the kangaroos. The shape of the kangaroo's heads, with pointed ears, long muzzles and sharp teeth, the body shapes and length of limbs as well as the tails with their white flashes, all resemble illustrations of foxes rather than kangaroos.

These pictures, however, reflect perhaps the final vision of Aborigines as noble savages, drawn at a safe distance from the scene of the action. It is significant that the illustrations were published in 1813, the same year as the great barrier of the Blue Mountains was first crossed, and European visions of the possibilities of Australia were radically altered. For the first time

Plate 4.3   John Heaviside Clark (1813) *Throwing the Spear*

settlers could break out of the confines of the coastal regions and open the vast interior of eastern Australia to exploitation. Australia was to be transformed from an Antipodean exile into a land of riches. The gentleman was to give way to the squatter, the woodman to the bushman and the vision of Aborigines was never to be the same again.

III

Many of the contemporary sources quoted so far have used a number of interesting terms not only to describe hunters and hunting, but also Aborigines and the countryside in which they lived. George Caley spoke of the inland Aborigines as 'Bush natives' (1966:178) and in fact the term 'bush', as used to describe the uncultivated hinterland of Australia, occurs increasingly from 1800 onwards. 'Bush', probably derived from the Dutch 'bosch', in the eighteenth century referred to country covered in natural forest which was uncleared and untilled. The term 'brush' was also used, as

Plate 4.4   John Heaviside Clark (1813) *Hunting the Kangaroo*

also was the word 'woods', and all these terms were in common use in America and the Cape of Good Hope settlement at the same period ('bush' in *OED*, and Mathews, 1951:225). In fact in Australia these three terms— 'bush', 'brush', and 'wood'—were all in use throughout the nineteenth century, with 'bush' eventually becoming the most common (Baker, 1966:ch. 4; Wilkes, 1978:65). The files of the Australian National Dictionary (in preparation) record many more usages of these terms from the early years of settlement.

In this connection one should also observe the term 'woodman'. It was the pseudonym of the letter writer on the Aborigines, and Barrington referred to inland Aborigines as belonging to the 'hunter or woodman' tribe. One meaning of this term in the eighteenth century was that of hunter, a person who hunts in a wood or forest (*OED*). One immediately recalls 'backwoodsman', a term common in America from the early eighteenth century to describe European colonists, along with 'frontiersman' (Mathews, 1951:59). The classic Australian term also springs to mind—'bushman'— but this term has very different connotations from the American. Why is this so?

Here we must distinguish, as does Russel Ward in his classic study of the Australian legend (1958:1-2 etc.; 1971:182), between the typical (ideal) bushman (and backwoodsman) and the average (actual) bushman (and backwoodsman). Both have accretions of myth: the bushman through the poetry of Lawson and Paterson and the backwoodsman through the novels of James Fennimore Cooper and others (Slotkin, 1973). In the idealised vision, the backwoodsman has a great deal of Indian culture and lore as part of his character, but in contrast the Australian bushman has little, or no, Aboriginality in his makeup. If there is a relationship between the ideal and the actual, then why should there be such a difference?

Ward has noted that the Australian bushman 'was callously brutal to the Aborigines to whom he owed so much of his knowledge' (1958:76). While this callousness toward Aborigines can be well documented, the indebtedness to Aboriginal knowledge about the country is more difficult to substantiate. As Ward indicates, the 'actual' bushmen developed after 1820 beyond the Blue Mountains, out onto the western plains. The skills utilised by bushmen were developed in response to the Australian environment. The skills included not just the ability to survive in a harsh environment but also the ability to exploit the country for economic return and the avoidance of control by bureaucratic governments in distant cities. Riding horses, cutting timber, splitting gumwood, managing bullock carts, shearing sheep etc., were not exactly indigenous skills of the Aborigines. As an early Australian song, *The Old Bullock Dray* (quoted in Ward, 1958:99), expressed it:

So it's roll up your blankets, and let us make a push,
I'll take you up the country, and show you round the bush;
I'll take you round the stations and learn you how to ride,
And I'll show you how to muster when we cross th' Great Divide.

It is perhaps indicative of this lack of knowledge of Aborigines that the very few Aboriginal language terms which entered the vocabulary of the bushmen and the later Australian dialect are nearly all derived from the Aboriginal language of the Sydney area, Dharuk. Though a few local terms were added to the English of new colonies in Victoria, South Australia, Queensland and Western Australia, most did not become part of the general Australian vocabulary. Terms such as 'corroboree', 'gin', 'gunyah', 'koala', 'nulla nulla', 'woomera', etc. are all Dharuk (Baker, 1966:ch. 15, Dixon, 1980:69-70); only the word 'kangaroo', collected by Cook from Guugu Yimidhirr speakers in northern Queensland (Haviland, 1974) and reintroduced to Australia by the first colonists in the mistaken belief that all Aborigines spoke the same language, has become enshrined in the general Australian vocabulary. It was Europeans who spread these mostly Dharuk terms across Australia so that Aborigines, living thousands of miles away from Sydney and speaking languages entirely different from Dharuk, incorporated these terms into their English and occasionally into their own languages (see also Donaldson, this volume). For their part the bushmen appear to have picked up very few additional terms from the hundreds of different Aboriginal languages and dialects they encountered in various parts of Australia. Most appear to have believed, as many Australians alas still do, that there was but one Aboriginal language on the continent and that the 'perverted and mangled' pidgin English used by whites in talking to Aborigines somehow neatly matched the 'childish babblings' of 'savages' (Strehlow, 1947:xviii, quoted in Dixon, 1980:71). By rejecting Aboriginal languages, the bushmen thus failed to comprehend the rich local knowledge that Aborigines could share with them concerning the country and the resources they had come to possess, and they failed to appreciate the Aboriginal sense of identity with the landscape and its mythology, expressed in ritual, song and dance.

This point concerning language is important for many reasons. It would appear to indicate that the strongest rapprochement between Aborigines and Europeans occurred in the very early years of settlement and, as Stanner has indicated, 'the collapsed romanticism turned into violence, the realism into indifference, and the sardonicism into contempt' (1977:23). From the outset of widespread European expansion into Australia the Aboriginal was denied a position in the vision of the landscape and a place in European/Australian culture. It was very different in America. Hallowell noted what he called the 'backwash of the frontier' in which the American Indian contributed substantially to American culture:

Our contacts with the Indians have affected our speech, our economic life, our clothing, our sports and recreations, certain indigenous religious cults, many of our curative practices, folk and concert music, the novel, poetry, drama, even some of our basic psychological attitudes ... (1957:231).

One could be naive and blame the Aborigines themselves for failing to find a place in the wider Australian culture and character from the outset of settlement. It could be argued that Aborigines are not American Indians, that they were merely hunter-gatherers who had little to contribute materially or spiritually to white 'civilisation'. Of course, such a point of view cannot be sustained; Aborigines certainly possess a considerable knowledge of the land and its resources, have a deep spiritual appreciation of it and could have shared this if Europeans had but listened. The answer to why Aborigines are not in the larger Australian culture or character must therefore be sought elsewhere. I would suggest that one needs to look to the nature of the early bushman himself and the context in which the major areas of Australia were settled in the nineteenth century.

As Ward (1958:ch. 4) has shown, the early bushmen were predominantly convicts or their immediate descendants, the so-called 'Currency Lads'. These men's backgrounds lie precisely in that area and period I have been discussing: the Sydney region between 1788 and 1810. Here they developed their own particular social and technical skills which they were later to use with such effect on the Australian frontier in the later nineteenth century. But these skills were developed with minimal contribution from Aborigines. While there were certainly some convicts who chose to take up the Aboriginal way of life, most kept themselves separate from both Aborigines and the ruling elite. Indeed, if we are to believe early accounts, Aborigines and the gentlemen and officers got on quite well together: sport in hunting being but one of their common interests. At the same time there is indisputable evidence of very bad relations between Aborigines and convicts from the first years of settlement, with killings on both sides. Aborigines were also used to track escapees and to inform on convicts, activities which certainly did not endear them to convicts and indeed violated one of the convicts' important moral codes: 'not informing on your mates'. So the early bushman took to the frontier not only a spirit of self-sufficiency and independence, but also a sense of disdain and deep distrust of Aborigines.

The context is equally important. Australia was not settled in the same way, nor at the same period as the Americas. Eastern America was settled from the seventeenth century onwards by yeoman farmers who in terms of technology and economy were not markedly different from their Indian neighbours. Hunting was an essential part of this economy for both Europeans and Indians and together they established a new economy, trapping. But Australia was settled in the throes of the Industrial Revolution and at a time of social turmoil. The settlement of the inland of Australia was achieved through the blatant exploitation of the country and its resources. There were no indigenous resources such as furs to be exploited on any scale, as there were in the Americas, and kangaroo skins were not as marketable as the golden fleece of imported sheep. The sealing industry had no real impact on the majority of mainland Aborigines. Nothing could stand in the way of quick profit and the pastoralism of the whites and the hunting and gathering economy of the Aborigines were soon at odds. For a brief moment the 'woodman' of the Sydney area, hunting for both profit and sport with Aborigines, may have resembled the American backwoodsman, but the bushman of the pastoral frontier of later years was a very different creature indeed.

IV

The 'savage sportsman' was a localised European image of the Noble Savage, created out of the larger European imagination, circumscribed by visions of the chase and tempered by actual contact with Aborigines in eastern Australia. But it was an image which was not to last for long, nor was it to make a major contribution to the development of Australian conceptions of character and place. The image of the bushman was an indigenous development, which was built in part on European notions, but had little in common with either the romantic associations of European literary traditions or the particularities of Aboriginal custom. It was created from an epistemological break with European mores and customs at a period when European attitudes and thought were in turmoil. Thus Aborigines in the European imagination gave way to new visions of Aborigines within Australia itself; the Australian imagination was to replace the European.

Acknowledgements

I would like to thank Fred McCarthy for references to Aborigines in the Sydney area, Joan Hughes of the Australian National Dictionary project for allowing me to consult entries on the early use of English in Australia, and Russel Ward for his comments on an earlier draft.

Bibliography

Baker, S. J.   (1966) *The Australian Language* Sydney: Currawong

Barrallier, F.   (1975) *Journey of an Expedition into the Interior of New South Wales 1802* Melbourne: Marsh Walsh

Barrington, G.   (1801) *A Sequel to Barrington's Voyage to New South Wales ...* London: C. Lowndes

——— (1810) *The History of New South Wales...* London: M. Jones

Caley, G.   (1966) *Reflections on the Colony of New South Wales* Melbourne: Lansdowne Press

Clark, J. H.   (1813) *Field Sports ... of the Native Inhabitants of New South Wales ...* London: Edward Orme [Reprinted as a supplement to *Foreign Field Sports, Fisheries, Sporting Anecdotes etc.*, London, 1814]

Cobley, J.   (1970) *The Crimes of the First Fleet Convicts* Sydney: Angus & Robertson

Collins, D.   (1975 [1798]) *An Account of the English Colony in New South Wales ...* Sydney: A. H. & A. W. Reed

Coombs, D.   (1978) *Sport and the Countryside in English Paintings, Watercolours and Prints* Oxford: Phaidon

Davey, L., M. Macpherson and F. W. Clements   (1948) 'The Hungry Years, 1788-1792' *Historical Studies* 3, pp. 187-208

Dixon, R. M. W.   (1980) *The Languages of Australia* Cambridge: Cambridge University Press

Hallowell, A. I.   (1957) 'The Backwash of the Frontier: The Impact of the Indian on American Culture' in W. D. Wyman and C. B. Kroeber (eds) *The Frontier in Perspective* Madison: University of Wisconsin Press

Haviland, J. B.   (1974) 'A Last Look at Cook's Guugu Yimidhirr Word List' *Oceania* 44, pp. 216-32

Hunter, J.   (1968 [1793]) *An Historical Account of Events at Sydney and at Sea, 1787-1792* Sydney: Angus & Robertson

Itzkowitz, D. C.   (1977) *Peculiar Privilege: A Social History of English Foxhunting 1753-1885* Hassocks: Harvester Press

Longrigg, R.   (1977) *The English Squire and his Sport* London: Michael Joseph

Mann, D. D.   (1811) *The Present Picture of New South Wales* London: John Booth

Mathews, M. M.   (ed.) (1951) *A Dictionary of Americanisms* Chicago: Chicago University Press

Miller, R. A.   (1979/80) 'Regal Hunting: Dryden's Influence on *Windsor-Forest*' *Eighteenth-Century Studies* 13, pp. 169-88

Munsche, P. B.   (1977) 'The Game Laws in Wiltshire 1750-1800' in J. S Cockburn (ed.) *Crime in England 1550-1800* London: Methuen

——— (1981a) 'The Game Keeper and English Rural Society, 1660-1830' *Journal of British Studies* 20, pp. 82-105.

——— (1981b) *Gentlemen and Poachers: The English Game Laws 1671-1831* Cambridge: Cambridge University Press

Rienits, R. and T. Rienits   (1963) *Early Artists of Australia* Sydney: Angus & Robertson

Robson, L. L. (1965), *The Convict Settlers of Australia* Melbourne: Melbourne University Press

Slotkin, R. (1973) *Regeneration through Violence: The Mythology of the American Frontier, 1600-1860* Middletown, Conn.: Wesleyan University Press

Stanner, W. E. H. (1977) '"The History of Indifference thus Begins"' *Aboriginal History* 1, pp. 3-26

_____ (1979) 'Caliban Discovered' in *White Man Got No Dreaming: Essays 1938-1973* Canberra: Australian National University Press

Strehlow, T. G. H. (1947) *Aranda Traditions* Melbourne: Melbourne University Press

Tench, W. (1789) *A Narrative of the Expedition to Botany Bay* ... London: J. Debrett

_____ (1793) *A Complete Account of the Settlement at Port Jackson* ... London: G. Nicol

Thompson, E. P. (1975) *Whigs and Hunters: the Origin of the Black Act* London: Allen Lane

Uhlig, C. (1970) '"The Sobbing Deer": *As You Like It* II.i. 21-66, and the Historical Context', in S. Schoenbaum (ed.) *Renaissance Drama* Evanston: Northwestern University Press

Ward, Russel (1958) *The Australian Legend* Melbourne: Oxford University Press

_____ (1971) 'The *Australian Legend* Revised' *Historical Studies* 18, pp. 171-90

Wilkes, G. A. (1978) *A Dictionary of Australian Colloquialisms* London: Routledge, Kegan Paul

FIVE

THE DARWINIAN PERSPECTIVE

D. J. Mulvaney

THE PREMIERS OF Victoria and South Australia in 1900 reacted positively to a petition signed by seventy-seven members of Britain's Liberal political and liberal academic establishment. It was organised and written by James Frazer, author of *The Golden Bough*, in an attempt to promote a transcontinental anthropological expedition by Spencer and Gillen. Frazer (1900) informed the two colonial governments that 'it is to Australia, more perhaps than to any other quarter of the globe, that anthropologists are now looking for the solution of certain problems of great moment in the early history of society and religion'.

Frazer wrote with the authority of forty post-Darwinian years of evolutionary theory, bolstered by the prestigious signatures of Asquith, Edward B. Tylor, James Lubbock (Lord Avebury), Francis and G. H. Darwin, John Evans, A. C. Haddon, Andrew Lang, W. H. R. Rivers and numerous other luminaries of natural and social science. To judge from the prominence of Australian exemplars in the writings of some of the signatories, and of the role which Aboriginal society played in the later influential models erected by Durkheim and Radcliffe-Brown, Frazer's pretentious document possessed some validity.

European scientific imagination was stimulated by Australian Aboriginal society, or rather by the preconceptions which armchair theorists brought to the analysis of anthropological data. Unfortunately, at a period when the racial superiority of Europeans was assumed and the right of colonists to supplant indigenes was justified in the name of progress, this scientific image of savage society both provided these doctrines with an academic underpinning and also influenced native welfare policies.

In several essays I have examined the influence of evolutionary theory in the Aboriginal context, and I restrict myself here to a few interpretative comments (Mulvaney, 1958; 1971; 1981). I have selected individuals as representative of diverse approaches by many scholars.

It was the apostle of Darwinism, T. H. Huxley, who first directed scientific attention to the presumed relevance of Australia for problems of human evolution. Writing in Lyell's *The Geological Evidences of the Antiquity of Man*, Huxley compared the recently discovered Neanderthal cranium with Australian specimens (1863: 86-9). He also observed that Aboriginal material culture resembled that of prehistoric Europeans. These hints were soon elaborated by others. Physical anthropologists assumed that the Aboriginal typified mankind at an early evolutionary stage.

The German anatomist, H. Klaatsch, typified evolutionary science of this era. Klaatsch visited Australia to study Aboriginal origins in the field. 'Many years previously I had begun my studies by examining skulls', he stated (1907: 577), 'and had noted the close similarity existing between the skulls of Australian aboriginals and those of primitive man in Europe, that was first pointed out by Professor Huxley'. It is relevant that he studied tree-climbing techniques, which were 'the rule amongst the primitive man-like apes'. Klaatsch also concluded (1923: 103, 108, 136), that Aboriginal language constituted 'fragments of the primitive speech of man', and that the race was a 'stationary remnant of primitive humanity'.

Few European colonists would have disputed his verdict. Klaatsch was a lecturer at the 1907 congress of the Australasian Association for the Advancement of Science. Another speaker was W. Ramsay Smith, later part-author of the influential entry on Aborigines in the first edition of the *Australian Encyclopaedia*. Smith (1907: 574) informed the audience that, of all human races, 'Australian aboriginals have furnished the largest number of ape-like characters. The more one investigates the truer does this statement prove to be'.

It was this uncritical enthusiasm of anatomists for collecting Aboriginal skulls which ensured such a mindless harvest of robbed graves during the early decades of this century. The present generation of prehistorians is paying a high penalty, for Aboriginal people regard excavations with disfavour.

If Aborigines were living physical relics from the dawn of human time, so too was their culture. Huxley merely had noted the parallels between present and past traces. Social evolutionists were more emphatic: 'living representatives of our common ancestors', pronounced Pitt-Rivers in 1867 (Myres, 1906: 50). Australian material culture stood in the same relation to that of prehistoric Europe, he concluded, as 'the mollusca of recent species to the mollusca of the primary geological period'. In his much quoted aphorism of 1865, Sir John Lubbock concluded that 'the Van Diemener and the South American are to the antiquary what the opposum and the sloth are to the geologist'. This was in his *Pre-Historic Times, as Illustrated by*

Ancient Remains and the Manners and Customs of Modern Savages, itself a significant title (1865: 336).

Pitt-Rivers treated artefacts as 'human ideas ... capable of classification into genera, species and varieties in the same manner as the products of the vegetable and animal kingdoms, and in their development from the homogeneous to the heterogeneous they obey the same laws' (1874: xii). Following his circular logic, he classified his types on a preconceived scale of progression, although all his specimens were approximately contemporary. Thus, Pitt-Rivers classed Australian weapons invariably 'lowest in the scale, because they assimilate most closely to the natural forms' (Myres, 1906: 11).

Comparable reasoning lay behind E. B. Tylor's belief (1893) that the Tasmanians were 'representatives of Palaeolithic Man'. Baldwin Spencer, the Melbourne biologist, had been Tylor's student and had assisted him to transfer the Pitt-Rivers ethnographic collection to its new Oxford museum. Not surprisingly, therefore, when Spencer produced a *Guide to the Australian Ethnographical Collection*, one year after assuming the honorary directorship of the National Museum of Victoria, he arranged his collections in the manner of the threads-and-patches vision of Pitt-Rivers: 'For example, the forms of shields used in different tribes are shown in one case, boomerangs in another, sacred ... objects in another' (Spencer, 1901: 5). In this manner not only visitors to European museums, but Australians also, were presented with a de-humanised and non-integrated display of Aboriginal society, in which simplicity rather than cultural complexity was the keynote. Visitors to Spencer's museum in 1901 were instructed that Aborigines 'may be regarded as a relic of the early childhood of mankind left stranded ... in a low condition of savagery'. In his time, Spencer was the acknowledged world authority on Aborigines, so it is significant that his enlarged *Guide* still presented the same simplistic interpretation into the thirties, and the display described survived the second world war (Spencer, 1901: 12; 1922; 13).

Understandably, Aboriginal mentality was held to parallel their primitive anatomy and elementary material culture. The journal of the Anthropological Institute in 1872 published a revealingly titled paper by C. S. Wake, on 'the mental characteristics of primitive man, as exemplified by the Australian Aborigines', in which discussion he included art. 'In all questions of morality, and ... the emotional nature', Wake concluded, the Aborigines were 'mere children', lacking powers of abstract reasoning. 'They represent the childhood of humanity itself, revealing to us the condition of mankind ... not ... long after man's first appearance on the earth' (Wake, 1872: 75, 79, 83).

Social theorists directed most attention to social institutions, with kinship, marriage systems and totemism being pre-eminent. Lorimer Fison and

A. W. Howitt became Australian postal anthropologists through the seventies and eighties. Their questionnaires were inspired by Lewis Henry Morgan, the author of *Ancient Society*, whose evolutionary stadial model influenced Engels to produce the Marxist classic, *The Origin of the Family*. Morgan encouraged the two Australians with the exhortation to Fison that 'in Australia . . . you are . . . nearer to the primitive condition of man than any other investigator'. Howitt, who had educated himself on Lyell, Darwin and Lubbock, was a receptive client (Mulvaney, 1971: 295).

After the death of Morgan, the partners later worked under the guidance of Tylor in a search for 'survivals' of custom; but it was the Spencer and Gillen team, under James Frazer's patronage, which most influenced overseas perception of the Aborigines. Significantly, Frazer said of their *The Native Tribes of Central Australia*, that it was 'a document of priceless value for the understanding of the evolution of human thought and society' (Frazer 1899: 281). Spencer was a scientist who evidently recorded what he saw and, therefore, Frazer inferred that his work was a strictly objective example of inductive method. Presumably it was his friend Spencer whom Frazer later had in mind when he disparaged romantic theorists such as Rousseau, by claiming for contemporary anthropology 'the soberer, duller task . . . in the patient accumulation of facts' (Frazer, 1905: 7). Certainly Frazer's savage Australians were devoid of nobility and even personality, as they acted out their fossilised lives in a primeval world of magic and taboo.

The apparent scientific basis of Spencer's work constituted its appeal to his generation of social theorists. Like them, he was trained in the first generation after Darwin. Yet, he was the embodiment of the fieldworkers described by Burridge, who 'do not go into the field with empty heads and without prejudice. They take with them what has been implanted in them; they go because of what has been implanted in them' (1973: 5).

Two letters from Baldwin Spencer to Frazer characterise the preconceptions which guided his methodology and preformed the 'facts' which Frazer and other armchair anthropologists assembled. It was in his first deferential contact with Frazer in 1897 that Spencer observed (Marett & Penniman, 1932: 9-10):

I need hardly say that the *Golden Bough* has been most useful to me. Of course Gillen and I have worked a great deal together up in the Centre, but most of the actual finding out of things has of necessity to be done by him. I send him up endless questions and things to find out, and by mutual agreement he reads no one else's work so as to keep him quite unprejudiced in the way of theories.

After their friendship had firmed, Spencer criticised the basis of A. W. Howitt's research amongst the detribalised people of Gippsland. Implicit in Spencer's comments is the assumption that his Alice Springs informants were 'uncontaminated' sources, despite the three decades of violent culture contact which must have exerted strong influences. In 1902, Spencer told Frazer that at the period when Howitt collected data about the mythological figures Baiame and Daramulun, 'the importance of securing minute and detailed information was really not realized, nor was it imagined that there were men without any so-called religious ideas' (Marett & Penniman, 1932: 76). A year later, Spencer emphasised that 'Howitt's own experience lies mainly amongst the most modified tribes . . . in fact in those days with no such work as yours and Tylor's to guide him, there was little to show him what to look for in this line . . .' (Marett & Penniman, 1932: 79).

Consider the significance of the emerged scientific perception of Aboriginal society. Obviously, it provided motivation and models for local researchers, while their data rewarded their patrons. By Edwardian times, Aboriginal society had emerged as the type of early man. Disembodied concepts and formulae drawn from Australia, chiefly via Howitt and Spencer and Gillen, played an essential role of presumed authentication in influential and widely read sociological and kindred works, such as James Frazer's *Golden Bough*, Andrew Lang's *The Secret of the Totem*, E. A. Westermarck's *The History of Human Marriage*, Ernest Crawley's *The Mystic Rose*, and R. R. Marett's *The Threshold of Religion*. In addition to the influence of Australian data on Durkheim and Levy-Bruhl, Australian ethnography entered the corpus of European Palaeolithic art through S. Reinach, and determined half a century of its interpretation (Ucko & Rosenfeld, 1967: 123-38).

At a less academic level, evolutionary anthropology offered comforting solutions for racist assumptions and prejudices long held by laymen. Symbolically, perhaps, in 1859 a Victorian parliamentary inquiry wearing the blinkers of protestant morality concluded that Aborigines were devoid of any religious concepts (Votes and Proceedings, 1858-9: 69-70). Frazer's 'scientific' world view of religious origins confirmed such preconceptions, because Aboriginal minds were steeped in his earlier magical stage. It is relevant that Baldwin Spencer emphasised magic; he never included religion as a subject entry in the index of any book.

It was a commonplace of European colonisation theory that indigenous people of lowly economic status should be dispossessed and that extinctions were inevitable. Humanitarians such as Florence Nightingale were concerned to find ways to preserve Aboriginal lives, but they obviously believed that there were both mystical and physiological reasons, together with cultural inferiority, which predisposed Aborigines to death (Nightingale, 1864: 552-8). After Darwin, the problem was converted into a law of nature. Pitt-Rivers expressed it frankly in 1867 when he spoke of 'the law which consigns to destruction all savage races when brought in contact with a civilization', and declared that 'The savage is morally and mentally an unfit instrument for the spread of civilization' (Myres 1906: 54). In Australia, Fison, Howitt and Spencer all shared the opinion that Aboriginal racial extinction would prove rapid and total. Despite their evident personal humanitarian concern, a pseudo-scientific assumption prevailed in their view of this outcome as inevitable (for example, Fison & Howitt, 1880: 185).

Such opinions accorded with popular anticipation, but they also provided its scientific justification. The shreds-and-patches evolutionary taxonomy effectively dehumanised Aboriginal society, so that even the rich and complex ceremonial and artistic life was misunderstood and assumed to reflect simplistic primeval minds. Hence, the great appeal of Spencer and Gillen to interpreters of European Palaeolithic cave art during the early decades of this century.

While the Australian anthropologists remained in contact with their informants (whom they frequently failed to name as persons), their individual case studies often contain circumstantial human details and cultural values. Not so with the European theorists, to whom anonymous savages were pieces in the jig-saw of social evolution. Data culled from Australia became social fact, discrete units, unrelated to the communities in which they originated. 'The prime want . . . is not so much theories as facts' claimed the assured Frazer, who never confronted a savage in his life (1905: 5).

This abstract manner in which Aboriginal Australia was perceived from Europe as a factual storehouse was exemplified by Tylor, in a letter to Spencer (1902). Spencer held that Aborigines made no connection between sexual intercourse and conception. 'I have been consulting . . . naturalists as to whether any mammal except man has any proveable knowledge of such connexion of the facts', Tylor stated, 'the opinion seems to be that only man recognises coition and birth as antecedent and consequent. If the state of mind of your tribes seem to go with that of the lower mammalia, the point is . . . vitally important to anthropology . . .'. Tylor previously had deplored the extinction of the Tasmanians more upon pragmatic than humanitarian grounds. 'Looking at the vestiges of a people so representative of the rudest type of man, anthropologists must join with philanthropists in regretting their unhappy fate . . . We are now beginning to see what scientific value there would have been in . . . a minute careful portraiture of their thoughts and customs' (preface to Roth, 1890: vii).

It is appropriate to close this sketch of Aboriginal Man's place in nature according to evolutionary anthropology, with an official government record. It illustrates the impact of Darwinian ideas upon the Aborigines during the fifty years following publication of *Origin of Species*.

The Commonwealth government sent Baldwin Spencer to Darwin for the year 1912 to frame recommendations for native welfare administration, following Commonwealth control of the Northern Territory. Spencer's report was tabled in Parliament during 1913. It contained many humanitarian recommendations, but the philosophy which informed it has a familiar ring. In formulating any programme, Spencer instructed Parliament, 'the mental and moral characteristics of the aboriginals . . . must be understood and taken into account'. He described Aborigines as 'a very curious mixture; mentally, about the level of a child who has little control over his feelings . . . no sense of responsibility and, except in rare cases, no initiative' (Spencer, 1913: 13-14).

The policy of paternalism, justified by the scientific evidence of anthropology, was thereby enunciated. The paternalistic message was taken, except that the government failed to provide the funding recommended by Spencer to implement his quite far-reaching, though authoritarian, policies. However, the social philosophy of the following half century of Aboriginal welfare drew much from the pseudo-science of Australian evolutionary anthropology.

Bibliography

Burridge, K. (1973) *Aborigines Observed* New York: Pergamon

Fison, L. and A. W. Howitt (1880) *Kamilaroi and Kurnai* Melbourne: Robertson

Frazer, J. G. (1899) 'Observations on Central Australian Totemism' *Journal of the Anthropological Institute* 28, pp. 281-6

_____ (1900) 'To the Government of Victoria', four-page petition, in author's possession

_____ (1905) *Lectures on the Early History of Kingship* London: Macmillan

Klaatsch, H. (1907) 'Some Notes on Scientific Travel amongst the Black Population of Tropical Australia in 1904, 1905, 1906' *Australasian Association for the Advancement of Science* 9, pp. 577-91

_____ (1923) *The Evolution and Progress of Mankind* London: Unwin

Lubbock, J. (1865) *Pre-Historic Times, as Illustrated by Ancient Remains and the Manners and Customs of Modern Savages* London: Williams & Norgate

Lyell, C. (1863) *The Geological Evidences of the Antiquity of Man* London: Murray

Marett, R. R. and T. K. Penniman (eds) (1932) *Spencer's Scientific Correspondence* Oxford: Clarendon Press

Mulvaney, D. J. (1958) 'The Australian Aborigines 1606-1929, Opinion and Fieldwork' *Historical Studies Australia and New Zealand* 8: pp. 131-51, 297-314

_____ (1971) 'The Ascent of Aboriginal Man: Howitt as Anthropologist' in M. H. Walker *Come Wind, Come Weather* Melbourne: Melbourne University Press

_____ (1981) 'Gum Leaves on The Golden Bough: Australia's Palaeolithic Survivals Discovered' in J. D. Evans and C. Renfrew (eds) *Antiquity and Man* London: Thames and Hudson

Myres, J. L. (ed.) (1906) *The Evolution of Culture and Other Essays* Oxford: Clarendon Press

Nightingale, F. (1864) 'Note on the Aboriginal Races in Australia' *National Association for the Promotion of Social Science Transactions* pp. 552-8

Pitt-Rivers, A. L. (1874) *Catalogue of the Anthropological Collection* London: Eyre & Spottiswood

Roth, H. L. (1890) *The Aborigines of Tasmania* Halifax: King

Smith, W. R. (1907) 'The Role of the Australian Aboriginal in Recent Anthropological Research' *Australasian Association for the Advancement of Science* 11, pp. 558-76

Spencer, W. B. (1901) *Guide to the Australian Ethnographic Collection in the National Museum of Victoria* Melbourne: Government Printer

_____ (1913) 'Preliminary Report on the Aboriginals of the Northern Territory' *Bulletin of the Northern Territory* 7

_____ (1922) *Guide to the Australian Ethnographic Collection in the National Museum of Victoria* Melbourne: Government Printer

Tylor, E. B. (1893) 'On the Tasmanians as Representatives of Palaeolithic Man' *Journal of the Anthropological Institute* 23, pp. 141-52

_____ (1902) Letter to W. B. Spencer 13 Nov. 1902, National Museum of Victoria, Spencer Collection, box 21-1/3

Ucko, P. J. and A. Rosenfeld (1967) *Palaeolithic Cave Art* London: Weidenfeld & Nicolson

Votes and Proceedings Legislative Council of Victoria (1858-59), Select Committee on Aborigines

Wake, C. S. (1872) 'The Mental Characteristics of Primitive Man, as Exemplified by Australian Aborigines' *Journal of the Anthropological Institute* 1, pp. 74-84

SIX

HEARING THE
FIRST AUSTRALIANS

Tamsin Donaldson

I

I HAVE CHOSEN to illustrate European responses to Australian languages with particular reference to two closely related languages of New South Wales. Between 200 and 250 distinct languages were probably being spoken at the time Europeans began to settle in Australia; my sample is therefore a small one. The history of responses to these two language is nevertheless revealing. Speakers of both languages encountered exploring Europeans relatively early, though the patterns of subsequent contact were to be rather different in each case. One, Wiradjuri, was once spoken in a number of dialects over a huge area, almost two-thirds of the length of the state, which soon became extensively settled by Europeans. The other, Ngiyampaa, is still spoken further to the west by a few people who grew up in an arid corner of their ancestral country where there are still no towns. Since the time of first contact, only a handful of people have published word-lists and a small amount of other linguistic information collected from speakers of these languages. This is fairly characteristic of what has happened right across the continent (Dixon, 1980: 8-17). While working with the Ngiyampaa speakers on their language over the last few years, I have gone through most of this material with them. With the help of their reactions, I shall try to reconstruct why the records for both languages are as they are.

A. D. Hope has a light-hearted poem in which he enjoys the sound of various place names. It starts:

> *I glean them from signposts in these country places*
> *Weird names, some beautiful, more that make me laugh.*

Later come the lines:

> *When the wrath of God is loosed upon Gilgandra*
> *And Gulargambone burns red against the west,*
> *To Sweet Water Creek at Mullengandra*
> *I shall rise and flee away and be at rest.*

(COUNTRY PLACES, 1975:59)

Of these particular places, Gulargambone is in Ngiyampaa country, while Gilgandra and Mullengandra, like a number of the others mentioned in the poem, are in Wiradjuri country. The sounds of such names strike the poet's imagination primarily as 'weird' rather than Wiradjuri; whether he finds them beautiful or comic, the playful associations that he creates for them are all derived from English-speaking cultural tradition. Gilgandra becomes another Gomorrah, and it is the connotations of the English name of Sweet Water Creek which allow the onomatopoeic interpretation of Mullengandra as a place of rest. But the names do not only have this sort of onomatopoeic power of suggestion. They also have etymologies, precise original meanings; as explained by the manager of a sheep run in Wiradjuri country in 1863:

When the white settlers overran the country they appropriated all the finest water-holes for their head stations, consequently these occupy what were at that time the chief camping grounds of the blackfellow and therefore possessed of native names.

Hence:

The present names ... have been derived from the original names of the 'camping places' of the blacks. These NAMES were ... *significant*, they recalled to mind some scene ... or event, or characterized the peculiarity of some leading landmark ... (Woolrych, 1890: 63).

Mullengandra and Gilgandra both end in -dra, an Anglicised version of the Wiradjuri suffix *-thurray* meaning 'having' or 'with'. *Maliyankaanhthurray* means 'with a small or young eaglehawk or eaglehawks', and *kilkaanhthurray* means 'with a water-hole or gilgai', in Wiradjuri. Gulargambone, *kilaakaampuwan*, ends in *-puwan*, the Ngiyampaa equivalent of the *-thurray* suffix, and means 'with young galahs'. Because there are still people who speak Ngiyampaa 'right through', as they put it, I have first-hand authority for Gulargambone; but the other forms have been reconstructed on the basis of regular correspondences between Ngiyampaa and what is known of Wiradjuri from the written records which are the topic of this paper. Wiradjuri descendants today use a few words and phrases tenaciously in private, but that is all.

The colonising context alone would explain the reluctance of the first white settlers, busy appropriating waterholes, to appreciate consistently the literal meanings, let alone the full local richness of association, of names of places in the Wiradjuri and Ngiyampaa country they were overrunning. Hence the unavailability of such associations to today's heirs to the legacy of the white settlers.[1]

But the mere absence of conflicting interests between colonisers and colonised would not have been enough for the former fully to understand the values reflected in the names—a positive readiness to learn and use the languages would have been required, an alertness for the unexpected. The truth of this will quickly become apparent if we consider the predicament of anyone who tries to use printed sources to find out the exact location and extent of 'Ngiyampaa country' and 'Wiradjuri country'. A likely first step would be to look at Tindale's map (1974). There one finds, not two, but four countries occupying the area west of the Great Dividing Range towards the Darling River, labelled Wongaibon, Ngemba, Weilwan and Wiradjuri. The explanation reveals how hard it has been for non-speakers of the languages to get apparently simple matters of nomenclature right. Wiradjuri represents today's Anglicised pronunciation of Wirraathurray—that 'with' suffix again, attached this time to the local word for 'no', *wirraay*.[2] Wirraathurray country is probably reasonably well represented on Tindale's map. But Ngiyampaa country properly has two dialectal subdivisions, the southern, Wangaaypuwan, the one 'with *wangaay* for "no"', and the northern, Wayilwan, 'with *wayil* for "no"' (-*wan* being a variant of -*puwan*, 'with', after an *l* sound). It is also probable, though not provable (Donaldson, 1980: 3), that Wirraathurray speakers on occasion called their language (and themselves) *ngiyampaang*. This may seem to add to the confusion, but in fact it provides a clue to its solution.

Throughout this area people once named themselves, their languages and their territories according to two different principles[3] for different social purposes. At one level, they used words like *ngiyampaa* which simply mean 'language'; and at another, words meaning 'with "no"' in the language concerned. The collectors of snippets of information from different areas who were Tindale's sources failed to realise this, though some gathered substantial hints. Tindale, following his sources, tried to find separate places on the map for all the names. To complicate matters, Aboriginal memory in different areas has selected names from different levels for survival. Ngiyampaa is now the predominant name in the west (some people who call themselves Ngiyampaa are unsure about whom to call Wangaaypuwan or Wayilwan); while in the east only the name Wiradjuri is commonly used. The situation is of course further confused when young people of Ngiyampaa and Wiradjuri descent, hoping to retrace more of their heritage, consult Tindale's map, and in turn lend their Aboriginal authority to its suggestions.

I would recommend people interested in getting a rough idea of Ngiyampaa and Wiradjuri countries to take a road map and look out for concentrations of names ending in -bon and -bone (that is, -*puwan*), and in -dra, -dry, thry, -gerrie, -jerra, -derra and the like (that is, -*thurray*), bearing in mind three points. Firstly, there were other ways of forming place names in Ngiyampaa and Wiradjuri than by adding the 'with' suffix to some other word or phrase. Secondly, not all names of Aboriginal origin are local; many stations in particular were named by their owners after other places in Australia. Thirdly, the single name Wiradjuri has been spelt at least sixty different ways so far!

We have seen how incoming settlers have depended on the Wiradjuri and Ngiyampaa languages for place names, as they have on other languages elsewhere in Australia. They also depended on them—or rather usually on Wiradjuri, since they met the more easterly Wiradjuri speakers first—for the names of various novel aspects of the world they were entering: new birds, trees, and so on. So in *kilaa* and *purraalka* galah and brolga may be recognised; in *pilaarr* and *wilkarr* belah and wilgah trees, in *kuwanhthaang* and *kuwarraying*[4] quandong and quarryhen or cockatiel.

II

Communication with the inhabitants of this new world was obviously important too, but not to the extent that the languages would be learnt 'right through'. Invaders and invaded each borrowed words from each others' languages into their own. But when it came to talk between them, the white settlers drew on a tradition already established in attempts to communicate with the people on the coast. This was the state of affairs in Sydney in 1796 according to David Collins, the English colony's Judge Advocate and Secretary:

Language indeed is out of the question; for at the time of writing this, nothing but a barbarous mixture of English with the Port Jackson dialect is spoken by either party; and it must be added, that even in this the natives have the advantage, comprehending with much greater aptness than we can pretend to, everything they hear us say. (1798:544)

It was this 'barbarous mixture' or nascent pidgin which Europeans took with them to try out on other people in other places as they moved inland and along the coast (see Urry, this volume; Dixon, 1980:69). In 1834 the Reverend Lancelot Threlkeld wrote in the introductory remarks to his pioneering grammar of the Lake Macquarie language:

It is necessary to note certain Barbarisms which have crept into use, introduced by sailors, stockmen and others who have paid no attention to the Aboriginal tongue, in the use of which both blacks and whites labour under the mistaken idea that each one is conversing in the other's language. (1834:xi-xii)

These 'barbarisms' have left their legacy among the Ngiyampaa people too. *Putyarri* meant 'good' in Port Jackson. The Ngiyampaa use a word *putyirriwan* to mean 'good' or 'handsome' in addition to the Ngiyampaa word *yatama*. When I first heard *kiyaman* in *kiyaman na mukaa yuwanha,* 'she's only *kiyaman* asleep' or 'pretending to be asleep', I laboured under the mistaken idea that it was of Ngiyampaa origin, only to be told that it was English. It comes from the slang word 'gammon', meaning 'lie' or 'humbug', via the early pidgin. The Port Jackson word *tiyin* gave rise to 'gin' in the pidgin, which lost ground to 'lubra' in English. But it survives in Ngiyampaa in the word *waatyin*, 'white gin' as opposed to 'black gin', the word normally used for reference to white women.

Already we have some clues as to why the published records for both Ngiyampaa and Wiradjuri should consist chiefly of word lists. Though they contain a small amount of grammatical material, there are *no* extended texts recording what their speakers used them to say, the closest thing being the very occasional attempt to transcribe the words of a short song. The limits for even the earliest attempts at communication were laid down by the invaders in terms of their perceptions of the usefulness of such communication and of effective forms it might take. The initiative for making the communication possible rested with the Aborigines, who, having grown up on the assumption of a normally multilingual world, and with a keen interest in language matters, did most of the learning. Europeans who have learnt to speak Australian languages have usually done so out of eccentric personal choice, not social necessity. Aborigines on the other hand had increasingly little option but to learn English—whatever variety of English or 'barbarous mixture' they were exposed to—and to restrict the use of their own languages. From the beginning it was hardly seen as of immediate practical purpose to anyone even to assemble word lists. The records which were published were not part of any enterprise aimed at making communication with the speakers of the languages more profound. They were compiled from quite different, asocial, motives—in accordance with a tradition well-established in Britain long before there was any question of meeting Australians, overrunning their countries, or deciding how and to what extent to attempt communication with them. Vocabularies were collected as specimens, for the sake of scientific enquiry.

III

The earliest published records came from explorers. In 1817 John Oxley passed through Wiradjuri country on an expedition undertaken by order of the British government. His instructions from the Secretary of State, which assumed the acquisition of scientific fact as the chief goal of exploration, derived ultimately from the 'Directions for Sea-Men, bound for far Voyages' issued by the Royal Society in 1666 (Sellick, 1982: 173). They enjoined him to obtain and carefully note down information of various kinds about the geography and the inhabitants of the interior; to collect specimens of the most remarkable animals, vegetables and minerals, and also a 'vocabulary of the language spoken by the natives whom he may meet, using in the compilation of each the same English words' (Oxley, 1820: 361).

Languages are the creatures of use in communication. Collecting information about them is quite a different task from collecting mineral or botanical specimens. If contact with their speakers is brief and superficial, the undertaking is 'obnoxious to many mistakes', as Banks noted in reference to his own attempts to collect words from coastal people 'when our acquaintance was of so short a duration that none of us attempted to use a single word . . . to them' (Williams, this volume).

It is clear from the instructions to use 'the same English words' in the compilation of each vocabulary that Oxley was asked to collect vocabularies first and foremost in order to make comparative study of the different Australian languages possible, rather than to help subsequent communication with the speakers of any particular language. But the communicative context in which a vocabulary is compiled inevitably affects not only its length and quality, but its usefulness for any purpose.

Oxley inserted a vocabulary of about thirty words in his journal shortly after describing the setting up of a depot on the Lachlan River 'in lat. 33.40.S., and in long. 148.21.E.'. This consisted of 'the few words of which we were enabled to obtain the meaning from the natives who occasionally visited us'. Of one visit Oxley wrote 'it was evident that some of the party had been at Bathurst, from their making use of several English words, and from their readily comprehending many of our questions' (1820: 8-10). Yet Oxley's own vocabulary shows every sign of having been collected in a similar fashion to Banks' coastal words, 'by signs enquiring of them what in their language signified such a thing' (Williams, this volume), but without Banks' interest in assessing the effect of the method on its results. The English column in Oxley's list contains mainly words referring to body parts and objects such as girdles and bones worn in the nose, which can be indicated by pointing or touching; and to a few other things which the visitors presumably brought with them, such as 'a kind of hornet's nest, which they eat'. The Australian column sometimes gives several equivalents for English words, without explanation. Most of the list is fundamentally recognisable as Wiradjuri, but only by those who know what to expect, since there are no explicit spelling conventions.

Captain Charles Sturt's exploratory expedition of 1829 was the first to travel through Ngiyampaa country. Equipped with similar instructions to Oxley's, he chose to ignore the one charging him to provide a vocabulary of the language of those he met. His interest is rather in 'the manner of communicating with them' from the practical point of view. He recommends, 'The great point is not to alarm their timidity: to exercise patience in your intercourse with them; to treat them kindly; and to watch them with suspicion, especially at night' (Sturt, 1833:179; 187-8).

Other excursions followed in the wake of settlement. Lieutenant Breton's *Excursions in New South Wales, Western Australia, and Van Diemen's Land* (1833) has a promising motto on the title page, which suggests that the author may be alert to the hazards of over-speedy attempts to discover and to interpret what he finds:

When obliged to have recourse to the superficial remarks of vulgar travellers, sailors, traders, buccaneers, and missionaries, we must often pause, and, comparing detached facts, endeavour to discover what they wanted sagacity to observe.

But when he comes to include in his account of his travels through Wiradjuri country 'the best specimen of a native idiom that I was able to procure', the result shows no significant advance over Oxley's word list. It consists of approximately the same number of words, like Oxley's mostly indicating parts of the body. There are also a number of words for birds and animals, which could have been elicited through English rather than by pointing. The social situation in which Breton was collecting was, however, markedly altered:

Near Bathurst I fell in with from 100 to 200 natives, who appeared to be on excellent terms with the colonists; but some serious disturbances had taken place a few years before, when many of them were killed. Discovering afterwards that it was in vain to contend with their antagonists they became quiet, and have remained so ever since (1833:193)

Breton relied for the bulk of his information about Aboriginal matters on the reports of other whites. The linguistic 'facts' which he collected for himself, turn out to be 'detached' not so much in the sense of cool enquiry intended by his motto as in the sense that they are unconnected to any prolonged or profound experience of their speakers' way of life or use of language.

Both the explorers and the travellers in territory recently settled by whites were on the move. They would scarcely have had any opportunity to familiarise themselves to any great extent with any one of the several dialects of the several languages whose speakers' territories they passed through, even if personally inclined to the attempt.

IV

There were quite different opportunities available to the next kind of language collectors to appear in Wiradjuri country, the missionaries. During the 1830s and early 1840s there was a Church Missionary Society mission at Wellington Valley, then at the limit of European settlement, but in an area where, as the missionaries complained, there were already about 2000 Europeans. These missionaries produced the first (and almost the only) attempts at a written grammatical description of Wiradjuri. (There were never any missionary institutions of this kind in Ngiyampaa country, nor was any vestige of grammatical information about Ngiyampaa published until the early 1900s.)

The 2000 local Europeans were not appreciative. One of the missionaries, Mr Watson, wrote a grammar and some gospel translation. This work was never published and was disposed of as waste paper on his death. However, he did provide some more highly valued information to Horatio Hale, later to achieve a scholarly reputation as a student of American Indian languages, who was the philologist on the United States Exploring Expedition at the end of the 1830s. Hale acknowledges Watson as follows:

during a fortnight passed at his house, Mr Watson not only gave every assistance in obtaining a vocabulary from the natives, but did us the unexpected favor of drawing up an account of the most important peculiarities of the language, modelled as nearly as possible on the grammar of Mr Threlkeld, for the purpose of comparison (Hale, 1846:482).

And this, he continues, constitutes 'a most valuable contribution on the part of Mr Watson, to the stores of philological science'. Hale was really the only person with any philological or linguistic pretensions who had shown an interest in the language so far. The other missionary at Wellington Valley, James Günther, who also wrote a grammar, never saw it published, though it was eventually edited for publication in 1892 (Günther, 1892). Günther summed up his labours as follows:

In reference to the cultivation of the aboriginal language, I would mention that I have collected the principal part of the Black's vocabulary, and alphabetically arranged it, as also composed a grammar, comprising the principal rules; but from want of sufficient exercise I am not able yet to speak the language fluently. I apprehend it will never be of very great use for religious instruction, for in its present state it is extremely deficient, and until the minds of the aborigines are more cultivated, the cultivation of their language will not proceed fast; during this delay their number will much decrease, and the remnant become more conversant with English (1842:1057-8)

The mission was then closed, as the missionaries put it, due to the 'vile interference of white men' (Gribble, 1884:75).

The motives behind Watson's and Günther's work remain essentially the same as those behind the explorers' instructions. Their results are much more solid than the explorers' occasional contributions. The published version of Günther's vocabulary runs to 40 double-columned pages, and for the first time grammatical information is provided—paradigms of verbs, nouns, pronouns—and sample sentences. This increase in information is obviously made possible by longer contact with Wiradjuri speakers. But notice that the attempt to establish a residential mission does not mean that Günther finds himself sufficient opportunities to communicate in the language to be able to speak it fluently. However, his admitted lack of fluency does not prevent him from making a number of immodest judgements. A language whose 'principal rules' could be adequately dealt with in a dozen pages of paradigms and lists of forms might well be regarded as 'extremely deficient'—except on a reading of 'principal' that owes everything to its presence in a report designed to impress the writer's superiors, and nothing to a respect on his part for the universal complexity of languages.

More importantly, Günther appeases his disappointment with Aboriginal reactions to his evangelical ambitions by appealing to three notions all of which were to continue to influence responses to Wiradjuri and Ngiyampaa for at least another century and more. From the notion that the languages of Aborigines were 'deficient', however ill-defined that notion might be, it followed not only that they would be of little use for teaching Aborigines, but also that little would be learnt from Aborigines by learning their languages. The other two notions, that Aborigines would 'much decrease' in number, 'and the remnant become more conversant with English', served to further rationalise a general reluctance to try to do so. Even the interest in collecting specimens of language for 'the purposes of comparison' goes into abeyance, and there is a gap in the published material until the last quarter of the 1800s.

V

Looking back from the vantage point of the turn of the century, C. Richards (of whom more later) commented that as Europeans would not acquire the native language, the blacks had to learn English, which they readily did. But the process was not quite so simple. For all their readiness, the blacks were not to be encouraged to use a variety of English 'cultivated' enough to forestall linguistically based adverse judgements on their minds and manners. Aborigines were still conventionally addressed in 'broken English' (R. & F. Hill, 1875: 103-5). Though the English that they spoke themselves soon developed its own grammatical complexities, much of its vocabulary continued to be drawn from words considered unsuitable in other contexts. However normal or neutral the connotations of such words became among the Aborigines themselves, they were always open to ridicule for using them.

Aboriginal people, then, became accustomed to denigration not only of their own languages, but also of their English. On the one hand, as the Parkes and District Historical Society (1969) put it, 'The "yabbering" of the blacks was a reference common among early writings of the Parkes District' where Ngiyampaa and Wiradjuri were probably both to be heard. On the other hand, their English was stigmatised and viewed in terms of a stereotype which made them appear ludicrous. (For a conversation with a Ngiyampaa person reported impressionistically and condescendingly in 'Jacky-Jacky talk', see Cherbury (1932).) This double disrespect generated amongst Aboriginal people enduring feelings of 'shame' about their native languages, which in turn reinforced the prejudices of the whites. Even today whites tend to misunderstand the nature of that 'shame'. If Ngiyampaa people say they are 'ashamed' to talk their native language—*kuyanpuwan*, 'with shame'—they are showing a culturally expected reticence about using it in an improper social context: with or before white people who cannot speak Ngiyampaa and might laugh at it. After the second world war migrants could be heard resolutely speaking languages other than English in the same country towns where Ngiyampaa people would not have dreamt of revealing that they had any knowledge of their own language. These newcomers assumed moreover that it would be valuable for their children to speak their native languages. Since that time, it has been easier for Ngiyampaa people to tell whites something of their feelings about the progressive restriction of their language, using rhetorical questions with complex reverberations, such as, 'The Dagos learn their kids their own yabber, so why are we shamed?'

VI

The gap in published material on Wiradjuri and Ngiyampaa did not come to an end in the last quarter of the nineteenth century because of any sudden growth of local white interest in learning the languages in order to speak them. It happened because of the burgeoning of an explicitly anthropological interest in Aborigines in general of the post-Darwinian kind discussed by D. J. Mulvaney (this volume), which was to last until the outbreak of the first world war. There was a revival of the scientific concern to collect facts about languages, with a new concentration on their possible usefulness in throwing light on the origins of man and society in general and of Australians in particular. In the context of a concern with primitive origins, the very notions of Aboriginal mental and linguistic deficiency which justified Günther in discontinuing missionary work in Wiradjuri suggested that Aboriginal evidence would be of particular interest. The notion that

Aboriginal numbers would decrease was rapidly becoming a conviction that Aborigines were unfitted to survive; and the task of linguistic salvage acquired a special urgency, in the words of a contemporary enthusiast, 'as this unfortunate, and, in my opinion, most ancient race will soon have ceased to exist' (Richardson, 1899:211).

In terms of aims, methods and scholarly carefulness there were basically three kinds of language collector during this period. The most ambitious were people who were making discoveries on their own account in particular parts of Australia, who felt that it was important to consider them in the light of comparative material from other Aboriginal groups. Sometimes they could get such material through correspondence with like-minded acquaintances, but very often they resorted to questionnaires which they sent out to magistrates, policemen, squatters and the like to complete by asking questions of the local Aborigines (see also Mulvaney's remarks on 'postal anthropologists', this volume).

Most of the investigators of Aboriginal society who sent out questionnaires were not primarily interested in language matters as such. More often they wanted details of kinship terminology or information on local marriage rules to test their theories of 'primitive' social organisation. A notable exception was Edward Curr, who felt that comparative study of Australian languages would provide the most reliable evidence of the past history of the Aborigines and throw light on their possibly Negro origins.

When Curr started his work he found there were only forty vocabularies available for the whole of Australia (the lack of interest in Ngiyampaa and in Wiradjuri since the close of the Wellington Mission had been parallelled elsewhere). Aiming to find common and widespread Australian words as a proof of the common origin of all Australian languages, he 'got a vocabulary printed out of a few common English words, which he managed to get filled in by stock owners here and there, other facts new to him becoming apparent from the collation of his little collection' (Curr, 1886-87: vol. 1, xiv). He altered and added to the original words as the work progressed, until the standard list had 124 entries, mostly nouns, with a few representatives of other word classes and a couple of phrases. He finally published 300 of these lists partly or wholly filled in by his correspondents, with equivalents in Australian languages. The finding which interested him most was that a couple of roots kept occurring through many of the lists as equivalents of 'woman' and/or 'mother', 'breast', 'milk', 'water', 'rain' (ibid.:30). Several of Curr's lists and answers to other investigators' questionnaires come from Ngiyampaa and Wiradjuri country, but none of the major enquirers worked there themselves.

The second kind of collector at this time was one who collected material directly when the opportunity arose, but was not predominantly interested in generalising from it, or in acquiring information to support a particular theory. The outstanding example is the surveyor R. H. Mathews, whose evidence for a number of Australian languages is the only evidence we have. He published information on both Wiradjuri and Ngiyampaa. His work on Ngiyampaa was until the last few years the most extensive published. He fed his findings into the journals of learned societies in England, France and Germany, often presenting them in a way that emphasised his diligence at the cost of suggesting that the languages themselves were somewhat insubstantial. For instance, he produced three publications based on material collected in Ngiyampaa country, each named by a different one of the names which appear on Tindale's map. In his preamble to his account of 'Ngēumba' he mentions the 'Wailwan' and the 'Wongaibon' (Mathews' spellings) and points out that 'The languages of both the tribes referred to have already been published by me' (Mathews, 1904). The 'languages' consisted of a couple of paradigms, a few chance remarks and a list of words—the longest being the 'Ngēumba' one of about 400.

Unlike Curr, Mathews had no principled theoretical grounds for choosing which words to list. Superficially his 'Ngēumba' words are all ones a newcomer to a society and its language might be expected to gather during time off from surveying, the nouns being subsumed under headings such as 'Family Terms', 'The Human Body', 'Inanimate Nature'. But a close look at the 60-odd terms referring to the human body reveals that as many as one-third concern parts which would have been considered far too private to have been included in a contemporary vocabulary of equal length intended for students of any language spoken in Europe, including glosses such as 'labia major' and 'noise made in copulating'. Examples of the same kind of preoccupation are commonplace not only in Mathews' work but throughout the history of vocabulary collection in Australia. A salutary one comes from a word list made at Caledon Bay by the ship's surgeon on the Flinders expedition which called there in 1803. There is an entry for 'cunnus' where the local equivalent is given as 'yacca': in the language of the area the word *yaka* means not 'cunt' but 'no!' The effect of including terms with sexual reference of a kind then thought offensive to female sensibilities, accompanied by suitably learned Latin glosses, was to lend an air of scientific authority to the word lists and to distinguish their collection as a masculine, scholarly activity in the tradition of the study of classical Greek and Latin.

In the last decade of the century a third class of collector appeared in print, contributors to a far from scholarly monthly put out by the Royal Anthropological Society of Australasia and called, from 1898, *Science of Man*. It published numerous highly speculative articles on popular evolutionary issues, often consisting of a jumble of unsupported propositions, such as that early women had more highly developed tongue muscles than men and so 'perhaps' were the first to learn to speak. It affected a practical concern for the collection of anthropological evidence by including any word lists sent in by the readership: people who came across information in the course of their work or got others to do so, policemen again, surveyors and so on; and people with personal recollections going back to before the development of a widespread amateur interest in anthropology who at last had an audience to share them with. These word lists result more often from an enthusiastic sense of urgency than from any understanding of language matters. They are full of internal inconsistencies; and isolated words from many different languages are often tossed in together without any indication of their sources, prompting an unfortunately unheeded letter of complaint from John Mathew: 'May I point out that to be of any service to students of philology the lists will have to be very carefully sifted, so as to ensure that the words are correct in form and genuinely local' (*Science of Man*, 23 July 1900:98-9).

C. Richards, who described himself as having been making enquiries among the Aborigines of the western district [of New South Wales] since 1856, planned to send in 2000 words of Wiradjuri, and was chiefly responsible for Wiradjuri almost dominating the *Science of Man* word lists for part of the period of its publication. His Wiradjuri lists are less informative than all this would suggest, partly because of faults in presentation and partly for another reason. Intellectually, Richards was a typical contributor, prepared to lace together a number of speculations of the day and assert them as evolutionary fact. His theory of the origin of language is onomatopoeic, the evolution of 'a language of endless variety from a few primitive sounds copied from nature' (23 January 1903:198). Since '[the Aboriginal] is more likely to bring us in touch with ancient times' (21 July 1902:98), Richards is anxious to prove that Aboriginal languages do indeed demonstrate his onomatopoeic principle. Instead of confining his arguments to articles, he illustrates them by contriving ingenious glosses for the words in his lists. For instance, the Wiradjuri words for 'wild clover', 'frost/ice', 'ironbark tree', 'spinal column', 'blindness' and 'buttocks'—to mention just a few—all begin, in his transcription, with the syllable 'moog-' or 'mog-': they must therefore mean something similar. So supplementary comments indicate that clover is 'cracked or divided'; frost/ice 'possesses to crack or divide'; the bark of the ironbark is 'deeply cracked'; there is 'something done to crack or divide' by the spinal column; blindness too is, in some unexplained way, 'cracked, divided'; and of course the buttocks 'are divided'. Not only is this sort of thing very hard to sustain: piercing, penetrating, tearing and exploding have to be added to this notion to cope with only a dozen more words which begin in the same way, and half still remain too intractable for comment. Worse, it also leads to errors in the basic glosses and the obscuring of genuine etymologies. For instance, '*Moog goo—Wood dtha*' (*muku wutha*) is translated as 'pierced or ruptured ear', hence 'deafness' (23 September 1902:34): in fact *muku* means 'blocked' of any kind of hole and so for that reason 'deaf' in conjunction with *wutha* 'ear'.

There was, however, one way in which Richards was quite unlike anyone else who had previously recorded material from Ngiyampaa or Wiradjuri, and quite unlike his fellow contributors to *Science of Man*. His most original achievement was to be the first ever to acknowledge his Aboriginal 'authorities' as such, to name them and supply short biographies.

The *Science of Man* fell on hard times and ceased publication in 1913. Thereafter the store of printed information about Ngiyampaa and Wiradjuri was increased by only a handful of words, most of them the incidental by-products of academic investigations into other aspects of Aboriginal life, and there was no prospect of a possible change in this situation until the end of the 1960s when Luise Hercus began to tape record speakers of Ngiyampaa (and of the odd word of Wiradjuri).

Before the *Science of Man* folded, there had been attempts to get govern-mental assistance. When this was not forthcoming, there was an editorial lament: '[The Anthropological Society's] is, of course, a national work and they should assist it, as after this generation the blacks, and other kinds of information, will have disappeared, and it will be lost for ever, although we could put it on record at small cost' (22 February 1904:2). The Ngiyampaa and Wiradjuri blacks did not disappear (let alone the blacks nationwide); their descent is numerous and socially cohesive, and has continued to call its sense of shared identity blackness. Nor were the blacks' languages being anything like as poorly transmitted from generation to generation as the editorial suggests, even if rarely used in the presence of whites. However, most Aboriginal languages of New South Wales now really are irretrievable as autonomous linguistic systems, whether for revival or for the record (with a correspondingly high symbolic and emotional importance being attached to surviving shibboleths and, increasingly, to black English). For such languages the *Science of Man* collections of words are, as Mathew predicted, largely useless, since one needs to know the language(s) concerned in order to make sense of them. If the living Australian languages are to be 'put on record' in a fashion which will give some satisfaction to posterity, black or white, a prerequisite would seem to be that non-native speakers involved in recording them need to be both able and willing to learn them 'right through', and, as that first white visitor to Ngiyampaa country, Sturt, put it, 'to exercise patience in . . . intercourse'.

Acknowledgement

The research for this essay was undertaken as part of the preparation of a Ngiyampaa dictionary, with funding from the Australian Institute of Aboriginal Studies. My thanks to Angus & Robertson for permission to quote from A. D. Hope's poem 'Country Places'.

Notes

1 Later, popular interest in Aboriginal languages was to focus on the meanings of place names surviving in Anglicised form as the names of towns. But there are still no satisfactory Australian place name dictionaries.
2 Or *wirray*. Outside quotations, the spelling system used for words from Ngiyampaa and other languages of New South Wales is the one adopted by Ngiyampaa people for the development of educational materials such as Johnson (1982). The sole exception is 'Wiradjuri' (instead of Wirraathurray, which occurs only in this paragraph), the Tindale spelling becoming popular among people of Wiradjuri descent.
3 More than two actually, but the others, and the names they give rise to, need not concern us.
4 The Ngiyampaa form is *kuwarrayi*. It is not clear whether the Wiradjuri equivalent ended in *ng*, as in 'si*ng*' or *ny*, as in 'ca*ny*on'. But its reinterpretation as 'quarryhen', with a final nasal, is an indication that the word was taken into English from Wiradjuri.

Bibliography

Breton, W. H.   (1833) *Excursions in New South Wales, Western Australia, and Van Diemen's Land, During the Years 1830, 1831, 1832, and 1833* London; Richard Bentley
Cherbury, C. P.   (1932) 'Rain-making in Western New South Wales' *Mankind* 1, 6, p. 138
Collins, D.   (1798) *An Account of the English Colony in New South Wales* vol. 1, London: T. Cadell Jun. and W. Davies
Curr, E. M.   (ed.) (1886-87), *The Australian Race* 4 vols, Melbourne: Government Printer; London: Trübner & Co.
Dixon, R. M. W.   (1980) *The Languages of Australia* Cambridge: Cambridge University Press
Donaldson, T.   (1980) *Ngiyambaa The Language of the Wangaaybuwan* Cambridge: Cambridge University Press
Gribble, J. B.   (1884) *'Black but Comely': or, Glimpses of Aboriginal Life in Australia* London: Morgan & Scott
Günther, J.   (1842) 'Annual Report of the Mission to the Aborigines at Wellington Valley, New Holland for the year 1841' *New South Wales, Governor's Despatches* 38

_____ (1892) 'Grammar and Vocabulary of the Aboriginal Dialect called the Wirradhuri', pp. 56-120 of Appendix to Threlkeld (1892)

Hale, H. (1846) 'The Languages of Australia' pp. 479-531 of *Ethnography and Philology*, vol. 6 of *Reports of the United States Exploring Expedition, under the Command of Charles Wilkes* Philadelphia: Lea & Blanchard; reprinted Ridgewood, NJ: Gregg Press, 1968

Hill, R. and F. (1875) *What We Saw in Australia*, London: Macmillan, extracted in B. Kingston (ed.) (1977) *The World Moves Slowly: a Documentary History of Australian Woman* Australia: Sydney, pp. 5-6

Hope, A. D. (1975) *A Late Picking: Poems 1965-1974* Sydney: Angus & Robertson

Johnson, D. et.al. (1982) *Ngiyampaa Alphabet Book* Dubbo:CAP Western Readers

Mathews, R. H. (1904) 'The Ngeumba Language' pp. 219-32 of 'Ethnological Notes on the Aboriginal Tribes of New South Wales and Victoria' *Journal and Proceedings of the Royal Society of New South Wales* 38, pp. 203-381

Oxley, J. (1820) *Journals of Two Expeditions into the Interior of New South Wales . . . 1817-18* London: John Murray

Parkes and District Historical Society (1969) 'Aboriginal Activity in the Parkes District' *Royal Australian Historical Society Newsletter* no. 84, p. 7

Richardson, T. L. (1899) 'Further Linguistic Information' *Science of Man* 21 December, pp. 211-12

Sellick, R. (1982) 'From the Outside In: European Ideas of Exploration and the Australian Experience' *Australia and the European Imagination* introduced by Ian Donaldson, Canberra: Humanities Research Centre, ANU, pp. 173-83

Sturt, C. (1833) *Two Expeditions into the Interior of Southern Australia, During the Years 1828, 1829, 1830, and 1831* vol. 1, London: Smith, Elder, & Co.

Threlkeld, L. E. (1834) *An Australian Grammar . . . as Spoken by the Aborigines in the Vicinity of Hunter's River, Lake Macquarie, &c. New South Wales* Sydney: Stephens & Stokes

_____ (1892) *An Australian Language as Spoken by the Awabakal, the People of Awaba or Lake Macquarie [near Newcastle, New South Wales]: Re-arranged, condensed and edited with an Appendix by John Fraser* Sydney: Government Printer

Tindale, N. B. (1974) *Aboriginal Tribes of Australia: Their Terrain, Environmental Controls, Distribution, Limits and Proper Names* Berkeley and Los Angeles: University of California Press; Canberra:ANU Press

Woolrych, F. B. (1890) 'Native Names of Some of the Runs &c. in the Lachlan District' *Journal and Proceedings of the Royal Society of New South Wales* no. 24, pp. 63-70

SEVEN

PROJECTIONS OF MELANCHOLY

Margaret Maynard

As EARLY AS the 1850s it was generally accepted that the Aborigines of the Australian mainland were dying out (Woolmington, 1973: ix). By the 1880s and 1890s, this belief had become a platitude of the Australian popular press. The forces of Darwinian selection (it was assumed) had been at work, and the wretched remnants of an inferior race—who were apparently past any hope of civilised redemption—were on the way out. The only thing that could be done for those who were passing away without so much as a struggle was to make their last days as free from misery as possible.

Such helplessness as they manifest stirs in us a feeling of pity, and we are moved by Christian philanthropy to give such help as will extend the vanishing point and allow them to glide off the stage rather than pass away abruptly.

Thus spoke the Melbourne *Age* in 1881 (13 January: editorial). The romantic assumption that the Aborigines would fade away, like a slowly dimming light, had an important effect upon visual representations of the Australian Aborigines in the late nineteenth century. The effect is particularly noticeable in the fine art representations of the late 1880s and the 1890s which are the topic of this essay. These representations contrast sharply with the caricatures of Aborigines to be found in the popular press in the same period: a contrast that reveals the ambivalence with which the Aborigines were regarded by other Australians. The caricatures reflect common beliefs about the degraded condition of the Aborigines, while the high art representations I shall be discussing show a nostalgic and melancholy regret for a race that appeared to be on the verge of extinction.

These high art representations were produced at a time when it was increasingly difficult for the average white Australian to see Aborigines in a traditional environment. At the same time Aborigines were being systematically excluded from many aspects of the new Australian society (Hartwig, 1972: 19). Aboriginal Protection Acts (passed in Victoria in 1869, in New South Wales in 1883, and in Queensland in 1897) banished them to reserves where they would be less of a nuisance, and allowed as comfortable a passing as possible (Rowley, 1974: 130). There was a wish to 'protect', and at the same time to exclude. Ambivalence is perhaps the chief characteristic of white Australian attitudes to Aborigines in this period, and it is therefore not surprising that it should also be evident in the visual arts.

The three painters responsible for most of the fine art images of Aborigines at this time are Tom Roberts, Benjamin Minns, and the Queensland painter Oscar Friström, who produced at least thirty works during the late 1880s and 1890s. Their representations form a group in that they are chiefly portraits. Standing figures are rare, though the works of Oscar Friström's brother Edward, who also portrayed Aborigines, include *Native Woman with Pole*, oil, 1893 (Queensland Art Gallery) and *Australian Water Nymph*, oil, 1897 (Queensland Museum), a full-length nude. Subject-paintings are almost non-existent except for Roberts' drawing from Murray Island (plate 8.11); and no pictures of the period show encounters between Aborigines and Europeans unless we stretch it to include Blamire Young's 1901 *Buckley Acting as Interpreter at Indented Head* (plate 8.20). The Aboriginal images of Roberts, Minns and Friström differ substantially from those in the work of (say) von Guérard, where nature is a dominating presence, in the sublime and picturesque traditions of European art. They have more in common with the earlier Bock monochrome portraits or the sculptured heads by Law of the 1830s, where individuals are portrayed without the wider context of a landscape or subject background.

Let us consider in detail one of these portraits by Tom Roberts, *Aboriginal Head—Charlie Turner*, painted in 1892 (plate 8.5). This work, bought at the time by the National Gallery of New South Wales, was regarded by the *Sydney Morning Herald* as a portrait painted with

so much strength and fidelity, that its value will grow year by year with the gradual disappearance from our midst of the original possessors of the soil. Thus it has a permanent, if melancholy interest, which justifies its inclusion in our national collection ('The Art Society's Exhibition: First Notice' 2 September 1892: 2).

Although aesthetic qualities were not ignored by this reviewer, the real value of *Charlie Turner* was thought to be that of an historical document, a gloomy record of social change. Other writers around this period argued similarly that realistic records of the apparently dying race would 'survive as historical documents when the true aboriginal type is lost' ('Between Ourselves' *Queensland Figaro* 5 August 1909: 13). Thus portraits of the Australian Aboriginal, like those of the American Indian, were invested with particular meaning (see information on Catlin in Parry, 1974: 83).

With this meaning in mind, we may consider Roberts' portrait of *Charlie Turner* more carefully. Virginia Spate in her important monograph on Roberts (1972) scarcely discusses his portraits of Aborigines (though these are considered in the thesis on which this monograph is based, and by Helen Topliss in this volume). Yet the *Charlie Turner* portrait supports and exemplifies Spate's general view of a change in Roberts' work in the nineties, to be seen in his increasing historicism and his increasing interest in the Australian outback and its heroic potential. The 'historicism' here, however, is far from simple. *Charlie Turner* is not an entirely naturalistic study. It presents instead an image of soulfulness, almost in the manner of seventeenth-century religious art (Rubens) or academic art-teaching (Lebrun, 1718, 1827). Something of the portrait's expressive quality had been glimpsed before in the lugubriousness of Rodius' Aboriginal portraits of the 1830s and the delicate wistfulness of Bock's watercolours. Roberts, however, by means of his references to earlier art, takes this expressiveness a stage further, creating a specifically romantic image of melancholy that responds to current sentiment about the Aborigines as a 'dying' race.

Charlie Turner's head and beard are brushed in roughly by Roberts in subtle and fairly dark tones, ranging from browns, crimson lake and grey purple, to almost black. The background of varied greys and blues is without detail. Reversing a standard academic formula for portraits of a light head against a dark background (a technique that Roberts does not favour in his informal portraits and one that would obviously not work with a black skin), the artist has produced something like an academic *tête d'expression*. The dark head is contrasted with a faint pink grey area touched in beside the head, which almost gives the effect of a nimbus. This coloration, combined with the minimal indication of neck and absence of body, results in a kind of disembodiment within the total area of the picture. Furthermore, the picture has no associations. We cannot identify this man with any particular social activity or any particular place. (It has not even been established where the portrait was painted—Topliss, this volume.) He exists therefore as a solitary and almost universalised symbol.

Why is it that Aborigines like Charlie Turner are normally represented in the fine arts by portrait heads rather than engaged in social or practical activities such as hunting or fishing? Photographers and illustrators often represent Aboriginal ceremonies, but painters virtually ignore them. The explanation for this lies partly in the nineteenth-century view that subjects for graphic representation were not necessarily suitable for oil paintings. It also lies in Australian painterly developments of the 1890s towards idealisation and national myth-making. Such developments made fine art portraiture especially responsive to the commonly held notion that the Aborigines were dying out, allowing a special meaning to be attached to the record of individual Aborigines who remained. Thus, ironically, the traditional upper-class art form of the portrait was used to imbue with dignity the 'fate' of a reputedly inferior race.

Bernard Smith has recently discussed the European mechanisms of forgetfulness that operated, in conjunction with social Darwinism, against Aborigines in the nineteenth century (1980: 17-25). His argument would be strengthened by a consideration of the way in which Aborigines are represented in the 1890s. Yet he makes no reference at all to such representations, almost implying that there were no nineteenth-century successors to what he calls the tragic *Tasmanian Aborigines* (1859) by Robert Dowling. I would like to argue that white Australian artists indeed

Plate 7.1 Oscar Friström (1898) *King Sandy—Moreton Bay*

painted tragic, dignified, and at times deeply sensitive portraits of Aborigines in the late nineteenth century. By concentrating on the melancholy heroism of their individual subjects, however, they failed to represent the collective plight of Aboriginal society. A solitary Aboriginal portrait head could pose no threat to established urban society, and occasion little if any questioning of conscience. The individual is perceived as a possibly heroic but essentially passive victim of the progress of evolution.

Few if any Australian paintings in this period were primarily concerned with the accurate depiction of social realities. The conventions of Aboriginal portraiture are not therefore in all instances unique, but this fact in no way lessens their interest. These conventions amount almost to a systematic iconography. The portraits for the most part ignore the subjects' social and physical environment. Often they show individuals with little or no clothing or ornament. The subjects are usually placed against a featureless or ill-defined background. Sometimes this is grey, turquoise, or blue, as with *Charlie Turner*; sometimes it can be quite intense in tone. Roberts' female portrait in the Dixon Galleries, identified by Helen Topliss as the *Maria Yulgilbar* of the 1895 Society of Artists Exhibition (plate 8.21), has a particularly brilliant background of Naples yellow that heightens the subtle dark tones of the woman's flesh.

Many of the portraits are composed frontally, as with Oscar Friström's *King Sandy—Moreton Bay*, of 1898 (plate 7.1), or in complete profile, like Tom Roberts' *Amehnam* (plate 8.7). Although profile and frontal portraits of Europeans are not uncommon, Aborigines are more consistently represented in this manner in the 1890s than are white Australians, the Aboriginal portraits often having the air of identification records or physiognomy studies. (Interestingly, a number of Charles Woolley's photographic records of the 'last' Tasmanian Aboriginals, taken in 1866 and similar in spirit to these later portrait-paintings, are also fully frontal or in profile.) There may also have been painterly reasons for preferring more abstract and simplified poses; and artists not bound by a commission would have enjoyed greater freedom to depict their subjects as they pleased.

Often the portrait heads occupy much of the picture space, and, like *Charlie Turner*, have little if any indication of a body below the shoulders or upper arm. Roberts' profile of *Amehnam* floats disembodiedly against a broadly treated, featureless background of grey to green turquoise. It is an extreme example, and may have been intended as a study for a larger work. With rare exceptions such as Oscar Friström's *Aboriginal Woman* 1898 (Brisbane Civic Art Gallery), the portraits of the 1890s almost never show hands. If arms are sometimes included, hands are carefully hidden. Roberts' *Young Lubra, Cape York* (plate 8.8) has arms that terminate just at the elbow. *Billie Millera*, 1894 (plate 8.19), is cut off slightly higher. The

Aborigines of the 1890s are represented in a state of passiveness. (For comparably passive representations of subject peoples in the Pacific see Bell (1982)). The conventions followed exclude all indication of their capacity for practical or social action.

The current anthropological interest in Aboriginal activities such as firemaking, basketwork and so on was an interest based on the observation of technology and collection of specimens. This kind of interest is reflected in photography and popular imagery but not in fine art of the period. Recent studies indicate that fine art representations of bush workers were similarly subject to 'editing' (Bradley & Smith, 1980). Artists were as little involved in representing the harsh specifics of workers' lives as they were in the real details of Aboriginal life. But in the case of the Aborigines, the detachment was of a different kind. The current view of the Aborigines as a dying race was a useful myth by which black society could be rendered ineffectual and unthreatening. The portraits of the 1890s reflect this view. The subjects carry no weapons and are non-aggressive. They are edited representations of truncated and inactive individuals.

At a time when it was difficult to see the Aborigines in their traditional environment or to have them pose for portraits, photographs provided useful documentation and compositional ideas. Thus some portraits of this period—excluding, it seems, those by Roberts—can be traced back directly to original photographs. This marks a further remove of the artists' experience of reality. The kind of alteration which is made to the original photograph in the final painting is added evidence of the way in which they manipulated their subject matter.

Nerli's smiling *Head of an Aborigine* (plate 7.2) is based on a photograph by the Sydney photographer Henry King which was reproduced as a postcard (plate 7.3). Here the expression is unusual with its cruel and taunting, almost animal-like, quality. For the most part expressions in portraits are tense but not aggressive, with a remotely sad, often brooding, look to the eyes. The portrait verges upon caricature; and the fact that it appeared as a *Bulletin* front page (10 October 1891: entitled 'The Original Landed Proprietor, on the NSW Boom Bank Smash') emphasises the difficulty of making clear distinctions between popular and high art depictions of Aborigines in this period.

Nerli, like the artists known to have worked from photographs, has altered his painting from the original. Apart from the change of expression, the changes effected, although slight, all contribute to a more formalised image that corresponds closely with the conventions under discussion. For example, Nerli has increased the size of the head within the space of the picture. On the bright green background he has added an intense yellow area of light behind the jaw and neckline. Compare this to the nimbus area

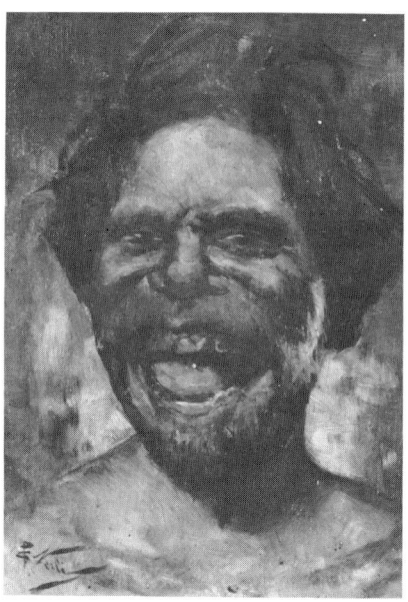

Plate 7.2   Girolamo B. Nerli, *Head of an Aborigine*

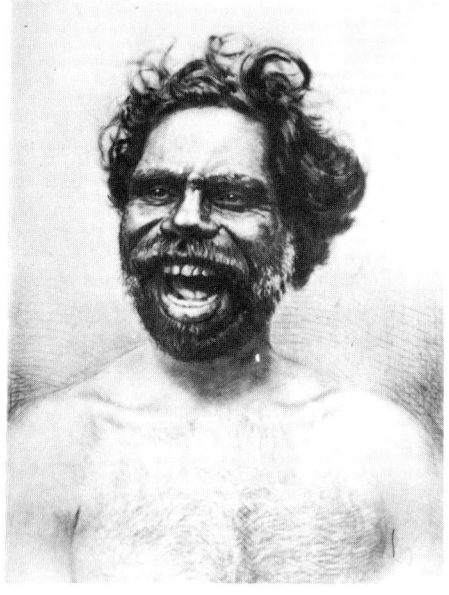

Plate 7.3   Henry King, *Australian Aborigine*

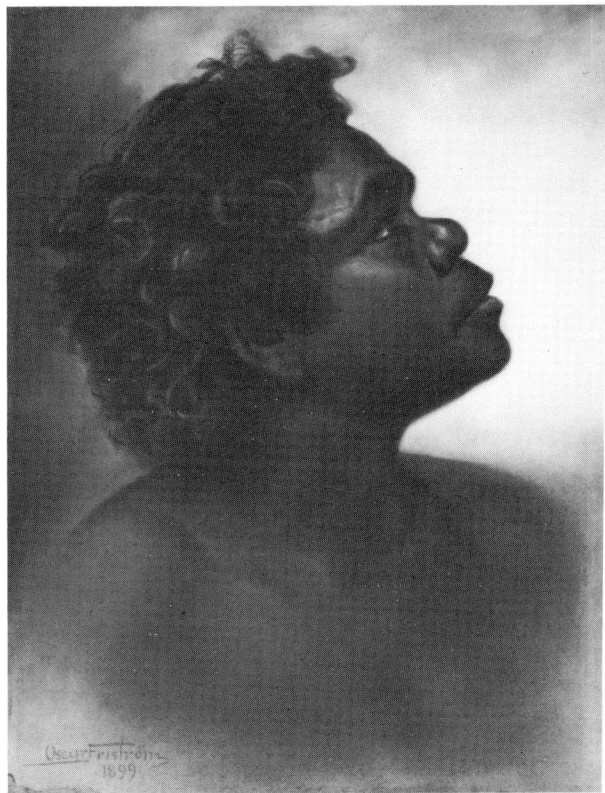

Plate 7.4   Oscar Friström (1899) *Head of an Aboriginal Woman*, **a copy of Friström's (1898)** *Female Aboriginal*

in *Charlie Turner* (plate 8.5), or to that behind Friström's *Female Aborigine*, 1898 in the Queensland Museum, of which plate 7.4 is a copy; it is a feature found with consistent regularity. Nerli has also altered the eyes and twisted the position of the head to one that is more frontal. Finally, he shows the man's shoulder fading out from the shoulder line, similar to Roberts' portrait but quite different from the King photograph. Something a little like this is found in the academic *étude de tête* (Nerli seems to have spent a year at the Florence Academy—Currie (1978: 55). For an illustration of an academic *étude de tête* see Boime (1971: illustration 4)). But what is most interesting is that this fading out is found in a great many other Aboriginal portraits of the 1890s, and can therefore be considered as an iconographical feature. While it derives very specifically from a popular technique of the day, it also reflects the way people thought about Aborigines at this period.

99

A photographic portrait study that softens and fades out toward the margins of a print is called a vignette, a technique first developed in the early 1850s. Vignetting was used, for example, by Charles Woolley for the magnificent sepia photographs he took of the 'last' Tasmanian Aboriginals. His photograph of *William Lanné* (plate 7.5) shows a head that dominates the photographic print and clothes that fade away to the sides and base. Published versions of Woolley's photographs, such as those in Bonwick's *The Last of the Tasmanians* (1870), also reproduce this fading out, a quite standard procedure for engraved portrait heads in newspaper illustration and of course for landscape views. The vignette device, although occasionally seen in other kinds of portrait, can be particularly closely associated with Aboriginal portraiture; as a decontextualising device, it mirrors in some ways white Australian social attitudes to Aborigines at this time. We find the device in Nerli's portrait, but also in many other works of various stylistic treatment.

Friström has deliberately introduced the vignette into his charcoal drawing *Aboriginal Male* (plate 7.6), and strengthened its curve with his flourishing signature, while a companion piece, *Aboriginal Female* (Brown & Maynard, 1978: figure 11) simply preserves the vignette effect of the original photograph by J. J. Preston. *Aboriginal Male* is based on a numbered Kerry photograph, *Narimboo Workii Tribe*. (Kerry's photographic firm had a widely advertised mail order business in Sydney for ordering postcards and photographic prints including Aboriginal subjects—Millar (1981)). Friström, like Nerli, has altered his drawing from the original photograph. He has twisted and strengthened his subject into a true profile, for example, and added the vignette effect. He has retained the strong furrowed brow, but overlaid the image with the large staring eyes of Lebrun's academic *tête d'expression*, *Attention* (Lebrun, 1718/1827). It is tempting to speculate on the reason for this kind of effect, which Friström does not seem to try for elsewhere. One could postulate some contact with academic art teaching, although Friström was essentially self-taught. The underlying motive remains uncertain.

The sense of a slow fading out, given visual form in the vignette, is something that is also expressed in contemporary descriptions of Aborigines. Terminology used in conjunction with their supposed demise often tends toward euphemistic words and phrases that emphasise a smooth transition from one state to another: 'fading', 'receding', 'retire', 'decay', 'wither', 'gliding off the stage', 'closing hour'. In discussing the work of Furphy, J. J. Healy makes an interesting point about the literary vignette in connection with 'A Vignette of Port Phillip' published in *Steele Rudd's Magazine* in 1906. Furphy's story concerns the tribal killing of Baradyak, an Aboriginal of the Upper Yarra, in the 1840s. Healy claims that in using this technique

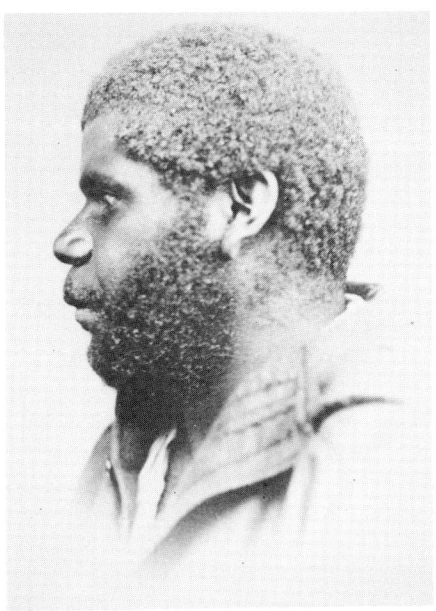

Plate 7.5   Charles Woolley (1866) *William Lanné*

Plate 7.6   Oscar Friström (1895) *Aboriginal Male*

of focusing on an incident in the past when there was contact between white and black,

Furphy had hit on one of the few artistic means for maintaining the only available focus for the European experience of the Aborigine. That experience attributed a momentary reality to the Aborigine during the phase of contact. Before that contact the Aborigine was outside of history; after it, he did not engage the serious attention of white Australians. There was, for Furphy, simply this central portion with a blurred surround (1978: 118).

The following description of the Aboriginal people by J. B. Woods, editor of *The Native Tribes of South Australia*, 1879, gives a further dimension to the literary vignette:

Without a history, they have no past; without a religion they have no hope; without the habits of forethought and providence, they can have no future. Their doom is sealed . . . (quoted Chase & von Sturmer, 1973: 7).

The Aborigines had no recorded history (in the sense familiar to Europeans), and were seen in the late nineteenth century to have no future. The vignette device seems to have been the most appropriate form in which an artist could record his doomed subject. The Aboriginal portrait thus becomes in more ways than one a melancholy focal point for contemporary ideas relating to the race.

The English names of Aboriginal subjects are frequently inscribed on the canvas of portraits in this period, and often their names in the local languages too, along with information on the locality of their tribes and the artists' names and dates. The recording of the subject's name was clearly done for historical purposes; the record of location was equally important, given the assumption that the people were dying out. Sometimes the information is detailed, as with Roberts' *Billie Millera* (plate 8.19), which is signed, dated and inscribed upper left, 'Billie Millera/ was a grown man/ in 46 when Ed. Ogilvie/ of Yulgilbar was the/ first white/ to see him' and 'Peanahgo'; and upper right, 'Billipimbah'. Not infrequently the local name is misunderstood or unrevealingly spelt, and in some cases we find a form of words from which no meaning can now be extracted. Rodius recorded on his 1830s prints the names of individual tribes and the date; hence there is some correspondence between the practice of painters and popular illustrators.

The phrase 'the last of', which appeared in illustration titles from the time of Truganini's death, is also sometimes appended to Aboriginal portraits of this period and on into the next decade. Portraits such as the one by Roberts listed as *Gubbie Wellington—one of the last Blacks of Corowa*, known only from a drawing (plate 8.1), reveal the fatalistic Darwinian stress on the notion of racial extinction.

Plate 7.7   Oscar Friström (1894) *Last of the South Australian Blacks*

Friström's painting, *The Last of the South Australian Blacks* (plate 7.7), probably painted in 1894, is in the same deeply pessimistic spirit. It is rather freely based on photographs of Tommy Walker of Adelaide, who was to die in 1910. It shows the familiar head fading out into rough, aggressive brush strokes. No arms are visible. Behind this last aged man gather his tribe, depicted as schematic, grey figures, moving in a dream-like procession. He stands almost as an heroic standard bearer, the hillside and non-functional spear doubling ambiguously as a flag. He is the last of his tribe, standing at the head of his race, a doomed victim of the progress of white civilisation. The final verse of Henry Kendall's 'The Last of his Tribe' is extremely close in spirit to the image of the old man whose forehead gleams with a golden, unearthly light:

> *Will he go in his sleep from these desolate lands*
> *Like a chief, to the rest of his race,*
> *With the honey-voiced woman who beckons and stands,*
> *And gleams like a dream in his face—*
> *Like a marvellous dream in his face.*

103

The fatalistic mood of this painting by Friström is found to some degree in the watercolours of Aborigines done by Benjamin Minns in Sydney, before his departure for London early in 1895. Minns, who was born and brought up in the Hunter River District, had close contacts with the Aborigines as a youth and his early works have a sensitivity toward them unfortunately quite absent in later work. According to Bertram Stevens, he was 'attracted to the Australian aboriginals as much by the sentimental interest attaching to the survivors of a fading race as by their picturesqueness' (Stevens, 1917). However true this claim may be, the circumstances of his interest in Aboriginal portraiture remain undocumented. (Strikingly indicative of Minns' ambivalence towards Aborigines, however, are the scurrilous cartoons he drew in the 1890s.)

Minns was living in Sydney by about 1884. His first exhibited works were portraits, genre and landscape. Only in 1894, following Roberts' precedent, did he begin to show Aboriginal portraits of which the first, shown at the Art Society of New South Wales exhibition, were *Types of New South Wales Aboriginals*, *Meditation* (*A Type of NSW Aborigine*) and *Aboriginal Girl*.

Types of New South Wales Aboriginals consist of three separate watercolours framed together intentionally as a triple portrait. Each individual portrait is inscribed with the date, the artist's name, the name of the person represented and the locality of the tribe. All three came from the coastal area of Bermagui, south of Sydney. They are inscribed, left to right,

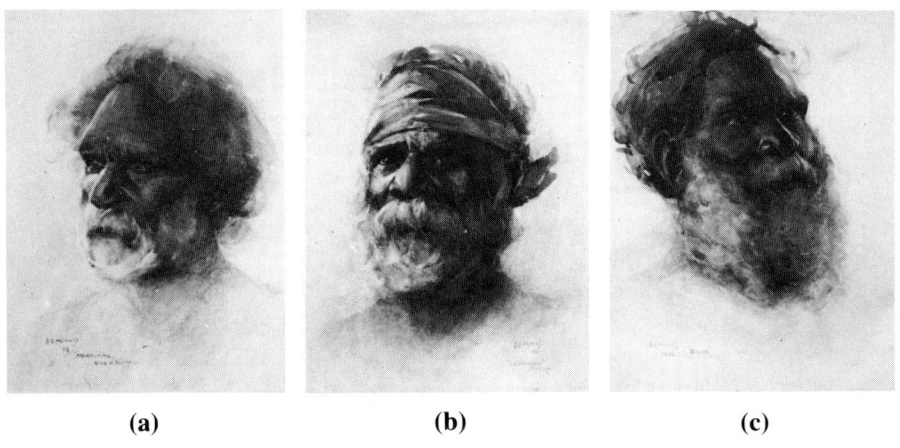

(a)　　　　　　　(b)　　　　　　　(c)

Plate 7.8   Benjamin Minns (1894) *Types of New South Wales Aboriginals:*
Plate 7.8(a) *Merriman, King of Bermagui*
Plate 7.8(b) *Coonimon, Bermagui*
Plate 7.8(c) *Droab, Bermagui*

'Merriman, King of Bermagui' (plate 7.8a), 'Coonimon, Bermagui' (plate 7.8b), and 'Droab, Bermagui' (plate 7.8c). Two years before Roberts had shown at the Society's exhibition three portraits framed together, *Church, State and the Law*, and Minns' formal triptych may well follow this substantial and historically relevant precedent. On the other hand, a Rodius lithograph such as *Natives of New South Wales, Biddy Salamander of the Broken Bay Tribe, Balkabra, Chief of Botany and Gooseberry, Queen of Bungaree* has three images on a single plate; we may again be looking at a derivate from popular art.

From their detailed inscriptions, the Minns portraits, like those by Roberts, seem clearly to be intended as factual records of particular people. But how factual are they? Minns' portraits are collectively described as *Types*, a word which suggests that the artist is attempting to depict certain universal or common characteristics found amongst New South Wales Aborigines. In representations of white Australians too in this period there is often a similar attempt to search out 'types' and universals: this is to be seen, for example, in depictions of bush workers and shearers. In the case of the Aborigines, this search for the 'typical' is not confined to the 1890s. Strutt talks of being commissioned to take the portraits of 'specially typical blacks' even in the 1850s (Mackaness, 1958: 30).

All three portraits in *Types of New South Wales Aboriginals* are painted on plain pale grounds. They all have eyes that focus frowningly on a distant goal, straining to see. There appear to be no bodies below the faint shoulder line. The right hand portrait of *Droab* shows a proud, thrust-back head, counterbalanced by a substantial, almost patriarchal, beard. Minns' watercolours are expertly handled. The red brown of *Droab* is tinged with blue shadows, and the hair freshly stroked in with delicate nuances of blue and purple. Two years later a *Bulletin* critic, however, had this to say about Minns' work ('Un-Artistic Artists—Yell the Second' *Bulletin* 19 September 1896: 12):

In any ordinary light there is no purple tint in an Australian aboriginal—or nothing like as much as Minns shows: and consequently to ordinary observers his aboriginal pictures appear wrong and untrue to the extent of his purple surplus.

This conservative critic believed in idealisation of nature, within the bounds of probability, which Minns' use of colour overstepped. In the reviewer's opinion, the chief value of these portraits of Aborigines was 'as realistic representations to be handed down to future times: and idealistic treatment would spoil their truth and lessen their value'. What he seems to be saying is that the sort of idealisation and colour harmony in Minns' work is not acceptable in portraits of Aborigines.

Four years earlier, the *Bulletin* critic in reviewing the exhibition in which *Charlie Turner* was shown considered Roberts' figure studies and single heads, although successful technically, to be not strictly speaking Australian at all:

Turning to the figure pictures that are not distinctly Australian, we find Mr Tom Roberts greatly in evidence. His contributions may fairly be termed 'pot-boilers', inasmuch as they are simply studies of single heads and figures. ('The Art Society of NSW' *Bulletin* 10 September 1892: 5)

Historical subject painting was seen as a suitable vehicle for nationalistic sentiment; portraiture was not. Australian artists, according to the conservative views of the *Bulletin*, should be handling grand, and not simple, themes.

The paintings of Minns, Friström and Roberts were not merely portraits, but portraits of Aborigines, and were thus doubly disqualified from acceptance into the traditions of grand idealising history painting. Roberts never painted an Aboriginal equivalent of *Shearing the Rams*, although some of his single portrait heads may have been intended for a larger historical piece that never materialised. Significantly, Roberts' first exhibited Aboriginal portrait, *An Australian Native* (present whereabouts unknown), was shown at the Centennial International Exhibition (1888-9), and a number of his Aboriginal studies were not sold but retained in his studio until 1900.

In seeking out Aboriginal subjects, Roberts was also searching for the rare and the exotic. By the 1890s there were few full-blood Aborigines left in New South Wales. In the north and west of Queensland, however, one could still find 'the race in all its primitive glory'; and Roberts' trip up Cape York Peninsula to the Torres Strait in July and August 1892 was partly a romantic quest (Bevan, 1894: 80-1; Topliss, this volume). Friström shared the same romanticism. It is not clear if he and Roberts knew each other, but by the 1890s Friström, although a far less accomplished painter, seems to have had some knowledge of Roberts' technique and subject matter. Friström showed two oil paintings of Queensland Aborigines at the Centennial Exhibition, however, and his earlier single heads of 1887 may well predate Roberts' interest in Aboriginal subjects. He rarely exhibited his Aboriginal portraits, except for a group from his own collection in 1909. It is known that Archibald Meston owned paintings of Aborigines by Friström (Isles, Love and Co., 1904) and his paintings are used as illustrations by E. M. Mjöberg (1918). But no commission details survive, and his attitude toward these works remains unclear.

Portrait images of Aborigines in the 1890s, practically ignored by Geoffrey Dutton in his study *White on Black* (1974), unite the romantically

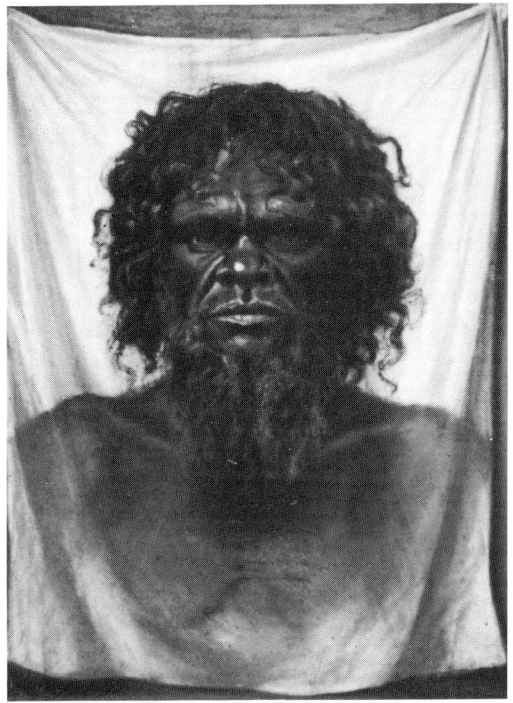

Plate 7.9 Oscar Fristrom (?late 1890s/early 1900s) *Portrait of an Aboriginal*

historical record of a 'dying' race with a formal codified iconography. The imagery draws on complex sources: upon popular tradition, academic prototypes and photographic models. Some images are more formalised than others. The gentle sympathy of Roberts' *An Aboriginal woman; Portrait of Maria Yulgilbar?* (plate 8.21) makes it very different from the many powerful, frontally posed, portraits by Fristrom of *King Sandy* and of *Catchpenny*, represented here by plate 7.1. Other paintings seem almost to have the intensity of icons: for example, Fristrom's oval-framed pastel *Aboriginal Woman and Child* of 1898 (Brisbane Civic Art Gallery), with its Raphaelesque overtones and its yellow, halo-like area behind both heads.

Fristrom's late *Portrait of an Aboriginal* (plate 7.9), undated, but possibly of the late 1890s or early 1900s, succinctly sums up the conventions of Aboriginal portraiture. This strange work, with its brilliant green ground, is the most melancholy Aboriginal portrait of the period. It is a pastel portrait of a frontally posed Aboriginal, detached from any social context. The face is depicted on a white Veronica veil, and the shoulder fades away in vignette-like manner. Like a holy relic, this Aboriginal sudarium is at once dignified and compelling: a symbolic representation of the Aboriginal as Christ. The artist has had no direct experience of the subject. For this is not simply a portrait of an Aboriginal, but a painting of an imprint of an Aboriginal face on a cloth: not an imprint made from first-hand observation, but one taken from a photograph (*Australian Aborigine. Queensland* by King). Fristöm's pastel thus encapsulates the romantic mythology concerning the tragic 'demise' of the Aboriginal race.

Acknowledgements

I would like to acknowledge the assistance of the Australian Research Grants Scheme in generously funding my study of 'Images of the Australian Aboriginal', of which this present essay constitutes a small section. Much of the initial ground work was undertaken in collaboration with Julie Brown, whom I would also like to acknowledge. My thanks to Helen Topliss for the inscription on *Billie Millera* and details of Roberts holdings in private collections, and to Nicolas Peterson for alerting me to a photograph of Tommy Walker. Humphrey McQueen kindly read the draft. Finally, I owe many details to the invaluable efforts of my research assistant, Birgit Culloty.

Bibliography

Bell, L. (1982) 'Artists and Empire: Victorian Representations of Subject People' *Art History* 5, 1, pp. 73-86

Bevan, E. (1894) 'Art at the Antipodes' *Antipodean* 2

Boime, A. (1971) *The Academy and French Painting in the Nineteenth Century* London: Phaidon

Bonwick, J. (1870) *The Last of the Tasmanians* London: Sampson Low, Son and Marston

Bradley, A. and T. Smith (eds) (1980) *Australian Art and Architecture. Essays Presented to Bernard Smith* Melbourne: Oxford University Press

Brown, J. and M. Maynard (1978) 'Painter and Photographer: Brisbane in the 1880s and 1890s' *History of Photography* 2, 4

Chase, A. K. and J. F. von Sturmer (1973) '"Mental Man" and Social Evolutionary Theory' in G.E. Kearney, P. R. de Lacey, and G. R. Davidson (eds) *The Psychology of Aboriginal Australians* Sydney: Wiley

Currie, B. (1978) 'Signior Nerli' *Art and Australia* 16, 1, pp. 55-60

Dutton, Geoffrey (1974) *White on Black. The Australian Aborigine Portrayed in Art* Melbourne: Macmillan

Hartwig, M. C. (1972) 'Aborigines and Racism: An Historical Perspective' in F. S. Stevens (ed.) *Racism, the Australian Experience* 2, Sydney: Australia and New Zealand Book Company

Healy, J. J. (1978) *Literature and the Aborigine in Australia* St Lucia: University of Queensland Press

Isles, Love and Co. (1904) *Catalogue of Australian Ethnographical Curios* 21 November

Lebrun, C. (1718) *Conférence...sur l'Expression Générale et Particulière* Amsterdam: De Lorme

Lebrun, C. (1827) *A Series of Lithographic Drawings Illustrative of the Relation between the Human Physiognomy and that of Brute Creation* London: [no publisher]

Mackaness, G. (ed.) (1958) *The Australian Journal of William Strutt ARA 1852-1862* Sydney: privately printed

Millar, D. P. (1981) *Charles Kerry's Federation Australia* Sydney: David Ell Press

Mjöberg, E. (1918) *Bland Stenaldersmanniskor i Queenslands Vildmarker* Stockholm: Albert Bonniers Förlag

Parry, E. (1974) *The Image of the Indian and the Black Man in American Art 1590-1900* New York: G. Braziller

Rowley, C. D. (1974) *The Destruction of Aboriginal Society* Harmondsworth: Penguin

Smith, Bernard (1980) *The Spectre of Truganini* Sydney: Australian Broadcasting Commission

Spate, Virginia (1972) *Tom Roberts* Melbourne: Lansdowne Press

Stevens, B. (1917) 'B. E. Minns' *Art in Australia* 2, [n.p.]

Woolmington, J. (1973) *Aborigines in Colonial Society 1788-1850* Melbourne: Cassell

EIGHT

TOM ROBERTS' ABORIGINAL PORTRAITS

Helen Topliss

WHILE DOCUMENTING ROBERTS' work for a catalogue raisonné (forthcoming) I came across a number of his studies of Aborigines and Torres Strait Islanders in private and public collections. My first task was to date them and to attempt to place them within the context of his other work which is known more widely. When I had combed my records for other such pictures and drawings, I discovered that there were some dozen works all done within the period 1890-95. As well as these extant pictures there are references to others in Roberts' article on his trip to the Torres Strait islands, entitled 'Going North' (1892a).

Not a great deal is known about these pictures. They have never been discussed as a group before. Nor have they been reproduced, except for the two which Geoffrey Dutton includes in his book *White on Black* (1974). When I first dated these works, I began to ask myself how these pictures were related to Roberts' work as a whole. I found that they belong to three distinct phases of his painting of outback subjects. The first two belong to the period of 1890, when he was working in the Riverina on *Shearing the Rams*, his first outback picture of heroic male labour; the second group belong to his trip at the end of 1892 to the Torres Strait islands via Cooktown; and the last two pictures belong to the period 1894-5, when he was working in north-eastern New South Wales near Inverell, where he painted *Bailed Up* and *In a Corner of the Macintyre*, and in the Clarence River area, where he painted *On the Timbarra, Reek's and Allen's Sluicing Claim* (plates 8.14−16).

The question that needs to be asked is whether the portraits of Aborigines and Islanders are incidental to his other outback pictures, and portrait commissions, or an integral part of what Roberts was trying to express about the particularity of Australian life. That he had conscious ambitions concerning his Aboriginal portraits is clearly implied in a letter he wrote to John Plummer, who was Secretary of the Society of Artists in Sydney. In December 1895, after he had completed all the portraits which I will be discussing here, he wrote to Plummer that he had been 'visiting parts of the colony and getting so far as Torres Straits and its Islands for studies of blacks' (1895c). Many years later Roberts claimed in a statement to the press in connection with his studies of Aborigines, 'I painted one in the Riverina, one in Sydney and several in Queensland. I thought they would have been an interesting record of a passing race' (1926). In this paper I am going to retrace Roberts' steps in order to establish a context for these pictures and to see if they can be claimed as an aspect of what I shall call his 'outback vision'. In drawing together all his representations of indigenous Australians, I will be relying on literary sources for works which have not yet come to light. And in order to understand their part in his oeuvre as a whole I will be comparing them with major works of the period and with other contemporary portraits.

Roberts' earliest identifiable portrait of an Aboriginal is *Gubbie Wellington*. Although its present whereabouts is unknown, a line reproduction was included in the 1890 catalogue of the Victorian Artists' Society, where it was exhibited with the caption 'One of the last Blacks of Corowa' (plate 8.1). Roberts must have painted Gubbie Wellington while he was

Plate 8.1   Tom Roberts (*c.* **1889**) *Gubbie Wellington—one of the last Blacks of Corowa*

Plate 8.2   Tom Roberts (1890) *Shearing the Rams*

working on *Shearing the Rams* (plate 8.2) which was painted in the Riverina at Brocklesby, near Corowa, on the station of Alec King and Alexander Anderson. *Shearing the Rams* was Roberts' first picture to express his new interest in the heroic aspects of the outback. This picture was to influence the direction he was to take over the succeeding decade, and the public reaction to it helped to set off a chain of pictures which are related to the same theme and place. The work was criticised in the *Argus* by the reactionary critic James Smith for being too specific and naturalist in style (1890). Roberts wrote a considered reply to this criticism where he expressed the necessity to depict 'a specific time and place' and where in his description of the outback and the various activities of the sheep industry he also anticipated his two later pictures *Shearing at Newstead* and *The Breakaway* (plates 8.3 and 8.4). In Roberts' own mind these pictures formed a kind of sequence or trilogy. In the letter Roberts connected sequentially the droving and rounding up of the sheep, the mustering in pens and the final herding of the sheep into the shearing shed. He conjured up the image of the golden fleece on the floor of the shed, three years before painting the picture popularly known by that name (plate 8.3).

In a number of public statements and letters to newspapers during this period Roberts spoke of the necessity of encouraging Australian artists. He

Plate 8.3 **Tom Roberts (1894)** *Shearing at Newstead*

Plate 8.4 **Tom Roberts (*c*. 1891-2)** *The Breakaway*

criticised the policy of the National Gallery of Victoria for not purchasing Australian works (1893). He was bitter about the fact that the trustees were uninterested in viewing a major work of Streeton's (1892b), and that they refused to buy his own *Shearing the Rams* which was purchased by a private buyer. He also emphasised the necessity of painting Australian themes. As President of the Society of Artists in Sydney, Roberts made a speech at its inaugural exhibition in 1895 where he repeated his view about the state of art in Australia, which he claimed was both melancholy and good: melancholy, because of the lack of patronage, but good in terms of the multiplicity of subjects for an artist to depict. The *Sydney Morning Herald* reporter quoted Roberts as saying that artists 'had the beauties of all the Pacific slope to paint—right away to the North where they were fishing for "bêche-de-mer", away to the far west, where gold was being mined for, and down to the southern coast, where pursuits were more agricultural . . . ' (Roberts, 1895b). It was crucial for artists to record the last colonial days for posterity: in twenty years' time nothing would remain. Roberts' own work in this period of the 1890s was concerned with recording the various aspects of outback life, particularly the agricultural pursuits which he mentions in his speech. He made one significant journey north to witness the bêche-de-mer fishing and pearl shelling industries, also noted in his speech.

The next Aboriginal portrait painted by Roberts is that of *Charlie Turner* (plate 8.5). This was exhibited at the Sydney Artists' Society in 1892, together with eight other portraits, forming his first contribution to this Society after his move from Melbourne to Sydney in 1891. The portrait was highly recommended by the reviewer, and it was bought for the Art Gallery of New South Wales. The reviewer wrote that it was painted with strength and fidelity and 'that its value will grow year by year with the gradual disappearance from our midst of the original possessors of the soil' (*Sydney Morning Herald*, 1892: 2). The melancholy note in the portrait is one which also enters photos of Aborigines of this and the preceding decades. Unlike other painters of the 1890s Roberts does not sentimentalise the features. Most of his portraits are sketches painted without attributes or effects; the interest seems to be focused on the features and the expression of the sitter. The directness of this head and the relative simplicity of the handling enable us to focus entirely on the features, particularly the eyes. The frontality of this portrait and the lack of any element apart from the head itself make it unusual even for Roberts' informal sketches. Compare it, for instance, with the 1891 portrait of *S. W. Pring* (plate 8.6), Roberts' friend and major correspondent of this period, where clothing is used to help set off the face. The focus rests on the features alone. Since the exhibition in which *Charlie Turner* was shown took place at the beginning of September 1892, I assume

Plate 8.5   Tom Roberts (1892) *Aboriginal Head — Charlie Turner*

that it was painted somewhere in New South Wales prior to his departure north. Although the portrait is dated 1892, Roberts was not in the outback that year, but he did spend the first few months of 1891 at Corowa.

Late in 1892 Roberts sailed up the east coast to the Torres Strait islands, stopping at various places before reaching Murray Island. There is no correspondence about this trip, and the only source of information is Roberts' long article which was published in four parts in the *Argus* from 12 November (1892a). I am relying on Roberts' own account of the journey in order to date the few portraits he painted en route. He sailed in a new ketch, the *Jessie*, where he took up a position as seaman in order to obtain free passage from Sydney to Cooktown. (His discharge certificate was amongst his papers.) In his record of the voyage, Roberts dwells on points of the coastline which recall events in Australia's early history, such as

Plate 8.6   Tom Roberts (1891) *S. W. Pring*

Captain Cook's first sighting of various landmarks. The *Jessie* was delivered at Cooktown where he may have painted *Amehnam* (plate 8.7), identified as a 'Port Darwin' belonging to the 'Woolna' tribe, one of the many names for the southern neighbours of the people of the Darwin area. Roberts has used virtually the same composition for *Amehnam* as he did for *Charlie Turner*, except that this is a profile portrait. The background and the spareness of style are the same.

Young Lubra (plate 8.8) was painted next at Somerset, Cape York. This is an unusual portrait in this context, as it is both a half-length portrait and more finished. The subject seems to be pregnant, but Roberts does not emphasise this, allowing the frame to interrupt the full line of the stomach. The portrait is inscribed as painted 'at Mr Jardine's place', Mr Jardine being presumably John Jardine, the first Government Resident appointed to the Torres Straits in 1864 (Haddon, 1935: 13). The first settlement was at

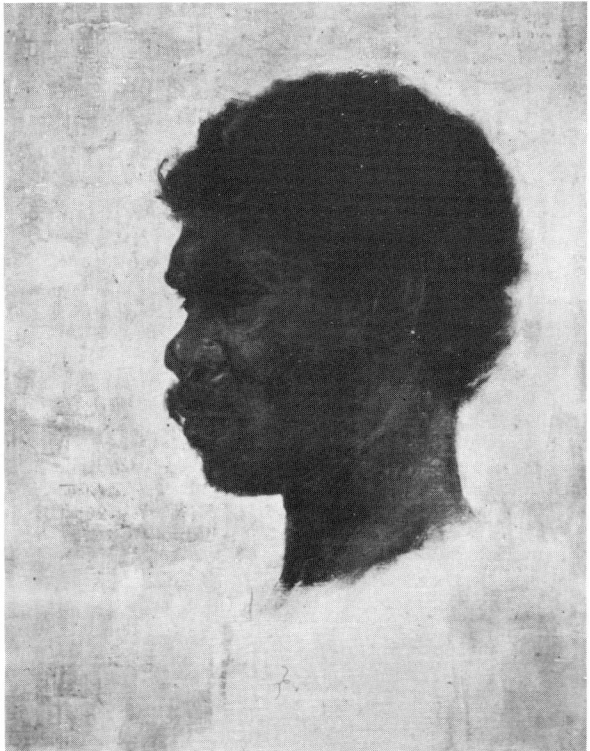

Plate 8.7   Tom Roberts (1892) *Amehnam*

Somerset and was later moved to Thursday Island in 1875 so that the Governor could better superintend the pearl shelling industry. Thursday Island was to be Roberts' next port of call. Most of Roberts' studies of Aborigines in this period have a pale grey or beige background which emphasises the skin tones, and in each of them he is at pains to concentrate on the features and on exact representation. The concern for accuracy and naturalism is what connects them to the outback pictures.

At Thursday Island Roberts describes the peculiar characteristics of the place and the multi-racial mix of people he describes as including 'Cingalee', 'Japs', 'Manila men', 'South Sea divers and boatmen of "all colours"', noting that 'there are three or four hundred white men to about two and a half thousand of "all colours"' (Croll, 1935: 211). What most clearly interested him during this trip was the observation of the different racial types. This emerges both in his narrative and in the remaining portraits.

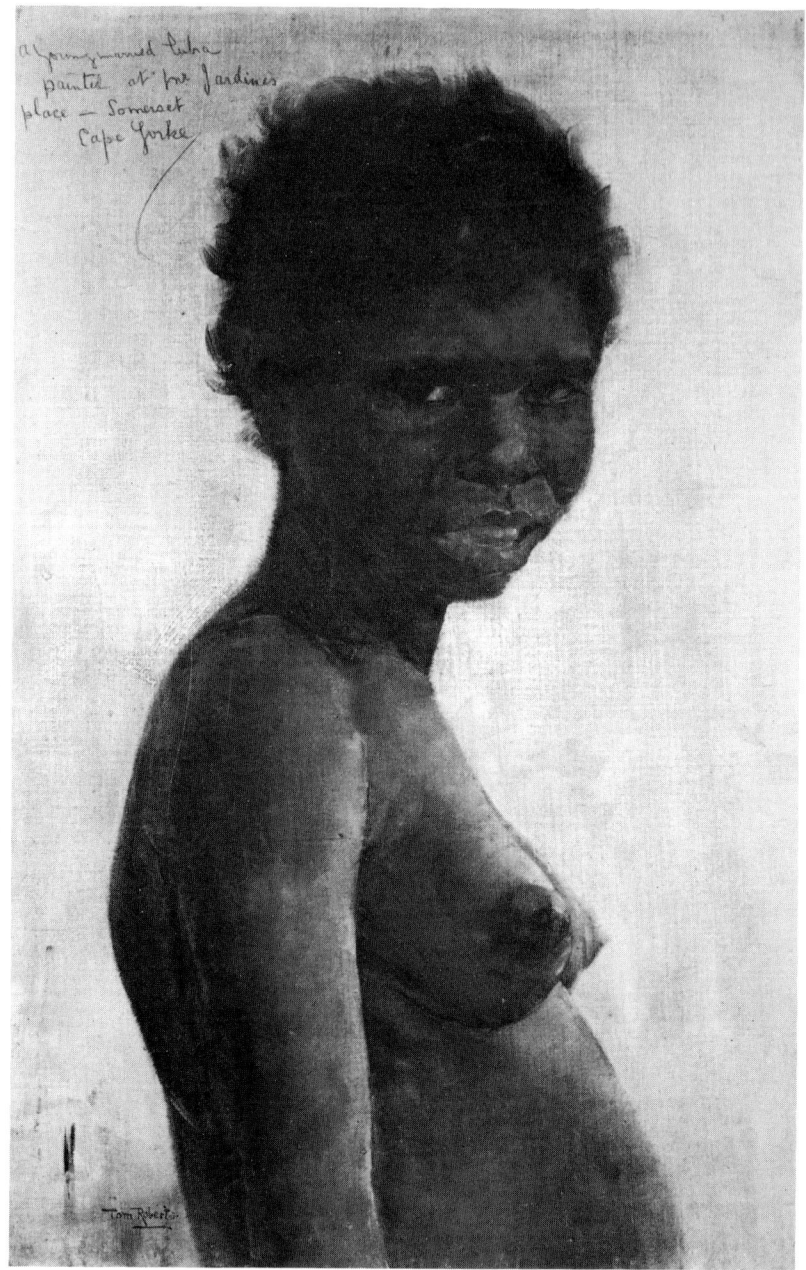

Plate 8.8   Tom Roberts (1892) *Young Lubra, Cape York*

Plate 8.9   Tom Roberts (1892) *John Douglas*

It was on Thursday Island that Roberts painted the portrait of *John Douglas* (plate 8.9), the Government Resident at that time. The portrait is a rapid sketch on wood. Its informality suggests that it was not commissioned (Roberts was to include this portrait in his series of twenty-three character sketches or panel portraits in his exhibition at the Society of Artists in 1900 (*Sydney Morning Herald*, 14 November 1900, p. 5). Roberts then accompanied John Douglas on one of his official visits to the islands. They travelled by steamer to Murray Island where they stayed and where Roberts read Professor Haddon's *Folk Lore of the Torres Straits* (Croll, 1935: 211-12). Alfred Cort Haddon had in fact spent five months on Mer or

Murray in 1888-89, where he recorded local rites and customs. Roberts' reading of this book, which he mentions in his article, testifies to his interest in the anthropology of the region. He writes about a wedding ceremony in great detail and the celebrations which follow, culminating in a '*kup kup*' or dance which continues throughout the night. Roberts also painted a couple of portraits which he describes graphically but which unfortunately have not survived. The first portrait was of a good-looking young man with semitic features. Roberts mentions his hair being decorated with red hibiscus, a white flower and feathers. After this he painted an elderly man called 'Dao' with a half-sad, half-wild expression (Croll, 1935: 213-14). The only works to remain of this part of the trip are a drawing at the Australian National Gallery, *Study of Natives*, and *Corroboree, Murray Island* (plates 8.10 and 8.11). It is possible that *Corroboree* has been misnamed, as the scene seems to be painted in daylight and the dancers are not visible. The '*kup kup*' referred to in Roberts' article took place at night with the flares of torches, and the night scene is particularly well described (Croll, 1935: 216-17). He notices the brilliant garments and dark limbs against the firelight and the intoxication of the movement and sound; none of this is relayed in this small sketch. The exotic effects detailed by Roberts in his narrative recall one of Gauguin's Tahitian

Plate 8.10   Tom Roberts (*c.* 1892) *Study of Natives*

pictures of the 1890s rather than this tame scene. It is a strange picture for Roberts to paint at this period, quite uncharacteristic in its lack of naturalism and definition (the hallmark of his outback pictures). It also does not have the varied brush strokes and fluidity of paint of the sketches of this period. The handling is flat and the colours are pastel shades more characteristic of his late works. Did the exotic scene which he described so well verbally prompt him to paint in a more impressionistic style than usual? Admittedly this would probably have been a preliminary sketch, but as such it is far less assured than his small Whistlerian impressions of the 1880s. This small picture with dappled areas of light and shade shows how unconvinced or untrained an impressionist he really was.

On his return journey Roberts stopped at Cooktown and Lizard Island where he watched the gathering of bêche-de-mer and pearl oyster shells. Here he mentions once more the interesting racial mix of 'Port Darwins, Binghis, Japs, Manila and Rotumah men'. A drawing in Roberts' scrapbook at the Mitchell Library of *Dick Rotumah* (plate 8.12) was presumably drawn here. Like the seated *Study of Natives*, it is a rapid thumb-nail sketch, done for the record. One of Roberts' finest portraits, that of *A Turbanned Man* (plate 8.13) in the National Gallery of Victoria, was probably also painted

Plate 8.11   Tom Roberts (1892) *Corroboree, Murray Island*

Plate 8.12   Tom Roberts (*c.* 1892) *Dick Rotumah*

here. It is undated, and there is no direct evidence of its provenance. But it has all the characteristics of Roberts' portraits of this period: the delicate tonal balance between grey background and the dark skin, as well as the grey of the clothes, and the crisp brushstrokes. It has a great deal in common technically with *Young Lubra* (plate 8.8). Further support for this dating comes from Roberts' description of the pearl shell divers, recruited, as he notes, from far and wide. His verbal portrait is very admiring: he refers to their nobility of bearing and he also records how they dress up at the end of the week's work to take part in festivities, at which time they 'are brilliant' (Croll, 1935: 216-17).

A Turbanned Man is probably 'a Manila man' (Croll, 1935: 220), dressed in what seem to be ceremonial clothes. The emphasis on dress can be contrasted with its absence from the Aboriginal portraits. The seriousness and nobility of the pose testify to Roberts' interest in the variousness of the people this trip was introducing him to.

In terms of period and context, the spirit in which the last-mentioned

Plate 8.13   Tom Roberts (*c. 1892*) *A Turbanned Man*

studies were undertaken would seem to be akin to that underlying Roberts'
general programme of making 'studies of blacks' all over the colony, which
he mentioned in passing in his letter to John Plummer. The value he set on
portraits such as these is also implied in his speech of 1895 at the Inaugural
Exhibition of the Society of Artists, where he listed various locations and
types of inspiration available to Australian artists.

Roberts' trip up north had interrupted his work in the pastoral outback.
In 1893 he went to north-eastern New South Wales to start work on
Shearing at Newstead (plate 8.3), and there he also made the first sketch for
Bailed Up (plate 8.14). The last group of Aboriginal portraits belong to this

period of 1894-95 and they were painted in the Clarence River area. *Shearing at Newstead* was painted at Newstead near Inverell, while *Bailed Up* was painted on the old Armidale to Inverell road, three miles from Newstead and two miles from Paradise station, where Roberts stayed with Russell Hughes. Another bushranging picture painted in the area is *In a Corner of the Macintyre* also known as 'Thunderbolt in an Encounter with the Police at Paradise Creek' (plate 8.15). Thunderbolt was the bushranger who held up the coach in *Bailed Up*. (This information is given by the son of Bob Bates (the coachman in *Bailed Up*) in an unidentified press cutting which has come to light among Roberts' papers.) As a sequel to *Bailed Up*, it is an example of how Roberts often worked in a programmatic way. 'Thunderbolt' was painted either at Newstead or at Russell Hughes' property, two miles from Paradise Creek. Another subject picture of this period is *On the Timbarra, Reek's and Allen's Sluicing Claim* (plate 8.16), describing an aspect of work on the goldfield along this tributary of the Clarence. While painting in the Clarence River area he stayed at another station, Millera, owned by Alexander Stewart. By 1894 Roberts was well

Plate 8.14   Tom Roberts (1895-1927) *Bailed Up*

acquainted with this part of New South Wales; he had a network of patrons there, and a number of stations he could stay at. It is worth noting that Roberts travelled constantly in north-eastern New South Wales from 1893 onwards. He stayed at some locations for months at a time, particularly at Newstead, the property of Duncan Anderson, who must have introduced him to other squatters in the area. In 1891 Roberts had moved to Sydney from Melbourne, presumably because of the end of the boom, the lack of patronage, and because of the unenlightened policy of the trustees of the National Gallery of Victoria who refused to buy contemporary Australian paintings.

The difficulty of finding patronage in the city helped to encourage Roberts' own propensity for the outback. During this period Roberts clearly found the outback and its connections with the 'heroic' past more appealing. (Some of the major works painted there were of the past and not of the present.) The big pictures he painted in the outback show a strong visual

Plate 8.15 Tom Roberts (1894) *In a Corner of the Macintyre*

response as well as an historical sense as can be seen in his careful reconstruction of a scene such as *Bailed Up*, which had occurred some 30 years before. (Roberts had old postcards of a Cobb & Co. coach at Inverell in order to help him paint the picture, as well as interviewing the old driver, Bob Bates, who recounted the famous hold-up.) Apart from his own sense of the colonial past, the outback clearly provided him with a number of patrons and a congenial way of life. His letters of the period refer to musical evenings, picnic races, tennis, and long rides on his own horse Black Bess. In late 1894, during the period when he was painting *On the Timbarra* (plate 8.16), Roberts rode from Tenterfield to Tabulam and down the Clarence.

A photo of Roberts on his horse, Black Bess (reproduced in Farwell, 1973: 323), was taken at Yulgilbar where he stayed in December 1894. Here he painted two Aboriginal portraits and the portrait of *Edward Ogilvie* (plate 8.17), one of the great property owners of the Upper Clarence area. Roberts described him as 'the chief aged 80 with no sign of mental failure, military type, in mind and physique' (1895a). Roberts painted him in the courtyard of his somewhat Italianate castle, as can be seen from the drawing of himself at work which Roberts included in the letter he wrote to his friend Pring (plate 8.18). Roberts' characterisation of Ogilvie is confirmed by the portrait which shows his erect, military bearing and his deter-

Plate 8.16 Tom Roberts (*c.* 1894) *On the Timbarra, Reek's and Allen's Sluicing Claim*

mination. Ogilvie was the first white man to explore the Upper Clarence River in 1840, where he took up 56 miles of land on either side, under the name of Yulgilbar. Ogilvie learned the local dialect of Bandjalang by kidnapping a boy called Pundoon, whom he returned to his people in 1842, thereby arranging a parley with the Aborigines of the area, who had until then been hostile. As a direct result of speaking their language he was able to make a treaty with them, allowing them their rights to hunt and collect honey in return for pasture for his sheep. Ogilvie described his encounter with these Aborigines in a long letter published in the *Sydney Morning Herald* (14 November 1842: 5). In this letter he wrote of the importance of

Plate 8.17   Tom Roberts (1895) *Edward Ogilvie*

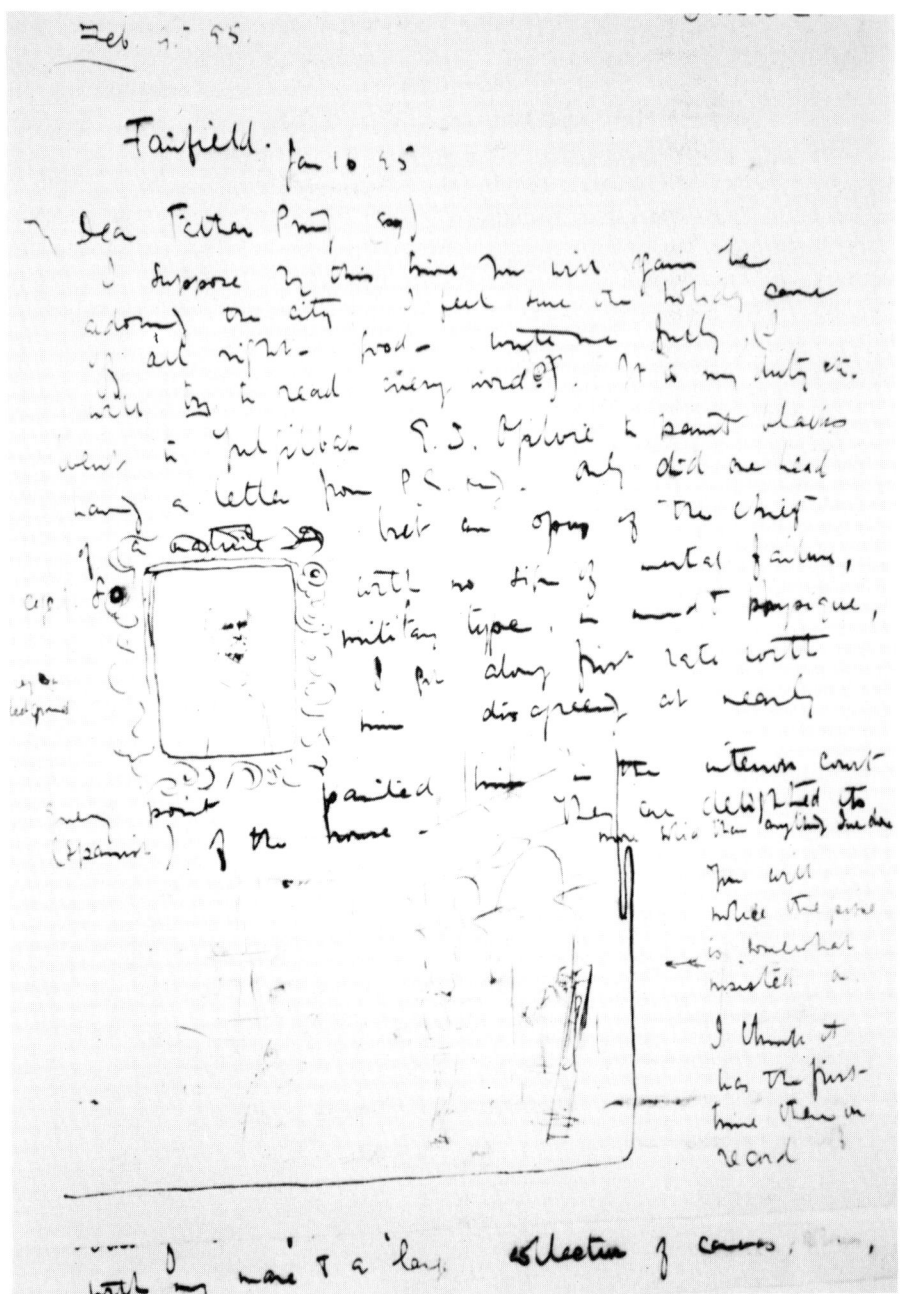

Plate 8.18   Tom Roberts (1895), *Roberts at Work at Yulgilbar*

peaceful co-existence, on the basis of his observation that Aborigines were placable and open to argument. Ogilvie's type of liberal humanism was to remain rare in this area. In the 1850s when Ogilvie's white station hands left for the goldfields he replaced them with Aborigines. *Billie Millera* (plate 8.19) may have been one of them, though the surname suggests that he worked on Alexander Stewart's station, Millera. Some of the Aboriginal workers at Yulgilbar were recorded in Ogilvie's station journal, which in 1852 contains the name Billy Milly (Prentis, 1972: 224). The picture is inscribed: 'Billie Millera / was a grown man / in 46 when Ed. Ogilvie / of Yulgilbar was the / first white / to see him'. This portrait is probably the one Roberts referred to in a letter to his friend Pring (1894). He relates that on seeing his portrait the old man could only see the likeness of a dog.

Roberts' portrait of Billie Millera is rather odd in its shrunken proportions and in its elongation of the face. But it is close stylistically to the northern portraits already discussed. Here he is concentrating on the profile and the contours of this craggy face. Roberts is looking for essential characteristics, unlike the photographer Lindt in some of his near-contemporary portraits of Aborigines taken around Grafton (Lindt, *c.* 1880). Both Lindt and Roberts are recording people living a changed way of life. Roberts chooses to depict them as individuals and as divorced from their environments; Lindt on the other hand surrounds his sitters with all the picturesque paraphernalia of

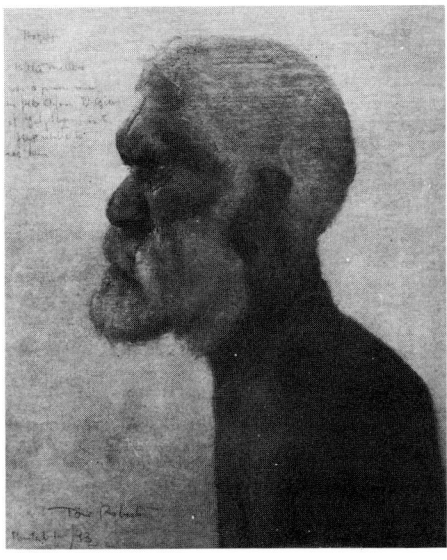

Plate 8.19　Tom Roberts (1894) *Billie Millera*

weapons and other materials related to their earlier life-style, but these are arranged artificially in a studio setting. Roberts as we have seen is interested in the essentials in all his Aboriginal portraits; this is perhaps unusual in a period when artists were increasingly returning to the 'noble savage' idiom, or developing aesthetic fantasies where Aborigines become spirits of the bush, as in Syd Long's pictures. Another comparison is provided by a fascinating large watercolour by Blamire Young (plate 8.20), which juxtaposes white man and Aboriginal in an exotic decorative frieze of elaborate detail and colour. *Buckley Acting as Interpreter at Indented Head* offers an aesthetically pleasing image of an historic event, however its beauty distracts our attention from the moral implications of the scene it represents. The exotic detail, brilliant colour, and art nouveau stylisation of figures make it difficult to interpret the picture. It takes some time for the viewer to disentangle the visual evidence and to locate Buckley, 'the wild white man', placed in a subsidiary position next to the prominent and central

Plate 8.20   Blamire Young (1901) *Buckley Acting as Interpreter at Indented Head*

figure of one of Batman's henchmen. Buckley is to be found behind this figure, where he is presumably translating the offers made by the white men for the Aborigines' land. The objects of barter are represented: the red cloth which joins the two groups, the beads seen hanging from the pocket of the central figure and the bags of flour on the left. This picture, like many others at the end of the century, emphasises aesthetic effect at the cost of historical concern. It is easy to neglect the moral dimension when looking at this beautiful watercolour. Its richness and stylisation mask the tragedy of Buckley's unwitting betrayal of the Aborigines with whom he has lived for nearly thirty-two years. There is a contrast here with the work of Roberts. Roberts was far less ambitious in his portrayals of Aborigines, both in limiting himself to his own experience and in choosing not to paint historical subject pictures. But he did express a sympathetic response to the condition of contemporary Aborigines. His portraits face up to the historical moment, and his concern to observe his sitters with accuracy and to inscribe their

portraits with information about them is evidence of an attitude which prevented him from resorting to the romantic images of noble savagery which were becoming current in the 1890s.

Roberts painted one other portrait in this area, called *Maria Yulgilbar* when it was exhibited at the Society of Artists in September 1895. This could be the same work as the unnamed portrait in the Dixson Galleries, Sydney (plate 8.21). I have discovered two drawings for this portrait in one of Roberts' sketchbooks in the Mitchell Library (n.d.: 99). Around one of these (plate 8.22), Roberts has attempted to write down a few words in Bandjalang. Some are recognisable as possible words of the local dialect, but none are useful in the interpretation of the drawing (Margaret Sharpe, personal communication). Possibly Ogilvie's own interest in the language prompted Roberts to record these words and also 'Peanahgo' (upper left) and 'Billipimbah' (upper right) on the portrait of Billie Millera. A photograph of 'Maria Charlie' (plate 8.23) shows someone who looks very like the sitter for Roberts' unnamed portrait in Sydney. This is taken from the Clarence River Historical Society archives. Even if Maria Charlie was not the sitter, there are strong facial resemblances between the two women, suggesting that they were related, and that the portrait was indeed painted in the Clarence River area.

What I think emerges from the study of these portraits and the larger context to which they belong is Roberts' historical sense and his avowed desire to record a specific time and place, especially in relation to certain outback areas in New South Wales. Roberts' outback pictures more than those of any other single Australian artist have become the foundation myths of a national identity. It seems evident from a review of his career in the 1890s that Roberts was thinking and working in national terms, and that he was on the lookout for representative subjects. In 1897, while camping on the Clarence River at Copmanhurst, he wrote to Pring in rhapsodic tones about the bush: and he added 'to think if one could express it all make others feel what beauty there is in it. Australia hasn't been fairly touched yet . . .' (Roberts, 1897). This letter was written after Roberts had painted all his outback pictures; towards the end of the century he was to be mainly employed in painting portraits.

Roberts' historical sense has already been recognised in his subject pictures. The same impulse can also be argued for his Aboriginal portraits. Of course they remain a fragmentary record, since he did not paint a subject picture concerning Aborigines, but they are not unrelated to the overall context which I have tried to outline. Certainly in his letter of 1895, already cited, Roberts reveals that he had set out to paint a number of portraits of blacks all over the colony. At the same time he was working on a much more homogeneous series of panel portraits of eminent figures, which

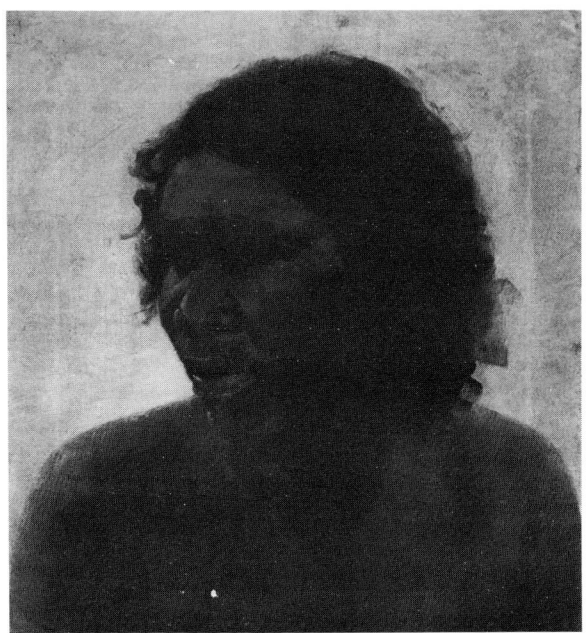

Plate 8.21   Tom Roberts (1894) *Portrait of an Aboriginal Woman: Maria Yulgilbar?*

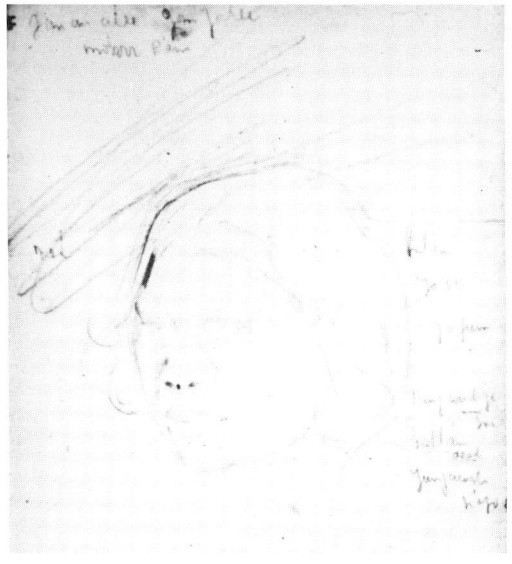

Plate 8.22   Tom Roberts (1894) *Drawing of Maria Yulgilbar?*

133

Plate 8.23 **(n.d.)** *Maria Charlie*

included politicians such as Edward Garran, musicians such as George Marshall-Hall and people of the theatre such as Dion Boucicault and Robert Brough. There were twenty-three portraits in all and Roberts hoped to sell them as a gallery of Australian types, noting on the catalogue handbill 'how interesting such a group would be to us now, of similar types of say, fifty years ago'. Sadly the pictures were dispersed, but Roberts' concern for the historical shows in his conviction that 'the interest of such a collection, if broken up, would be to a great extent lost' (Roberts, 1900). Later, from London, Roberts corresponded with Deakin about the importance of setting up an Australian gallery of politicians connected with Federation and even offered to come out to Australia for six months to carry out the work. In 1910 he wrote to Deakin that 'it disturbs me to think that most of you are likely to go on till the inevitable comes, and leave behind nothing that will give the future anything that will show what you all were as men to look at . . .' (Roberts, 1910).

Roberts' record of Australian Aborigines can be seen as reflecting the same historical sense, and certainly would have been by contemporary viewers convinced that Aborigines were 'a passing race'. These portraits can be claimed as a fragment or aspect of his 'outback vision'. They are images of individuals caught at a specific moment, whose distinct personalities are portrayed with absolute naturalism.

Acknowledgement

I am indebted to Stephen Crawford for sending me the photograph of Maria Charlie (plate 8.23) from the Clarence River Historical Society's archives.

Bibliography

Croll, R. H. (1935) *Tom Roberts* Melbourne: Robertson & Mullens

Dutton, G. (1974) *White on Black: The Australian Aborigine Portrayed in Art* Melbourne: Macmillan

Farwell, G. (1973) *Squatter's Castle: The Story of a Pastoral Dynasty; Life and Times of Edward D. S. Ogilvie: 1814-96* Melbourne: Lansdowne Press

Haddon, A. C. (1890) 'Legends from the Torres Straits', *Folk Lore* 1, pp. 47-81, 172-196

Haddon, A. C. (1935) *Reports of the Cambridge Anthropological Expedition to Torres Straits* vol. 1, Cambridge: Cambridge University Press

Lindt, J. W. C. (c. 1880) *Album of Twelve Photographs of Australian Aborigines* Grafton (La Trobe Library)

Ogilvie, E. D. S. (1842) Letter *Sydney Morning Herald* 8 July, p. 3

Philipp, F. and J. Stewart (eds) (1964) *In Honour of Daryl Lindsay: Essays and Studies* Melbourne: Oxford University Press

Prentis, M. (1972) 'Aborigines and Europeans in the Northern River Regions', MA thesis, University of Sydney

Roberts, T. (1890) Letter *Argus* 4 July, p. 10

—— (1892a) 'Going North' *Argus* 12 November, p. 13; 19 November, p. 4; 3 December, p. 13; 10 December, p. 4; reprinted in Croll, 1935: 208-23

—— (1892b) Letter *Argus* 30 November, p. 7

—— (1893) Letter *Argus* 30 September, p. 14

—— (1894) Letter to S. W. Pring, 8 December, Mitchell Library MLMSS 1367/2

—— (1895a) Letter to S. W. Pring, 16 January, Mitchell Library MLMSS 1367/28

—— (1895b) 'Society of Artists: Close of the First Exhibition' *Sydney Morning Herald* 21 October, p. 3

—— (1895c) Letter to John Plummer, 4 December, Mitchell Library MS ar. 48

—— (1897) Letter to S. W. Pring, 16 January, Mitchell Library MLMSS 1367/2

—— (1900) *Exhibition and Sale of Paintings by Tom Roberts: Previous to his leaving Australia* Sydney, 14 November; Society of Artists

—— (1910) Letter to Deakin, in Philipp & Stewart, 1964:173

—— (1926) 'Then and Now: Changes in Art: Tom Roberts Impressed' *Sydney Daily Telegraph* 8 June, p. 11

—— (n.d.) Sketchbook vol. 6, Mitchell Library

Smith, J. (1890) Leader column *Argus* 28 June, pp. 8-9

Sydney Morning Herald (1892) 'Art Society's Exhibition: First Notice' 2 September, p. 2

Topliss, H. (forthcoming) *Tom Roberts: A Catalogue Raisoné* Melbourne: Oxford University Press

NINE

THOMAS DICK'S
PHOTOGRAPHIC VISION

Isabel McBryde

THOMAS DICK'S WORLD was not the cosmopolitan circuit played by the intellectual leaders discussed in some other chapters of this volume. It was that of a small port and fishing town on the far north coast of New South Wales, Port Macquarie (figure 9.1). Here his grandfather had settled in 1841 after migrating from England. By profession Thomas Dick (plate 9.1) like other members of his family, was an oyster farmer, or 'culturist', to use the term of the time. His political arena was that of local and parish government, his scientific arena the practicalities of oyster culture and the contacts they gave him with museum and state fisheries scientists in Sydney.

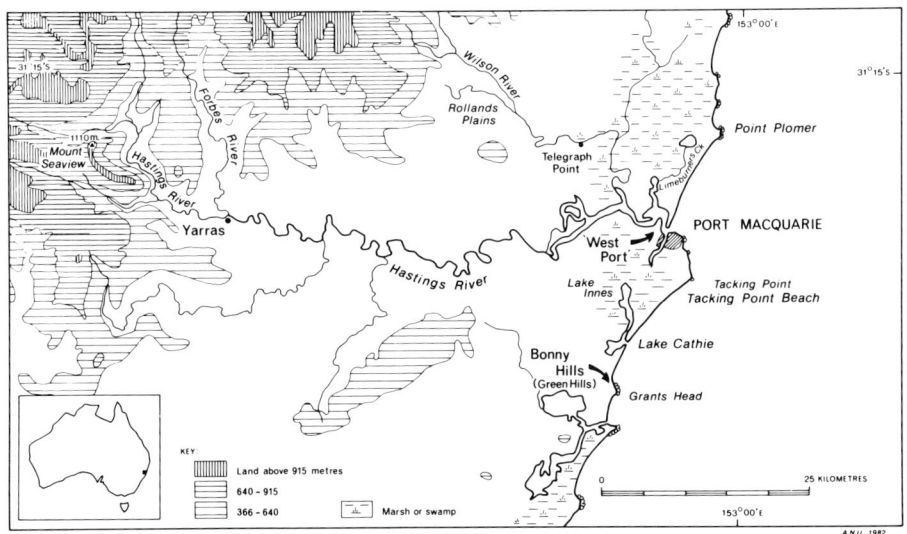

Figure 9.1 *Port Macquarie and the Hastings River district*

137

Plate 9.1a *The photographer photographed: Thomas Dick and friends* **from Port Macquarie and Sydney picnic at Yarras on the Hastings River. Photograph was taken by T.C. Roughley** *c.* **1916-1917. Dick pours tea from the billy. On his right sits Les Horsfield, the owner/driver of the Ford which was the car used for many photographic excursions**

His interests in natural history, in local history, and in the culture of the region's Aborigines were intense and all-embracing. Photography provided a medium for illustrating his ideas; he has left a magnificent visual record of Aboriginal life in the Hastings district. In this work we may see him both reflecting, and reacting to, intellectual movements originating in Europe and colouring Australian perceptions of the Aborigines at that time.

Dick's photographic record survives only in fragmented form. Several museums and libraries hold print collections, two have sets of surviving glass negatives, while some negatives and prints remain with members of the family. However, these comprise but part of the original record. Matching surviving negatives to the print collections leaves disturbing discrepancies. We must be grateful to the Australian Museum for its decision forty years ago to acquire a substantial number of negatives portraying Aborigines (McCarthy, 1947: 426). This, with Dick's sending of print sets to Cambridge and to Brisbane in the 1920s, has preserved the Aboriginal record more

Plate 9.1b *Studio portrait of Dick by Eden Photo Studios, Sydney*: somewhat less
successful as a portrait than Dick's study of his Aboriginal colleague (plate 9.7a)

effectively than other aspects of his work. Consistency of style, and the
involvement of the same group of Aboriginal participants during the period
of photography do help us to recognise Dick's Aboriginal photographs. A
substantial coverage of other aspects of local history may well have existed,
but its components await research and recognition, if they survive.
Recognising the work of individual photographers where negatives are not
identified can be very difficult, since it depends on knowledge of the style
and equipment employed, and also of the localities or subjects portrayed. It
is inconceivable that Dick used his photographic talents only in the service
of his interests in Aboriginal culture. However, for other subjects he may
well have adopted a different style to convey his interpretation. The
dispersal of the collection is tragic. Tragic also is the loss of so many
negatives, and of the accompanying documentation. At present I am
preparing a catalogue of existing components of the collection, and studying
the Aboriginal record.

Dick's Aboriginal photographs created between 1910 and 1927 pose a number of questions. First, the visual record must be assessed and interpreted. This may be done within several contexts: the history of photography as a visual art in Australia; the practice of ethnographic photography at the time; or in terms of the ethnographic information which may be encapsulated in the visual record, judged independently of the purposes of its creator. From this follow questions relating to Dick's motivation and aims. What led the oyster culturist to become ethnographic photographer? Were his aims documentary, or artistic and interpretative? His work is certainly of high quality, both technically and artistically; dimensions other than the documentary and ethnographic are relevant. It reminds one not only of the control of technique demonstrated by the contemporary photographers of Kerry and Company (Millar, 1981) but also of the conventions of lighting and composition used by the innovators of the Pictorial School—Cazneaux and Deck in Sydney, and Nicholas Caire in Melbourne (plates 9.2, 9.3, 9.4). Dick's photographs also evoke something

Plate 9.2 *Fishing in the still waters of the tidal creeks, Hastings estuary.* **Composition and lighting add emotion to this evocative scene**

of the haunting atmosphere of the portrayals by Curtis and Latham of American Indian life (Curtis, 1972; McLuhan, 1973; Gidley, 1976 and 1979). What is Dick's perception of Aboriginal culture? Does he consciously display it in his photographic record?

The elements of his perceptions of Aboriginal society are elusive entities, for little has survived of his writings. Much has to be inferred from the visual record itself. Thomas Dick died suddenly on 13 May 1927, his fiftieth birthday, drowned off Tacking Point Beach (figure 9.1) where he took so many of his Aboriginal photographs. It is thought that immediately after his death his widow destroyed his artefact collection, his paper on the Aborigines, and many of his negatives. None of his document collections or writings on the history of local Aborigines and on their culture survive, nor

Plate 9.3 *Study of canoes.* **This is evocative in its use of tonal variation and reflection. The fires placed on pads of clay in the canoes are well documented for the region, and were noted by Cook at Botany Bay in 1770. The canoes were made of bark from the Stringybark (*Eucalyptus agglomerata/E. globoidea*) or a mahogany (*E. acmenioides/ E. resinifera*)**

Plate 9.4 *On the upper reaches of the Hastings.* **Back lighting again is used to effect, but here creates a sense of movement and action. Photograph taken between Yarras and Mount Seaview**

can his artefact collections now be traced. The typescript for his history of Port Macquarie, however, together with a number of negatives and prints remained in the family for many years.

Letters written during the last few years of his life hint at poor health and diminished activity (cf. Roderick, 1952: xx-xxi). Until then his life had been excessively busy, devoted to civic and church affairs and to the family oyster-growing business. He was a man of energy and initiative, seen as an 'achiever', with considerable independence of mind. From his practical knowledge of coastal ecology came contact with scientists in Sydney, who regarded him as 'a keen observer of nature' whose 'data should not be despised' (Baker, 1915: 277). The Dick family were respected as expert oyster culturists by officers of the State Fisheries. They consulted Thomas Dick regarding several of their projects; for example, when advising the South African government on oyster growing and the transport of live oysters. The Fisheries Annual Report for 1915 contains a paper discussing his observations of oyster-spawning (Dick, 1916). Visits, specimens and information were exchanged between Dick and R. T. Baker, Curator of the Technological Museum in Sydney, and with T. C. Roughley, an expert on coastal fish species. Baker refers to Dick's observations in his paper on mangrove ecology, and uses his photographs to illustrate several points (Baker, 1915: see plates xlvi and xlvii). By 1914 Dick was beginning to make his detailed studies of Aboriginal activities. In that year he seems to have made his commitment to photography, purchasing, with advice from Baker and Roughley, the first of his large format Thornton Pickard cameras. Later his standard range of equipment included a Ruby Reflex and two Thornton Pickards. In 1915 Baker presented Dick's paper on Aboriginal shields to the Royal Society of New South Wales. This was a fascinating technical account, incorporating evidence from his father's observations of earlier days. It was published in the Society's journal (Dick, 1915) and Dick was elected to membership. His sponsors were men of power in the Society: Baker and Smith of the Technological Museum and Hedley of the Australian Museum. Later relations with the Society seem less happy; after several unsuccessful attempts to place papers on various natural history topics he resigned his membership in 1923. His letters to the Society mention his paper on the history of Port Macquarie Aborigines, but there is no evidence of its ever having been submitted.

By 1923 he had created a file of over 500 glass negatives, recording different aspects of Aboriginal life in the Hastings district. He had also acquired a considerable collection of artefacts characteristic of the local area: spears, shields, clubs, boomerangs, spear throwers and hafted hatchets. Some of these were the work of his informants, others came from a collection made by his father. He used them in the photographic record, making it a valuable source for material culture studies (plates 9.5, 9.6 and 9.17). In addition he made substantial collections (about 6000 pieces) of stone artefacts from local archaeological sites, especially the coastal middens and workshop areas. His comments on these in letters to the Australian Museum (1918/1919) reveal a sophisticated awareness of technological aspects which was not appreciated. He pointed out that the collections included several total production sequences, which he had photographed *in situ* before collecting, also that he could provide information on the sources for the raw materials involved. Such aspects, he felt, endowed the collection with considerable educational value. These points were not accepted by the museum ethnologist of the time, who was concerned only with cabinet specimens of designed tools and unique items. He remarked that waste material was found in abundance on all such sites, and so by definition did not comprise 'implements'. The crated artefacts were returned to Dick after

Plate 9.5 *Instructing a young man in tribal lore*. **The three main Aboriginal contributors to the record, acting out the elders instructing a young man**

several years in store at the museum. This unhappy exchange was not repeated; Dick's next overtures to a state museum were directed to Queensland. One wonders whether the strained relations between his patron Charles Hedley and the Australian Museum's hierarchy at this time played a part in the rebuff.

To artefacts and images Dick added the written word (Ewers, 1976). For the centenary of Port Macquarie in 1921 he prepared a series of articles on local history, published in the town newspaper. They were based on documentary material collected by his father (Roderick, 1952: xx-xxi; *The Voice of the North*, 10 May 1921, 8). In this history he refers to his manuscript on the Hastings District Aborigines and their culture (unfortunately, the document has not survived).

. . . to me the history of this fast-dying race has always been of intense interest. It is generally admitted that their origin goes back to very remote times, and my imperfect study of them at even this late day, convinces me that they were badly

Plate 9.6 *Portrait with weapons*. **A posed portrait, of a type rather than the individual. This may have been taken at the time of Port Macquarie's centenary celebrations, 1921. These included a procession, stage managed by Dick, and headed by his Aboriginal informants decorated for the occasion (see *Voice of the North* 10 May 1921, p. 8)**

misjudged and at times very hardly treated by the first white invaders of their ancient domain. The time has passed unfortunately for gaining anything like a comprehensive knowledge of this stone age people, but much may yet be recorded that should prove of interest to those seeking information relative to the primitive races of mankind. Racial antagonism and the struggle to maintain a foothold on this continent in the early days of settlement, afforded neither time nor inclination for intelligent study of the original inhabitants. They cannot be judged by their few degenerate descendants of today, who it must be remembered, have arrived at their present pitiable condition as the direct result of contamination by the vices of civilization, which they are mentally ill-equipped to combat. (*Old Port Macquarie* no. 22, 4 June 1921)

In 1923 he said of this work:

I set out years ago to collect and write the history of these Aborigines, and get together, not only a fine collection of photos, but also a fine collection of implements etc., and not the least was a remarkable amount of information.

I went into the mountains with them, gained their confidence and their secrets connected with their laws, and in some instances the information was only given with the understanding that it would only [?not] be published until after death.

I was fortunate for some of the old men were most intelligent and they recognised that their race was run, as it were, so they gave me under the conditions named, the history of their race.

Now by these means I secured all of the marks on the sacred trees, and their meaning, all of the rules of the 'Waipara' or man making ceremony.

In all their doings these primitive people followed nature, and when the whole is written a very interesting record will be made available to those interested. I do not known when I will bring out the work for I am now too much handicapped ... (Letter to Longman, Director, Queensland Museum, April 1923)

These comments reflect familiarity with prevailing academic views of the period on the Aborigines—the inevitability of Aboriginal decline, both in culture and in population, and their contamination by the 'vices of civilisation'.

Dick's sympathies are evident, also his regret, but he offers no hope of a new future for the Aboriginal communities of his region. His interests seem firmly directed to the past. The Aboriginal subjects could perhaps be seen merely as 'representatives' of the passing Aboriginal culture, as stereotypes (plates 9.6 and 9.7(a)). Yet there is also his strong respect for the practical skills of the Aboriginal hunter, and the understanding of these gained from close association over many years. As well as being 'types' the Aborigines he portrays are people, are individuals. He is often at pains to correct their popular image as members of 'the low race of people' which he associates with Darwinian theories and with Darwin's comments on the Australian Aborigines which he considered based on a small sample from the 'poorest' area. (Captions to prints sent to the Queensland Museum in 1923.)

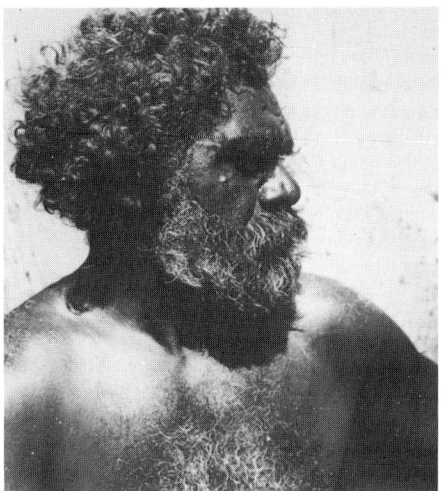 

Plate 9.7(a) *One of Thomas Dick's Aboriginal colleagues—Murray*: an interesting portrait study, but still conveying less individuality than many of the action photographs of the same man. Dick's comments on a print of this photograph sent to the Queensland Museum indicate that he intended it to portray 'the type' of the Aborigines of NSW

Plate 9.7(b) *Portrait of Murray*. Lionel Lindsay's perception gives insights into the present, while Dick's perspective was to the past

The photographic record was compiled over many years on trips to the bush made with his informants, to re-enact events and activities in the appropriate settings. His son Ray Dick, who went on these trips as a young boy, has vivid memories of the hiring of the car, the piling into it of artefacts, Aborigines and camera gear before driving into the bush. The Aboriginal informants, or associates, comprised five men and two women, with their children (plate 9.9); they were employed for the occasion. Two of the men were elderly (plate 9.5). They would have had considerable knowledge of pre-contact life. All but one came from the Hastings district. In the bush they engaged in specific activities, such as canoe-making, shield manufacture, fishing, hunting and gathering (plates 9.8 to 9.12), while Dick photographed. So the record is not of Aboriginal life of the early twentieth century, the life of the fringe camps and settlements, but a re-enactment of traditional life (plate 9.13).

These points may be rather neatly demonstrated in the comparison of plates 9.7(a) and 9.7(b), both portraits of Dick's Aboriginal colleague

Murray. Each in its way is also a statement about the dispossessed Aboriginal minority in rural New South Wales at that time. Dick's photographic portrait (plate 9.7(a)) was intended to show 'the type' of the Aboriginal, to demonstrate that this was far removed from the popular preconceptions of a 'low race of people'. The image is also a projection of the past, heavy with nostalgia, yet at the same time it is a successful portrait of that particular man. The other portrait of Murray (plate 9.7(b)) is a sketch with colour wash by Lionel Lindsay (Port Macquarie Sketchbook— Dixson Library ZDL PX68 f16 dated 19 October, 1916). Lindsay visited Port Macquarie in 1916 as a guest of Dick (Ray Dick personal communication) and while there compiled a delightful series of sketches of the convict period buildings and coastal scenery. That of Murray contrasts with the Dick photographic study. Yet the differences are not only those imposed by medium. The Lindsay sketch embodies a different perception of Aboriginal people, as well as of Murray himself. Less formal than the Dick portrait it portrays a lively personality. We even seem to be given a glimpse of Murray's own view of his world. Did both subject and artist share a sardonic sense of humour? Here we have a portrayal of the present life of the Aboriginal, the life of the dispossessed, the dweller on the fringes of European society. This is summarised in the sketch's title—'Murray-drunk. Tom Dick's pet aboriginal'. The nostalgia, that regret for lost cultural traditions of the past that permeates Dick's images, is absent. In its place is uncomfortable present reality. Yet the individual merges even here into type specimen, though of a different cultural situation, or so it would seem when we read the caption with its hint of a denial of individual humanity.

The photographs form several distinct categories. There are enactments of activities such as hunting, fishing, gathering (plates 9.8 to 9.12), camp life, ceremonial, fights and such highlights as the sighting from the cliffs of Bonny Hills (Green Hills) of the *Endeavour* as she sailed the east coast in 1770. On this negative the ship has been added in retouching (plate 9.14). Then come the series of 'stages of production' showing shield and canoe manufacture, hut construction and stone tool manufacture (plates 9.15 and 9.16). These were recorded in admirable detail, involving many negatives for each series. Some physical effort must also have been involved for all concerned in setting up these series, especially those taken up river on the Hastings between Yarras and Mount Seaview (see figure 9.1, and plates 9.4 and 9.13). These series are now difficult to re-assemble in entirety given the dispersal of negative and print collections, but what may be put together is of great value (plates 9.17 to 9.20 which come from three separate sources). In addition there are two groups, involving fewer negatives, comprising portraits and posed set-pieces of human figures (plates 9.9 and 9.10). These seem to me less successful than the other photographs, but this may reflect

Plate 9.8 *Subsistence activities—gathering nuts of the Macrozamia*, a cycad whose fruit provided valuable flour, but only after careful and laborious preparation had removed dangerous toxins (cf. plate 11.1)

Plate 9.9 *Subsistence activities—gathering pipis (*Plebidonax deltoides*)*, ocean beach shellfish species, on Tacking Point Beach

Plate 9.10 *Subsistence activities—gathering oysters (*Crassostrea commercialis*)* from the mangrove (*Avicennia marina*) areas of the tidal creeks in the Hastings estuary

Plate 9.11 *Subsistence activities—fishing with the multi-pronged fishing spear* **in a tidal creek lined by mangroves (***Avicennia marina***)**

my own aesthetic judgement and the values of the 1980s rather than any real variation in the quality of Dick's record.

From Dick's comments on his Aboriginal research and the captions to some prints we may infer that he envisaged three distinct purposes for the record. First, he sees the educational value of the photographs. They are 'instructive', capable of correcting misleading information found in the literature on the subject or popular misconceptions. He is also aware of the importance of the detailed record of activities and technological processes as an end in itself. Careful planning, patience and much work was required from both Aboriginal participants and photographer to achieve comprehensive coverage of these, to record all 'stages of production' (plates 9.17 to 9.20). However, Dick stresses a third aim, 'to produce scenes described by the early explorers such as John Oxley', (Dick, 1923). Many prints bear his captions referring to 'the time of Oxley' or to Cook, as exemplars of European incursion into Aboriginal Australia (plate 9.14). The

151

Plate 9.12 *Subsistence activities—fishing with set nets.* **This photograph provides rare information. It records a mode of fishing not noted by the ethnohistorical sources, but posited by archaeologists who have studied the fish bones from excavated middens in the region (Coleman, 1980). Dick's notes on this print sent to the Queensland Museum in 1923 read 'driving fish to set nets on the Hastings. The nets were made with twine made from Kurrajong bark'**

captions also convey regret for a lost life-style, nostalgia for an Aboriginal Arcadia, as well as sympathy for the present 'pitiable condition' of the Aborigines and respect for their traditional skills. He refers to 'beautiful river scenes where the native once lived his free and happy life' (plate 9.4), 'hunting in their own native land and bush' (plate 9.21). According to his son, Ray Dick, it was concern for the losses sustained by the Aborigines in culture-contact that inspired his father to embark on the photographic record. There is considerable emotion expressed here, in words and in images. For Dick this third aim may have transcended the other two.

Interpretation then was consciously involved, and the interpretation was largely the photographer's. However, it seems that we must regard his informants as genuine co-workers in this venture, contributing knowledge as well as acting their parts. Dick is not an ethnographic observer recording

Plate 9.13 *Gathering stems of grass trees (Xanthorrhea),* once used for spear shafts, in the upper river country near Yarras

Plate 9.14 *A re-enactment of the sighting of Cook's Endeavour* navigating the east coast, symbol of European incursion into an Aboriginal Australia. Taken from the cliffs at Bonny Hills (Green Hills). The ship has been added in retouching the negative

activities in progress about him, but is deliberately eliciting, then using the knowledge and skills of his informants and subjects to create a visual record of the past, located in the appropriate settings, with appropriate players using correct and appropriate 'props'. Such a project could only succeed with the co-operation and confidence of the Aboriginal participants, evidenced by their mien in the photographs, and in the long continuance of the project. To many of the non-Aboriginal citizens of Port Macquarie in the years during and after the first world war it must have seemed at the very least an eccentric programme.

Photographic re-creation of an ethnographic past, the posing of subjects and providing 'props' (sometimes appropriate, sometimes wildly misleading) were common features of ethnographic photography at the turn of the century, especially in America (Scherer, 1975; Blackman, 1980). E. S. Curtis provided costume for his subjects, occasionally even wigs for those

Plate 9.15 *Stone flaking*. **This is well illustrated in Dick's record, also workshop areas. Anvil percussion is consistently shown rather than free hand knapping. The use of fire in preparing stone material for reduction is also a feature of photographs in this series. The photograph shows one of the pipi middens (*Plebidonax deltoides*) Dick recorded on Tacking Point Beach.**

who had adopted the short-cut hair styles of the white man (Blackman, 1980: 71). This became a point of contemporary criticism. Curtis would argue that the cedar bark capes used for his north-west Indian studies were especially made by skilled workers. Certainly they were no longer commonly made or used, but they were appropriate for an image of pre-contact times, as were the furs provided and the abalone shell nose rings. 'Curtis wanted to capture more of the past than was there' (McLuhan, introduction to Curtis, 1972: xi). Similarly Dick persuaded his associates to let their beards grow before photographic sessions (R. Dick, personal communication). These conventions of posing the subject with appropriate accessories were common in earlier Australian photography; they can be seen in the Aboriginal photographs taken by 'the great Lindt' in Grafton in the 1870s

Plate 9.16 *Experimenting in making stone artefacts by flaking and grinding:* **preparation for photographic session? This garden scene would appeal to the experimental archaeologists who litter their laboratories and gardens with waste flakes and cores**

(Lindt, 1875). His studies show also the technical constraints of wet-plate photography. Obviously there were technical constraints for Dick too, working in the bush with large format glass plate cameras, but not of this dimension by the second decade of the twentieth century. Yet some criticisms were made of his posed pictures. Baker reported to him that the Royal Society's referees for his 1915 publication excluded 'the plate where Aborigines were posed for shield cutting as they considered this was "hardly a true ethnological picture"' (Baker letter, 39/1898, 28 October 1915). Baker did not concur with their judgement, assuring Dick that he regarded his prints as 'splendid specimens of the photographic art as well as valuable ethnographic studies.' (Baker letter, 41/1418, 4 December 1916).

Developments in photography late in the nineteenth century, especially dry-plate processes, permitted new ethnographic roles for the camera, exploiting its potential for comprehensive, non-selective recording. Dick's work must be assessed in the light of contemporary perceptions of these. In the 1890s both im Thurn and Portman in papers to the Royal Anthropological Institute urged the use of photography to augment the written record (im Thurn, 1892/1893; Portman, 1895/1896), while in 1898 the British Association for the Advancement of Science established a committee for the collection, preservation, and systematic registration of photographs of anthropological interest. Portman, a colonial administrator with strong anthropological interests, had already produced a fine record of Andamanese Island life and material culture. He stressed that photography could supplement oral testimony, as well as give authentic records of manufacturing processes (1895/1896: 76). For him the documentary, technical and professional aspects were vital—'accuracy is what is required. Delicate lighting and picturesque photography are not wanted'; nor are 'fuzzygraphs' (1895/1896: 77, 81). Im Thurn, also an administrator/ anthropologist, claimed it the duty of travellers to record 'the fast fading primitive phases of life'. They should use their cameras to provide an accurate presentation of 'primitive folk regarded as living beings', shown with their objects of everyday use (1892/1893: 184, 197). The stress both these writers lay on the accuracy and comprehensiveness of the record perhaps ignores the obvious and necessary selections that are made by any successful photographer. Nonetheless their points were new, were well made, and important. We have no direct evidence of Dick's having read these articles, but it is not unlikely, and he does use the term 'primitive phases'. Their philosophies and aims would have been congenial to him; certainly he followed many of their precepts in his practice.

The concern of most ethnographic photographers of this period was to record a vanishing way of life (Davis, 1980). Yet this in itself offers considerable scope. We may have the documentary record, made by the photographer who wishes to remain an observer, to provide visual documentation of what happens around him, aiming at comprehensive, non-selective and objective coverage. Or we may have the interpretative record, in which the photographer uses his artistic skills in creating images to present a particular view of the present or a re-creation of the past. Curtis' photographic portfolios for his twenty volumes of the *North American Indian* were records of this latter kind. Supreme artistic and technical skill with careful planning of scene and subject were devoted to conveying a vision of Indian life and values, as well as a sense of the tragedy involved in the destruction of that life (Coleman, introduction to Curtis, 1972).

Curtis said of his photographs of American Indians:

These pictures were to be transcriptions for future generations that they might behold the Indian as nearly life-like as possible as he moved about before he ever

Plate 9.17 *Stages of production — building a bark shelter (1).* **Valuable series were made by Dick showing what he termed 'stages of production' in manufacturing or construction processes. Only parts of one set were published, of the shield series (see Dick, 1915), but others form invaluable and irreplaceable sets. Here we see four shots of the series showing the building of a shelter from the bark of the swamp ti-tree (*Melaleuca leucadendron*). Shelters of this kind are described in the literature for the area, and the ti-tree provided ideal bark for the purpose. Note the range of equipment shown in 9.18**

Plate 9.18 *Stages of production — building a bark shelter (2)*

Plate 9.19   *Stages of production — building a bark shelter (3)*

Plate 9.20   *Stages of production — building a bark shelter (4)*

Plate 9.21 *Kangaroo hunt up-country*: **a posed shot with stationary quarry long dead**

saw a paleface or knew there was anything human or in nature other than that he himself had seen (quoted Blackman, 1980: 71).

Of Indian life:

Alone with my camp fire, I gaze about on the completely circling hill-top, crested with countless campfires, around which are gathered the people of a dying race. The gloom of the approaching night wraps itself about me. I feel that the life of these children of nature is like the dying day drawing to its end; only off in the West is the glorious light of the setting sun, telling us, perhaps, of light after darkness (Curtis in 1905, quoted by McLuhan, introduction to Curtis, 1972: viii).

But as Coleman says, Curtis aimed not just to create images of Indian life, but images *about* Indian life, imposing on these images his 'interior vision of what they were and what they symbolised' (Coleman, introduction to Curtis, 1972: vi). The success of his portrayal, according to Coleman, derives from the coincidence of his vision with that of his subjects.

Like Curtis, Dick was concerned to create a pre-contact image, and provided authentic facilities for this. He was also, like Curtis, ready to use his artistic skill as a photographer to create the 'mood' and atmosphere of this lost period (plates 9.2 to 9.4). He used lighting and picturesque scenery in a way the more rigorous Portman would have deemed inappropriate (plate 9.21). To this extent he has created a type rather than recorded existing reality. His vision is one of nostalgia for the time when Aborigines lived and hunted freely in their own lands. It was a world irrevocably lost to the north coast by the 1920s, so an Arcadian rather than a Utopian vision. This, together with his avoidance of recording the present life of his informants, is in itself a powerful reflection of the ideas of many students of Aboriginal society and culture at the time.

If we compare Dick's work with that of contemporary photographers of the Aborigines this deliberate presentation of a vision of pre-contact society is his distinguishing feature on the conceptual level. His use of the artistic conventions explored by the photographers of the Pictorial Movement is also distinctive in the genre. It marks him as deserving a place not only in the history of ethnographic photography, but in the development of photography as an artistic medium in Australia. A survey of the work of his contemporaries emphasises the point. The photographers of Kerry and Company recorded Aboriginal camps and Aboriginal personalities on commission for the owners of the great station properties of New South Wales or for the postcard trade. They recorded a present reality; or part of it. In the 1890s Kerry himself made a series of the bora ceremony held on 'The Mole' near the Macquarie Marshes. This is magnificent documentary photography of high quality. However, it is the external record, ethnographic photography of the kind advocated by Portman and im Thurn and practised in Australia by Spencer (Mulvaney, 1982). Dick's work also differs from the self-conscious portrayal of the 'exotic' and 'primitive' found in the enactments photographed by the cameraman who produced the Australian series for George Washington Wilson for the British postcard market. The closest in style and aims seems to be the Cairns photographer of the 1920s, Alfred Atkinson.

In spite of the deliberate refusal to make an outsider's record of existing reality, Dick's deep local knowledge, his long association with his informants, and their readiness to share knowledge with him, have given his record an authenticity and range rarely found in the work of others. He created a full series of stages of production, and recorded in detail everyday subsistence activities, activities indeed often ignored by observers, including contemporary ethnographers (see plate 9.14 and Coleman, 1980). Building on his own knowledge and that of his associates, he attained to a considerable degree the solid ethnographic record he saw as secondary to his re-creative aim. Given the history of contact in northern New South Wales, by 1915 such a record could only have been achieved by the methods Dick attempted. Yet this record is more than its presentation of ethnographic information, more than a visual display of great beauty in the photographic arts. Its images offer an interpretation of Aboriginal life that was a unique co-operative creation of Aboriginal and non-Aboriginal students of the Aboriginal past.

Acknowledgements

In research for this paper I owe many thanks to members of the Dick family in Port Macquarie, especially Mr Ray Dick, also to Mr Uptin of *Port Macquarie News* and to the Hastings District Historical Society with its documentary files in the care of Mr F. Rogers. In Sydney Ms Keenan of the Museum of Applied Arts and Sciences provided guidance to the correspondence between Dick and Baker, Dr Lampert to his correspondence with the Australian Museum, and in Brisbane Mr Quinnell to that with the Queensland Museum. Dr Urry advised on interests in the Anthropological Institute, London, at the end of last century, and Mr Grimwade of the Cairns Historical Society, on the life and work of Alfred Atkinson. Mrs Goodrum of the Australian National University drew the map (figure 9.1). The Trustees of the Australian Museum, the Board of Trustees of the Queensland Museum, the Curator of the University Museum of Archaeology and Ethnology, Cambridge, and the Principal of the Australian Institute of Aboriginal Studies, as well as Mr Ray Dick in Port Macquarie, all kindly gave permission for use of prints in their collections. Plate 9.7(b), the Lionel Lindsay sketch of Murray (Dixson Library ZDL PX68 f16), drawn in 1916, is reproduced here with the kind permission of the Trustees of the Mitchell and Dixson Libraries, Sydney, and of Mr Peter Lindsay. My thanks to Ms Rhodes, Dixson Librarian, for much kind help, and to Mr Brian Bird for producing the copy print used for this plate. Mr Howard Hughes, Photographer of the Australian Museum, Sydney, who has the care of the major surviving collection of Dick's glass negatives, provided fine prints used for many of the illustrations reproduced here. To him, and to all those mentioned, my debt is great and is gratefully acknowledged.

Bibliography

Anon.   (1921) 'History of St Thomas' Church: How it was Built' and 'Port Macquarie Centenary' *Voice of the North* 10 May, p. 8

Baker, R. T. (n.d.) Letters in the letter books of the Museum of Applied Arts and Sciences, Sydney

—— (1915) 'The Australian Grey Mangrove' *Journal and Proceedings of the Royal Society of NSW* 49, pp. 257-81

Blackman, M. B.   (1980) 'Posing the American Indian' *Natural History* 89(10), pp. 69-74

Coleman, J.   (1980) 'Fish Bones for Fun and Profit' in Ian Johnson (ed.) *Holier Than Thou* Canberra: Department of Prehistory, Research School of Pacific Studies, Australian National University, pp. 61-75

Curtis, E. S. (1972) *Portraits from North American Indian Life* Introductions by A. D. Coleman and T. C. McLuhan, USA: A. and W. Visual Library Outerbridge and Lazard

Davis, S. (1980) Foreword to Roslyn Poignant *Observers of Man* London: Royal Anthropological Institute

Dick, T. (1915) 'The Origin of the Heliman or Shield of the New South Wales Coastal Aborigines' *Journal and Proceedings of the Royal Society of NSW* 49, pp. 282-8

_____ (1916) 'The Spawning of the Common Oyster' Appendix to *Annual Report on Fisheries NSW for 1915*, pp. 51-3

_____ (1920-1) *Old Port Macquarie*, series of articles on local history published in the *Port Macquarie News*; typescript in the collections of the Hastings District Historical Society, Port Macquarie

_____ (1923) Letters to Longman, Director of the Queensland Art Museum, Queensland Museum correspondence files

Ewers, J. C. (1976) 'Artefacts and Pictures as Documents in the History of Indian-White Relations' in J. Smith and R. Kvasnicka (eds) *Indian-White Relations* Washington: Harvard University Press, pp. 101-11

Gidley, M. (1976) *The Vanishing Race: Selections from E. S. Curtis, The North American Indian* Newton Abbot: David & Charles

_____ (1979) *With One Sky Above Us* Exeter: Webb & Bower

Lindt, J. W. C. (1875) *Aboriginal Natives of the Clarence River District, NSW*, Album of photographs, Grafton, in Mitchell Library, Sydney

McCarthy, F. D. (1947) 'An Analysis of the Large Stone Implements from Five Workshops on the North Coast of New South Wales' *Records of the Australian Museum* 21(8), pp. 411-30

McLuhan, T. C. (1973) *Touch the Earth* London: Abacus

Millar, D. P. (1981) *Charles Kerry's Federation Australia* Sydney: David Ell Press

Mulvaney, D. J. (1982) Introduction to R. Vanderwal (ed.) *The Aboriginal Photographs of Baldwin Spencer* South Yarra: John Curry, O'Neil on behalf of the National Museum of Victoria Council

Portman, M. V. (1895/1896) 'Photography for Anthropologists' *Anthropological Institute Journal* 25, pp. 75-87

Roderick, C. (ed.) (1952) *Ralph Rashleigh or the Life of an Exile* by 'Giacomo di Rosenberg' (James Tucker), Sydney: Angus & Robertson

Scherer, J. C. (1975) 'You Can't Believe Your Eyes: Inaccuracies in Photographs of North American Indians' *Studies in the Anthropology of Visual Communication* 2(2), pp. 67-79

Thurn, E. F. im (1892/1893) 'Anthropological Uses of the Camera' *Anthropological Institute Journal* 22, pp. 184-203

TEN

THE POPULAR
IMAGE

Nicolas Peterson

IN THIS PAPER I want to examine the way in which photography contributed to the construction of a popular image of Aborigines in the first two decades of the twentieth century, as a first step towards a more general analysis of the social significance of photographs of Aborigines. I have chosen these two decades because they are the first period in which there was widespread popular usage of photographs in the form of picture postcards. This particular usage of photographs partially resolves some of the many practical and theoretical issues facing any such sociological analysis.

Among the more practical problems are those arising from the huge quantities of images, the impossibility of dating most of them accurately, the lack of any indication as to how widely circulated and seen they were, and the frequent absence of information on the photographer, the content or the context of the picture. The theoretical issues are of some importance because limited consideration has been given to photography by social scientists so far, with the consequence that there are few theoretical frameworks or modes of analysis readily available (but for a perspective on photographs of Aborigines see de Lorenzo, 1980). The result is clear in the texts of the many new books recycling old images. Rarely do they rise above the descriptive; the authors, like the public, being swept along by the apparently unassailable actuality of the images which they tend to treat simply as evidence of how things were. Even where there is a determined intellectual attempt to grapple with the illusions of the mechanical eye, their impact on our daily lives or their refractive value to the sociologist, the best analyses usually turn out to be intellectually, sociologically and analytically thin, as Becker (1974) comments.

When we set out to discuss the way in which photographs either mirror or influence social attitudes, we may find ourselves in fact merely analysing the attitudes or procedures of particular photographers or their publishers. The way in which people commonly respond to pictures is in any case highly variable: when asked to describe what we see in a picture, we often switch

164

between comments on content, aesthetics, and technique, seeing the picture sometimes from an observer's viewpoint and sometimes from that of its subject (Machotka & Spiegel, 1979). In any discussion it is difficult to keep such responses completely separate. When looking at photographs from an earlier period there is the further complication that we are tempted to introduce modern readings into the original contexts.

Here I propose to begin the analysis by building on Rochelle Kolodny's work (1978). She has suggested that professional photographers of anthropological subjects can be shown, from their own writings, comments, and images, to have been working more or less explicitly within one of three ideological frameworks which act to structure their perception and images. I shall try to show that enough of these perceptions are encoded in postcard images for the viewer consciously or unconsciously to adopt them as the framework in which they read other meanings into the picture. It then becomes possible to look at the relative prevalence of these different contextualising frameworks at one point in time and their change over time. The conjunction of these frameworks with contemporary public concerns should in some measure account for the images selected for postcards.

Three ideological frameworks

The three frameworks Kolodny distinguishes are: romanticism, realism and the documentary (1978: 36-9, 33-106). (Instead of 'romanticism' she in fact uses the term 'primitivism', which she argues to be a specific sub-category of romanticism. To follow her usage might be construed as an endorsement of ethnocentric views.) Each of the frameworks is grounded in a set of philo-sophical and cultural propositions about the nature of the world which have been explicitly articulated in writing and images by many photographers since the 1840s. She distinguishes four aspects to these frameworks: assumptions about the nature of the world as defined through the role of the image; assumptions as to the connection between these definitions and our cultural categories; assumptions about the ideological frameworks they uphold; and finally assumptions about the functions of such frameworks.

Romanticism in photography, Kolodny argues, is associated with the belief that the camera reveals the world of essences (Sontag, 1977:96) which connects it with the domain of art. This in turn links it to a belief in idealism and a redemptive ideology. It was, and is, the dominant mode, in her view (1978:75), in photography of anthropological subjects, resolving contradictory feelings towards other cultures by transforming them into aesthetic phenomena and in so doing decontextualising and distancing them. If she is correct about this mode generally being the most prevalent, then the Aboriginal images stand in marked contrast in the period under consideration.

Realism is the popular view that photographs capture the world as it is. Photography in this view may be linked with science and with other forms of empirical enquiry: it is assumed not to transform the objects it records but merely present them to our scrutiny. As a consequence its images may come to provide a norm for judgements of the way things are. Holders of this view are however deceiving themselves with the assumption that photography works in an ideological vacuum free from cultural meanings. Impressed by the actuality of the image, they fail to consider the social and political circumstances which made its creation possible.

The documentary framework is associated with the belief that photographs can have a practical effect on everyday life. They may inspire action to improve the world or they can be used to salvage remnants of a changing world perceived as getting worse. As such it is connected with social science and technology, planned change and a belief in progress. As Sontag says (1977:108), such meanings depend heavily on captions or accompanying prose that attempt to firm up the political and moral associations of the image, which again draws attention to the fact that photographs cannot serve as uncontaminated evidence. Often too, as both Sontag and Kolodny point out, the aestheticising tendency of a photograph can operate to neutralise the distress it is intended to convey. Thus, as Kolodny emphasises, the three frameworks are not mutually exclusive. They are interrelated in complex ways while nevertheless remaining distinct ideological orientations explicitly articulated by photographers in their talking and writing and in the images they capture.

Kolodny does not actually apply her analysis to any substantial body of work so she does not deal with the practical problems related to matching a set of images to her frameworks, yet a secure basis for such an analysis can only be found by testing it on a set of images. It is as such a set that picture postcards become significant.

The rise and significance of the postcard

Between 1902 and 1914 the western world was swept by a craze for buying, sending and collecting picture postcards. The numbers of cards were enormous: 866 million were posted in the United Kingdom in 1909-1910, or over twenty cards per man, woman and child (Staff, 1966/1979:91). Closer to home, 14 million were posted in the same year by New Zealanders, or fourteen per man, woman and child (Knight, 1971:89). Australia was also caught up in the craze although no similar figures are available. However, in New South Wales 1 734 340 postcards were mailed in 1902, the year postcards started to proliferate. This was one postcard for every eighty-six letters posted in the state. By 1906 there had been a dramatic rise in the absolute and relative numbers of postcards to letters posted and this was well before the peak of the boom around 1910. In that year 12 621 096 postcards were posted or one postcard for every nine letters, which was over nine postcards per head of population (Australia, 1910:1932; Clark, 1963:154). The actual consumption of postcards was much higher, however, as many were bought and kept and others sent singly or in batches within an envelope. In the case of the 291 Aboriginal postcards from this period on which I have based my analysis only 27 per cent were sent through the post although another 10 per cent were written on.

It is not difficult to account for the enthusiasm. Since its inception, photography had had a powerful fascination, but at first the technology of making and developing pictures confined its popular use to the studio, and the absence of techniques for the mass reproduction of photographs also prevented the wide circulation of images except as transformed into engravings. It was not until the last decade of the nineteenth century that printing technology started to overcome the latter problem. The world's first newspaper to be exclusively illustrated by photographs was published in 1904 (Knight, 1971:147). Although Australian books and weekly magazines carried photographs at this time, it was only in 1908 that the *Sydney Morning Herald* published its first photograph, showing the arrival of the Great White Fleet of the American Navy, and such were the printing problems that someone unkindly suggested it should have been captioned 'Sydney on a dark and stormy night' (Walker, 1976:228−9).

While progress in printing leapt ahead during the 1890s, particularly in Saxony and Prussia where the majority of the world's pre-1910 postcards were printed, it was the alteration of the United Kingdom postal laws in 1902 that unleashed the flood. The back of the postcard might now be divided into two so that it could carry a substantial message as well as the address, and the picture on the front be expanded to cover the whole card. Thus postcards became a major vehicle for the wide dispersion of photographic images of every kind; and because they were used and collected by people of all classes they had an impact on the imagination of many people.

The vast majority of postcards were (and still are) commercially produced by people seeking to make a profit, raise funds and/or publicise a cause. Since the producers are mainly photographers or companies with access to vast quantities of images, those that are made into postcards have been selected because they will sell. As such it can be presumed that they are a distillation of the images of most contemporary interest, so that some cultural significance resides in the themes selected, the relative proportions on each theme, and the imagery.

A third significance is that all postcards have a varying degree of additional contextual and sociological information which greatly enhances the possibilities for locating some of their contemporary meaning. Almost all postcards carry captions and, usually, information on the publisher. Where the card has been used, a range of other information may be available, including the sex and place of residence of the sender and addressee, the date of posting and the views, explicit or implied, of the sender of the image.

The following analysis is based on 291 postcards which I judge to have been produced between 1900 and 1920. While it is not a random sample, I believe it to be a reasonably accurate reflection of the range and variety of postcards available during this period, probably representing over one-third of the total, judging by the rate of my discovery of new images while forming the collection.

Are the three ideological frameworks encoded in the postcards?

The only question I will investigate here is the extent to which the three frameworks Kolodny suggests photographers of anthropological subjects work in are encoded in the postcard images. Once one moves beyond the image to include the caption and any written text, the intentions and perceptions encouraged by the publishers and senders enter in, raising a host of other issues which can only be dealt with in a more extended analysis, although I will make passing references to the captions.

The easiest orientation to pick out is the romantic one. In all cases it involves a decontextualisation of people by photographing them against blank backgrounds or recontextualising them in formal poses in their 'natural surroundings'. Unsurprisingly this orientation is reflected in most studio shots (plate 10.1) which tend to portray single individuals and which are very much the work of professional photographers about whom Kolodny is principally writing. The decontextualising tendency, along with a generalising tendency, is evident in the captions. Thus of forty studio photographs only three give the name of the person photographed, while most are captioned in terms such as, 'Aboriginal chief/warrior/medicine man' or 'Aboriginal-South Australia'. The generalising tendency is even more explicit in a less common style of captioning which introduces the word 'type' or 'typical', as in 'Exceptionally Fine Type of NSW Aboriginal' or 'A Type of Aboriginal Lubra, NSW'. Recontextualisation has to be understood in the light of the fact that Aborigines known to the public at large were largely fringe dwellers (plate 10.2). Thus, placing people in real or simulated

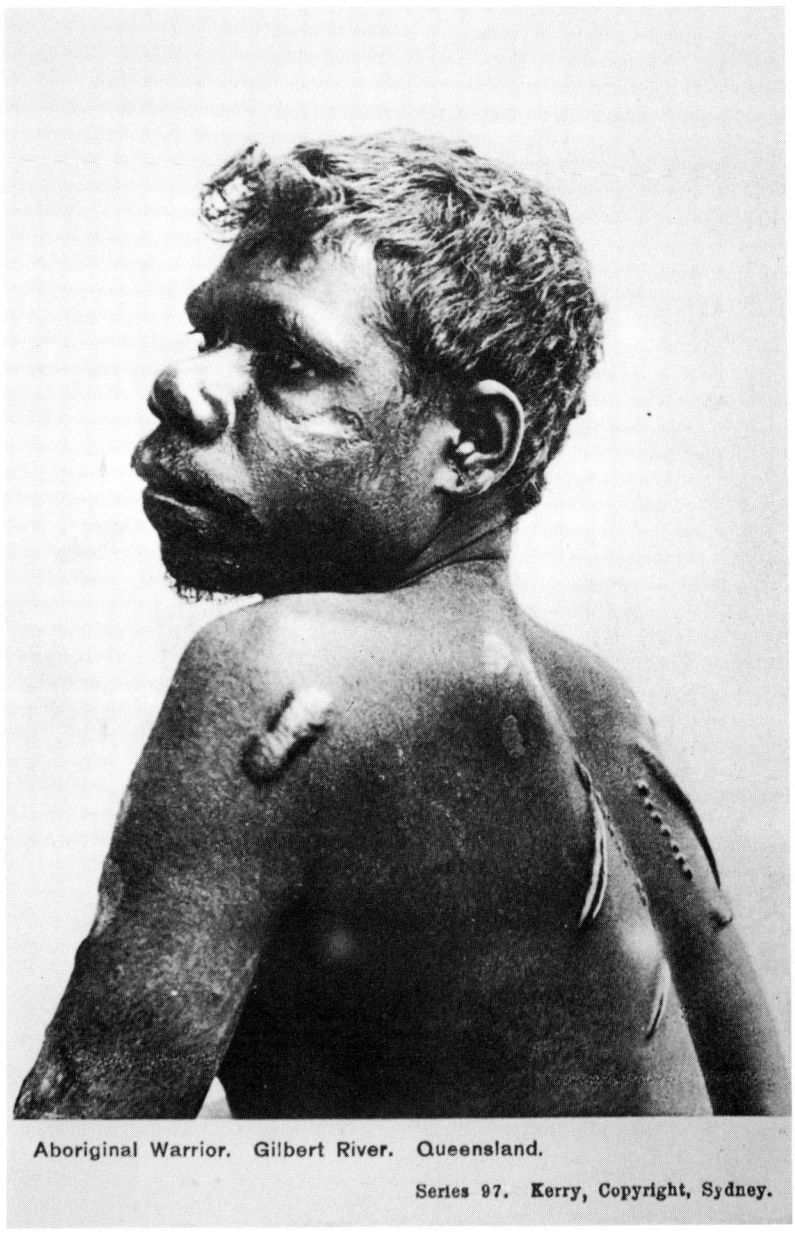

Aboriginal Warrior. Gilbert River. Queensland.

Series 97. Kerry, Copyright, Sydney.

Plate 10.1 *'Aboriginal Warrior, Gilbert River, Queensland'*. **A typical carefully posed studio shot from 1890s in the romantic vein.**

HUNTING FOR TUCKER. ABORIGINAL LUBRA, N.S.W.
[Star Photo. Co., Copyright.

Plate 10.2 *'Hunting for tucker: Aboriginal Lubra, NSW'.* **The formal pose and unlikely combination of weapons—women rarely use spears and boomerangs—underline the recontextualisation, contradicting the implied observation of daily activity suggested by the caption**

GATHERING WILD BIRDS EGGS.
Series 49 — Aboriginal Mystic Bora Ceremony.
Kerry (Copyright) Sydney.

Plate 10.3 *'Gathering wild bird's eggs: Aboriginal mystic bora ceremony'*. **Kerry was privileged to see this bora ceremony held on the lower Macquarie River, western New South Wales, in 1898. Although in one sense documentary—catching a passing way of life—the caption implies the romantic framework as does the careful posing**

bush and dressing and arming them as they were thought to be dressed and armed at contact is a recontextualisation underlined by the very formal poses.

In one or two instances one might hesitate whether to assign postcard photographs to the romantic category or to the documentary. Kerry's widespread and popular photographs of an Aboriginal bora ceremony, for example (plate 10.3), seem partly concerned to capture a certain way of life before it disappears. However, the formal poses, the romantic captions and Kerry's own comments which indicate he felt he was getting a privileged view of rites normally hidden from Europeans, as indeed he was (Kerry, 1899), all suggest that he was working within the romantic framework.

Most of the photographs in this category are fairly straightforward portraits of one sort or another, with the consequence that a passive mood pervades them. One common pose, however, is active. This is the threat posture with raised club or spear in one hand and often a shield in the other (plate 10.4). Such poses not only display fine musculature to advantage but have a vaguely heroic impact, evoking the courage of men lightly armed taking up their own cause fearlessly.

Aboriginal Warrior throwing Boomerang

Kerry & Co., Sydney.

Plate 10.4 *'Aboriginal Warrior Throwing Boomerang'*. **The active nature of the body posture also enlivens the facial expression by contrast with the boredom betrayed in many of the passive poses**

Plate 10.5 *Seated man*. **Although the background is virtually blank the clothes and front-on posture make this uncaptioned postcard a typical picture in the realistic framework**

Nakedness is also an essential feature of photographs in the romantic mode, although not confined to those in this framework. Generally the loins are covered with something passing for a traditional dress item or discreetly with cloth.

Interestingly the majority of photographs in the romantic mode were taken in the 1880s and 1890s and few actually made during the postcard boom years, which means that people like Kerry were not only deliberately using old photographs but that almost all of them are in untinted black and white.

The majority of postcard photographs are framed by the realism ideology. A wide range of themes are included but portraits of individuals and groups predominate. Several features unite these photographs. Nearly all show Aboriginal people in European clothing (plate 10.5) frequently in some kind

PALM LEAF MIA MIA, N. QUEENSLAND.

Plate 10.6 *'Palm Leaf Mia Mia, N. Queensland'.* **This rather dull picture places people squarely in front of their dwelling on the fringe of a banana plantation. Although the people are naked this is clearly within the realistic framework**

of context such as a camp. The general poverty is evident and the contrast with the aesthetic emphasis of the romantic framework is underwritten by the low aesthetic appeal of the often poor photographs sometimes made less attractive by shoddy colouring (plate 10.6). We may wonder why anyone should ever have wished to buy such postcards. A tentative answer to this problem will be offered at the end of this paper.

The 'realistic' photographs tend to be just as posed as those of the romantic variety, but in a very different way. Realistic posing is nearly always the same, presenting a direct front-on view of a sitting individual or of a standing group, often lined up in front of a dwelling (plate 10.7). As Sontag comments (1977:37-8) of Arbus's portraits, such posing gives a sense of solemnity, frankness and full disclosure of the subject's nature. The posing thus underlines the empiricist ideology with its emphasis on concreteness—all is exposed to be seen—and immersion in the present social reality (Kolodny, 1978:50). Conjoined with this, in the context of photographs of Aborigines, is the feeling that the people have surrendered to the camera and been subjugated by it, which the images frequently confirm. The social inequality and the authority of the photographer are betrayed most clearly in the removal of the tops of women's dresses which

Plate 10.7 *'Aboriginal Camp'*. **A typical line-up photograph of people in front of their camp**

are often folded down (plate 10.8). Certain photographs of naked or partially naked Aboriginal women in this period seem deliberately erotic in intent. In this photograph, however, the arrangement of the clothing seems primarily designed to accentuate racial difference.

Within the realism framework come postcards showing many activites such as fishing and tree climbing. In all of these people are dressed in their everyday European clothing, which suggests that the photographers were watching people in the course of daily life rather than seeking to document a disappearing way of life (plate 10.9).

For the most part the captions reinforce the emphasis on the descriptive and specific: 'Blacks in Camp: Port Victor'; 'Wilmot Strahan in his Mia Mia, Warrnambool, Vic.'; or 'Australian Aborigines fishing'.

Finally there is the poorly represented documentary framework. Two orientations are included within this: the concern to document a disappearing way of life, and the desire to inspire action to improve the situation. Although there was a widespread belief that Aborigines were dying out, none of the postcard images betray a consistent concern with documenting a disappearing way of life. Such an interest seems to have come much later and is in any case only easily discernible in a substantial set

TYPICAL ABORIGINAL LUBRA, N.S.W.

[*Star Photo. Co., Copyright.*

Plate 10.8 *'Typical Aboriginal Lubra, NSW'* **Subjugation by the camera—apparent from the arrangement of the clothing**

Plate 10.9 *'Aboriginals and bark canoes'*. **A fine photograph of Lake Tyers by W.H. Cooper illustrating a common theme**

Plate 10.10 *'Missionary and native helper'* **and** *'A native child'*. **The juxtaposition of these two images is the work of the publisher. Without evidence of the photographer's intention, the moral overtones derived from their juxtaposition cannot be attributed to him but he must surely have intended the tutelary pose. This postcard along with the one in plate 10.11 make up half the images from the sample that might be classified within the documentary framework**

Plate 10.11 *'Point McLeay Mission, Jubilee 1859-1909'*. **Read, as a missionary worker at Point McLeay, probably intended the moral message in this photograph even if he did not pose the tableau. Although this would place the image in the documentary—social improvement—framework, Read was not a professional photographer.**

of images (see McBryde on Dick in this volume). Without reference to a text or caption it is almost impossible to place the isolated images of individual postcards within this framework. There are, however, a number of images that have moral overtones. All of these are associated with missionary organisations. Such overtones are clear in the case of the paternalistic pose of a white pastor with his hand on the shoulder of a young Aboriginal man (plate 10.10), and even more strikingly in the highly structured image taken during the celebration of Point McLeay's first fifty years which polarises pagan and Christian (plate 10.11). Pictures of a white teacher sitting with children in a bucolic setting and of a supervised tug-of-war carry fainter but still discernible moral overtones. Like the cards reproduced here, they are not trying to inspire, but simply to document change, and the role which whites have played in it.

Conclusion

From this brief discussion it can be seen that the romantic and realistic photographic frameworks are clearly encoded in the images chosen for postcards in terms of four contrastive features, as set out below:

Romantic framework	*Realistic framework*
Decontextualisation— blank backgrounds	Contextualisation in contemporary living situation
Recontextualisation— bush settings	
Naked or in traditional attire	Clothed more or less completely in European attire
Considered posing, rarely front-on	Front-on artless posing
Absence of European artefacts	Presence of European artefacts

At least two of these features are required firmly to situate any image within one or other framework. As noted above, the documentary framework is not proven in the images without support from a text.

Within the set of 291 postcards considered over 80 per cent fall within the realistic framework. Why? The period of nation building before the First World War went hand in hand with the establishment of the white Australia policy. That policy was widely debated at all levels of society, and enshrined in legislation. The threat posed by non-white immigrants was perceived as both racial and economic, endangering the purity of the 'white race' and the standard of living. The economic threat related to the low wages which non-white people would work for, wages they could only accept because they tolerated an unacceptably low standard of living. Although Aborigines did not feature directly in the debate surrounding the policy it seems likely they were part of the evidence that many people, consciously or unconsciously, drew on to support these views. The predominance of images in the realistic framework showing impoverished, run-down shanty dwellers may have been obscurely consoling, bolstering ideas of racial superiority implicit in the white Australia policy and confirming that it was as well to keep other non-whites out, given the way they lived. Whites were seeing what they wanted to see. There were plenty of more aesthetic and ennobling pictures being taken of Aborigines in this same period by people such as Spencer and Gillen, Basedow and others which could have supplemented the old studio shots issued by Kerry, Lindt and the like, but they were confined to books and the weekly magazines.

There is another aspect to the interest in images of Aborigines which is harder to document. It was widely believed that Aborigines were slowly but surely dying out at this period. The realistic images may have eased white consciences about this process, by documenting the low status of Aborigines and implying they were on the wane. For those more charitably disposed towards the Aborigines, the prospect of their extinction evoked a romantic melancholy best tapped by the generation of painters discussed by Margaret Maynard in her essay in this volume, but also present in some of the postcard images.

Acknowledgements

I would like to thank Harvey Feit for drawing my attention to Kolodny's work and arranging to make it available to me and Rochelle Kolodny for her detailed and helpful comments. I have also greatly benefited from the interest and comments of Howard Morphy, David MacDougall, Judith MacDougall and Rosalind Peterson.

Bibliography

Australia   (1910) *Royal Commission on Postal Services: Minutes of Evidence* vol. 2, Melbourne: Government Printer

Becker, H.   (1974) 'Photography and Sociology' *Studies in the Anthropology of Visual Communication* 1, pp. 3-26

Clark, M.   (1963) *A Short History of Australia* Melbourne: Macmillan

De Lorenzo, C.   (1980) 'An Interpretation of Some Photographs of Australian Aborigines' *Working Papers on Photography* 6, pp. 32-7

Kerry, C. H.   (1899) Note in *Journal of the Royal Society of New South Wales* 33, pp. xxvii-xxviii

Knight, H.   (1971) *Photography in New Zealand: A Social and Technical History* Dunedin: John McIndoe

Kolodny, R. L.   (1978) 'Towards an Anthropology of Photography: Frameworks for Analysis' MA thesis, Department of Anthropology, McGill University

Machotka, P. and J. Spiegel   (1979) 'Construction of Pictorial Meaning' *Studies in the Anthropology of Visual Communication* 5, pp. 115-31

Sontag, S.   (1977) *On Photography* London: Allen Lane

Staff, E.   (1966/1979) *The Picture Postcard and its Origins* London: Lutterworth Press

Walker, R. B.   (1976) *The Newspaper Press in New South Wales, 1803-1920* Sydney: Sydney University Press

ELEVEN

ORDERING
THE LANDSCAPE

Rhys Jones

I am as free as nature first made man,
Ere the base laws of servitude began,
When wild in woods the noble savage ran.

JOHN DRYDEN, *THE CONQUEST OF GRANADA*, PART I (1670)

IT WAS XENOPHON in the fourth century BC who brought to the European imagination the word 'paradise', originally a term for the walled parks and gardens of Persian kings and nobles. There is a sense of dichotomy deep within our history between the pleasures of an ordered space, cultivated within, and the terrors of a confused wilderness without; a garden of Eden as opposed to the desert; the place of man as opposed to the realm of nature. Henry VIII reversed this order when he built inside the garden of his Nonsuch Palace an area called, even then, a 'wilderness'; albeit a somewhat whimsical one, consisting of a stage forest with alleys of fruit trees and clipped evergreens shading ferns and flowers; with life-sized replicas of wild animals located amongst the bushes; and for unwary visitors, a booby-trap water spray (Scott-James & Lancaster, 1979:27).

Untamed man in an untamed land

In the English medieval world there were to the west and north lands held by people living under quite different, and to the Anglo-Norman mind, difficult to comprehend legal and cultural systems (Scott & Martin, 1978). Some lay quite literally 'beyond the pale', the other side of the ditch and dike defenses of the Dublin Quadrilateral. The nature of this Celtic world is evoked by the seventeenth-century antiquarian and diarist, John Aubrey. Describing a Britain before written history, he tries to

imagine then what kind of a countrie this was in the time of the ancient Britons. By the nature of the soil, which is a sour woodsere land, very natural for the production of oakes especially, one may conclude that this . . . was a shady dismal wood: and the inhabitants almost as savage as the beasts whose skins were their only rayment. The language British . . . the boats . . . basketts of twigges covered with an oxe skin: which the poore people in Wales use to this day . . . . They were two or three degrees, I suppose, less savage than the Americans (Aubrey, *c.* 1656, in Powell, 1949:1-2).

The discovery of the New World had presented to the European mind whole systems of peoples and cultures totally different from any that they had previously encountered. The Aztecs of the central valley of Mexico may have lacked the use of the wheel and metals and they had almost no pastoral animals to milk or to eat, yet they were agriculturalists with neat gardens of maize and beans often irrigated by complex systems of water ditches. Their large-scale society with its armies, its totalitarian theocratic government, its pyramids and other huge ceremonial structures and even the practice of wholesale human sacrifice by priests to appease the gods would nevertheless have had analogues described in the pages of the Old Testament—perhaps a Pharaonic Egypt or a Baal-worshipping Phoenicia beyond the western ocean.

More difficult to comprehend were the people who lived by hunting and gathering their food. These practised no agriculture and lived in groups no larger than those of extended families. They possessed no property beyond the items of immediate use which they carried around with them such as spear, digging stick or net bag, and they seemed to wander at random through the countryside moving from camp to camp, possessing no land, and related to no specific place. Such hunters and gatherers were the inhabitants of a vast extent of the eastern seaboard of the Americas from the foggy shores of Newfoundland past the languid isles of the Carribean or the densely forested mouths of the Amazon as far south as Tierra del Fuego. Their lands, the great forests and plains which they occupied, were seen as a wilderness: an empty land worked by no human hands, a vast *terra nullius*, land belonging to no one. For colonists wishing to take over this land, a doctrine such as the one proposed by John Locke in his *Two Treatises of Government* in 1690 was highly convenient. Since this was a wild country which was not previously owned, it was available to anyone who wished to enclose it. This doctrine soothed any conscience made uneasy by the act of usurpation. Whatever may have been the cynical dictates of colonial policy, there was also a genuine failure of the sixteenth- and seventeenth-century European mind to perceive the nature of the economy and social government of hunting societies. In the absence of detailed ethnographic descriptions, recourse was made to the notion of an Eden of mankind, child-like and innocent before the Fall, or to that of men physically fully formed but mentally only half-groping towards human intelligence.

Later writers were also to take as a poetic device the contrast between the manicured and ordered landscape of agriculture with its stout yeomanry of peasant farmers, and the chaos of the wild lands occupied by hunters. The contrast is eloquently expressed by Oliver Goldsmith in his *Deserted Village* of 1770 where

> *Sweet Auburn! loveliest village of the plain,*
> *Where health and plenty cheered the labouring swain*

is juxtaposed with images of the American wilderness:

> *Those matted woods where birds forget to sing...*
> *Those poisonous fields with rank luxuriance crowned...*
> *Where crouching tigers wait their hapless prey,*
> *And savage men more murderous still than they;*
> *While oft in whirls the mad tornado flies,*
> *Mingling the ravaged landscape with the skies. (351-8)*

It was such ideas that Europeans brought with them when they first tried to perceive Australia, that one continent, entirely occupied by hunters and gatherers. Although Aborigines or the smokes of their fires were everywhere to be seen, the explorers dismissed or ignored the Aborigines' relationship with the land; rather the land itself was seen as the quintessence of wilderness, a place not owned or affected by man. These perceptions have been well discussed by Bernard Smith (1960:158-76), and it suffices here to give only an illustrative example. François Péron believed that he saw in southern Tasmania a pristine and untouched landscape which he described as consisting of 'immense forests of trees that seem coeval with nature itself, and where the sound of the axe was never heard' (1809:181). Péron was referring here to the fact that the Tasmanian Aborigines, unlike those of the Australian mainland, did not possess edge-ground hatchets, but were restricted to the use of hand-held flaked stone tools for cutting. Aborigines were considered as merely observers of such scenes, and they were often depicted as such in the early watercolours and etchings; they had no systematic relationship either intellectual or ecological with the terrain itself. As M. M. Robinson wrote in an ode read before Governor Macquarie in 1816, the Aborigines had been

> *For Ages doom'd in Indolence to roam,*
> *The rocks their Refuge, and the Wilds their Home!*

The view that Australia was a wilderness unowned and economically or ecologically unaffected by Aborigines has been dominant throughout the period of European colonisation right up to the present time, and it still influences opinion and policy as can be shown by the following three contemporary examples.

In 1971 Mr Justice Blackburn delivered judgement on the famous case of *Milirrpum and others* versus *Nabalco Pty Ltd and the Commonwealth of*

Australia (17 *F. L. R.* 141) at the Supreme Court of the Northern Territory, where Aboriginal clans of Yirrkala in north-eastern Arnhem Land were claiming ownership of land which had been ceded as bauxite leases to a mining company according to a Northern Territory Ordinance but with no reference to the Aborigines who lived there. Mr Justice Blackburn ruled that the Aborigines did not, according to British and later Australian law, own this land. To own it, one had not only to have some formal title; one also had to work it, to use it. Property required the union of land and labour. According to his Honour this was not the case with the Aboriginal plaintiffs, even though they had demonstrated systematic social links between clans of people and certain defined tracts of ground, and had also indicated how in the recent past they used the resources of this land for food and material possessions. The judgement of Mr Blackburn was that the Aborigines 'have a more cogent feeling of obligation *to* the land than of ownership of it'; and, in a celebrated phrase, 'it seems easier on the evidence to say that the clan belongs to the land than that the land belongs to the clan' (17 *F. L. R.* 141; see also Hookey, 1972, Stanner, 1979:275-94).

An immediate political consequence of this stark statement of the legal position was a change in the law of the Northern Territory, then under the jurisdiction of the Commonwealth Government. Under the Aboriginal Land Rights Act 1976, all existing Aboriginal reserves and certain other unalienated Crown Land would either be granted to or could be claimed by Aborigines according to certain procedures. In the latter category, one of the first successful land claims was made for a large area of the Alligator Rivers flood plains and escarpment country immediately to the west of Arnhem Land proper. This area, which also has within it deposits of uranium ore, is of great potential for tourism and has major natural history values; so following an intensive judicial enquiry (Fox, 1977), the title of ownership was transferred to the traditional Aboriginal owners, who then immediately leased it for a hundred years back to the Commonwealth Government, to run the area as a National Park. This is the Kakadu Park, planned to be managed under the most enlightened policies concerning recognition of Aboriginal values and needs. Yet was there some slip in an administrator's pen, or was it the subconscious expression of an old idea that led the Director of the Australian National Parks and Wildlife Service to write in his Foreword to the first published draft of the plan of management that the 'Kakadu National Park has been described as an *untamed wilderness*' (my italics; Ovington, 1980:v), and that the management plans would 'ensure the retention of the wilderness character whilst providing for the needs of the traditional Aboriginal owners'.

The political struggle for land in Australia is of course a continuing process. Recently in an attempt to limit Aboriginal claims, the Northern

Territory Government ran a publicity campaign in the southern States with one of its main points being that land returned to Aborigines to be used by them in a traditional way would thereby become 'unproductive'. As Chief Minister Paul Everingham put it in an address to the National Press Club in Canberra, 'one of the most worrying aspects of the future extent of land rights is the ability to convert currently *productive* leases to inalienable Aboriginal freehold, as a result of their purchase by Aboriginals' (my italics; 1982:5).

Obverse views

To me, the most salient aspect of the 'Age of Discovery' was that almost everywhere in the temperate regions, with the exception only of certain small islands such as those of Bass Strait and the Falklands, the discoverers struggling through the surf were met on the beaches by other people looking at them from the edges of the trees. Thus the same landscape perceived by the newcomers as alien, hostile or having no coherent form, was to the indigenous people their home, a familiar place, the inspiration of dreams. The fifteenth-century Welsh poet Tudur Penllyn expressed this dichotomy well, as from his 'shady dismal wood' he contemplated the manicured red-soil plains of England, but advised his country-man, the guerrilla Dafydd ap Siancyn (David Jenkins) that:

Dy gastell ydyw'r gelli,	(which I translate as)
Derw dol yw dy dyrau di.	*Thy castle is the copse,*
Da yw ffin a thref ddinas	*Oak glade thy towers*
Gorau yw'r glyn a'r graig las;	*Good is the urbane edge of cities*
Gwylia'r trefydd, cynnydd call,	*Better the glen and the shining rock*
A'r tyrau o'r tu arall	*Watch those towns, formal and fat,*
	And turrets from inside out.

(PARRY, 1962:169-70)

It is time we tried to look at an Australian landscape through Aboriginal eyes.

The Gidjingali and the Blyth River Plains

The Gidjingali[1] are an Aboriginal people who live on the coastal plains of the Blyth River which flows into the northern coast of Arnhem Land (figure 11.1). This river which they call *an-gatja wana* or 'big river' has an estuary two kilometres wide at its mouth, and it is tidal more than 30 kilometres upstream. This great sluggish stream of grey water snakes its way across a flat flood plain, with the main watercourse and subsidiary billabongs and

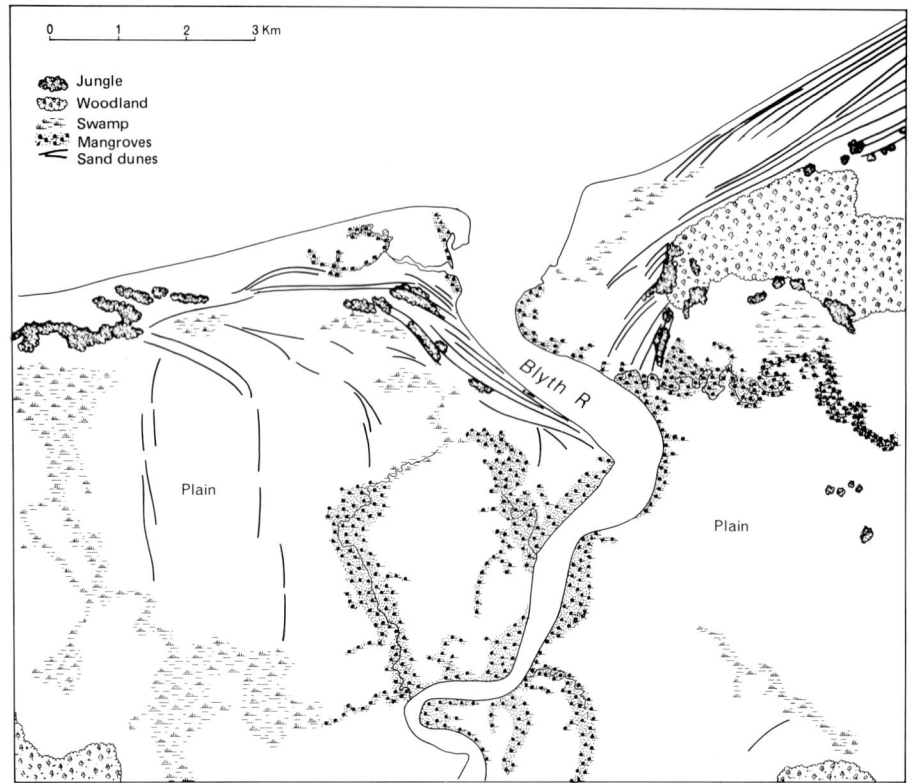

Figure 11.1 *Coastal plains of the Blyth River* **in northern Arnhemland. This is the terrain owned by the Gidjingali people, and indicated are the main ecological subdivisions of this landscape**

drainage gutters lined with mangrove thickets, so dense with their tangle of aerial roots that from the river all view of the low land behind is blotted out by walls of dark green. From the perspective offered by an aeroplane flying above this country (figure 11.3), all such relief is blotted out and the country has a vaguely organic look like the cytological cross-section of some gigantic kidney. However, with an eye trained in geomorphology, one sees a large flood plain of recent origin—certainly less than 6000 years old and formed after the sea reached its present level, having over the previous several thousand years risen from its glacial low level due to the steady warming of the world's temperature. For a while there would have been a wide hollow bay indented into a low sloping land of laterite-capped rocks clothed in eucalypt woodland. Then quickly, the river adjusting to its new

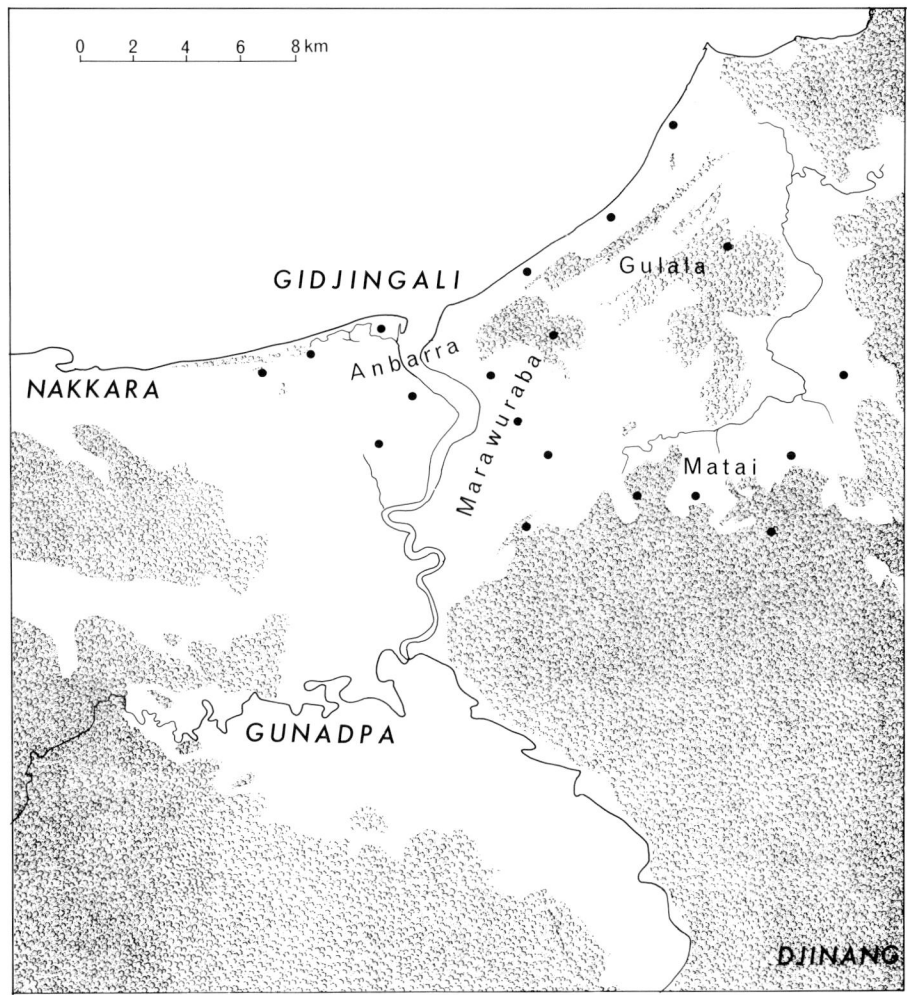

Figure 11.2 *Coastal plains of the Blyth River: Gidjingali territories*. **The dots indicate the location of the core territories of the main land-owning units of the Gidjingali people. Also shown are the locations of the four named communities of these people and the lands of neighbouring language groups. (Information after Hiatt 1965, Jones 1980 and Meehan 1982)**

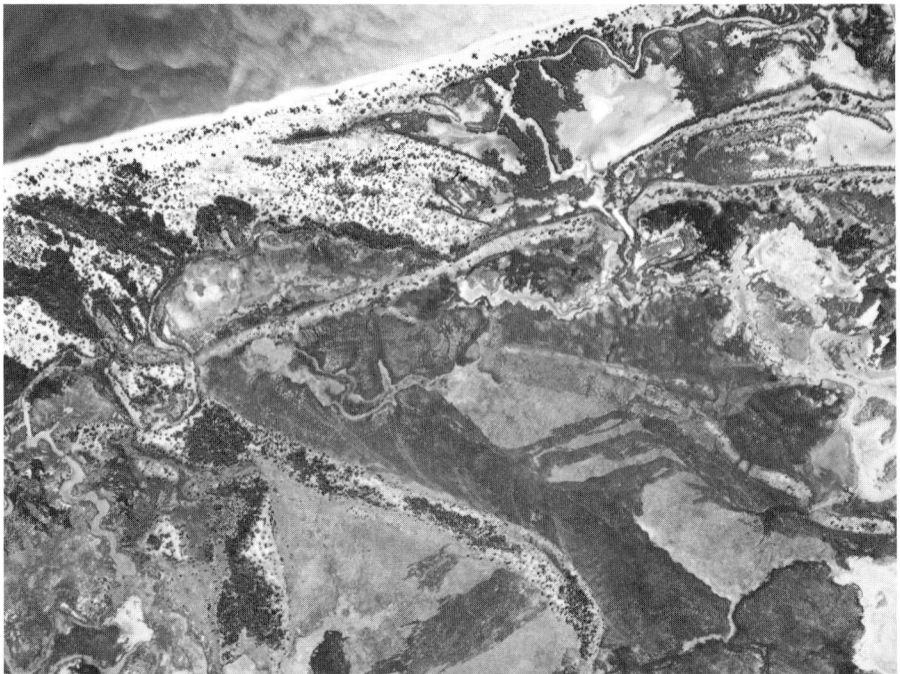

Figure 11.3 *Blyth River mouth*: **aerial photograph of coastal dunes and black soil plain west of the river mouth. This country is that of the Djunawunya land owning group as shown in figure 11.4**

base level filled the bay with clays to form a rapidly prograding flood plain. Old river courses formed temporarily during this phase of deposition, only to be left fossil by the formation of some new clay or shell bank. Their old courses can still be traced, their beds filled with fresh water during the wet season to remain as long sinuous swamps during the following dry. On the seaward side of the flood plain would have been coastal sand dunes, and as these were overtaken by the advancing flood plain, they have been left as parallel sand ridges up to several kilometres inland from the present coast. At low tide, the future sand dunes of this still-advancing coast can be seen as low sand banks and shoals, pale green under their shallow veil of water.

This landscape with its salt flats shimmering in the heat of a vertical sun seems to the uninitiated as barren as the coast of north-western Australia did to William Dampier 180 years ago: 'the Land I had seen as yet was not very inviting, being but barren towards the Sea, and affording me neither fresh Water, nor any great Store of other Refreshments' (1729:149). The great coastal estuaries of tropical Australia have blocked the attempts of

Europeans to colonise them since the middle of the last century, yet they constituted perhaps the richest of all terrains in Australia from the point of view of Aboriginal hunters and gatherers.

The flood plain of the Blyth River and its surrounding coastline, comprising a total area of only 400 square kilometres, is the country of an entire people (figure 11.2). They speak their own language, divided into several dialects, and they conceive of themselves and are seen by neighbouring peoples as a self-contained polity, one of the Aboriginal 'nations' of Australia. At the time of effective European contact in the middle of this century there were some 300 Gidjingali-speaking Aborigines, the number having nowadays increased by about a hundred (Hiatt, 1965:19). Within this language community there are four main sub-groups, each of whom speaks a distinctive style of Gidjingali. The Gulala people occupy the long beach strand east of the mouth of the Blyth River as far as Cape Stewart. The Matai, who take their name from the flowers of the *Eucalyptus miniata*, have their estates situated in the open savanna forests inland to the east of the river, and the Marawuraba live in the wetlands adjacent to the east bank of the river. At the river's estuary, especially on its western shore, are the estates of the Anbarra, whose very name denotes them as people of the river mouth. To the south of these Gidjingali communities live the Gunadpa on the inland edge of the flood plain and within the woodlands to the south (figure 11.2). They speak a language which is mutually intelligible with Gidjingali, and therefore technically a dialect of the same speech community, though both groups assert a separate identity from each other. Outsiders often refer to all of these people as Burarra. To their west along the coast live the Nakkara people, approximately 200 in number, speaking a totally different language, indeed possibly of a different language family; to their south are the sparsely distributed Rembarrnga in their hard rocky country of interior Arnhem Land; to the east the Djinang speakers of the swamps of the Goyder, and beyond them the various speech communities of north-eastern Arnhem Land who call themselves Yolngu. Thus over an area of only 20 000 square kilometres of central and eastern Arnhem Land is a level of linguistic diversity almost equivalent to what one might expect from an entire continent were we thinking from a European model. Yet this pattern of groups of people numbering some 300 to 600 people and each speaking a different language was characteristic of the whole of Aboriginal Australia.

Land and people

The populations supporting such languages may seem very small to people who come from speech communities numbering many millions, yet the

Gidjingali with a total density of 1.4 square kilometres per person and (within the Gidjingali) the Anbarra community, with 0.5 square kilometres per person or seven people per kilometre of coastline, constituted one of the highest population densities in the whole of Aboriginal Australia. The first thing to learn about the Aboriginal perception of landscape therefore is that every person lived in a small speech community in a territory surrounded by lands belonging to other people who spoke different languages and who defined themselves as belonging to different polities.

The size of this territory varied inversely with the richness of the country and its capacity to support people. In relatively rich areas such as the coasts of Arnhem Land and Cape York, the mouths of the large rivers of New South Wales and of the Murray, such tribal territories were as small as the 400 or so square kilometres of the Gidjingali. Conversely in the arid interior desert country such as that of the Warlpiri or the Pintupi, population density was as low as one person per 100 square kilometres, and so the total territory might extend to the order of 40 000 square kilometres. People did sometimes travel beyond these limits, but unless sanctioned by neighbours, this might be dangerous, exposing the traveller to the perils both of secular punishment for trespass, and more insidiously to the dangers of supernatural retribution through inadvertently wandering onto 'dangerous' places due to ignorance of the religious geography of distant places.

Thus the core of one's geographic perception was kin-based, its centre the country belonging to one's own people. This was often expressed by people defining themselves according to the special characteristics of this core territory, and distinguishing themselves from strangers who came from different kinds of country. Thus the Anbarra men, sitting during the heat of the day under the shade of the gently rustling Casuarinas growing just above the high tide mark, defined themselves as the people of the *djaranga*—the sand or beach. Their neighbours to the immediate south with whom they shared a language and had strong bonds of intermarriage and religious co-operation such as the Matai, they referred to as people of the *malpi*—the woodlands or forest; yet looking at the distant blue smoke haze rising from the horizon far away they would point with their lips and say there were the men who live in the *gun-gurrema* or 'stone' country, a dangerous place inhabited by sorcerers. It is an Anbarra-centric view of landscape that I wish to present in this paper.

Land systems

The Anbarra define elements in the landscape according to terms which incorporate a series of different attributes. In this sense theirs is similar to the 'land systems' approach developed by CSIRO scientists after the Second

World War (Christian & Stewart, 1953). In defining their different land forms, the Anbarra amalgamate a suite of characteristics of a particular land type, such as the bed-rock or soil, the drainage characteristics, the vegetation: both dominant forms and special categories, such as edible, useful or dangerous species, and in some cases the animals present. Each land type has a name which, when used, conveys all of this useful ecological information to the listener. I will give some examples together with their main economic resources.

Starting from the inland margin of their country (figure 11.1), we have the *malpi* or open woodland. This develops on poor stony slopes capped with lateritic gravels which flank the flood plains and is dominated by the stringy bark and woolly butt eucalypts, *E. tetrodonta* and *E. miniata* respectively. The former provides sheets of bark easily removed by ring-barking the trunk, which are used for a wide variety of purposes ranging from roofing material for huts to surfaces for painting. The trunks of the trees are slender and straight with a typical diameter of about 25-30 cm, but they are deceptive in that many have their centres eaten out by termites whose great mound nests of grey clay stand like megaliths between the trees. Accordingly the Aborigines use these naturally hollowed-out trunks as logs for coffins or for the tubes of drone-pipe musical instruments. Bees use these hollowed trunks too, and the nests are cut open with hatchets, nowadays made from steel but in living memory from igneous stone with a ground-down edge.

The understorey to the *malpi* woodland varies, but often this is dominated by a small fan palm *Livistonia humilis* whose pith can be eaten after being beaten and soaked. Of greater importance is the other understorey, found especially on the east side of the river, the cycad (*C. media*), whose 'nuts', though in a fresh state carcinogenic to man, can be processed by a complex series of procedures including drying, leaching, fermenting and baking, to produce a dense, slightly cheese-smelling 'cake', which was one of the carbohydrate staples of the Gidjingali (plate 11.1). Other plants with edible tubers grow unobtrusively amongst the litter of the forest floor, and occasionally distant crashes can be heard as a kangaroo (*M. antilopinus*) moves away from the voices of approaching hunters. In general, however, the Anbarra regard the *malpi* as an inhospitable place, dry and lacking sufficient concentration of food to support major camp sites. They view it as a place to be passed through quickly as they travel from prime locations of this inland country, such as the small swamps that fill natural depressions in the ground, or the streams with their waterholes and well-drained sandy soils. In some senses then the Anbarra see the *malpi* as we would a 'wilderness'. A man referred to as *an-malpi* is seen as wild or unsophisticated; quite literally, a backwoods man.

Plate 11.1 *Gidjingali women preparing Cycas media nuts* **during the dry season 1972. They are cracking the husks with wooden mallets and anvils, and the kernels are being left out to dry under the sun before further leaching and baking to remove poisons within them. The carbohydrate material will be ground into a flour and baked to form 'loaves' of** *natjo*, **most of which are given to men taking part in major ceremonies**

Beyond the woodlands are the flat and open flood plains referred to as *kapal*. These are seasonally flooded, but at the height of the dry season the black clays become brick hard and deeply cracked. When wet, they are clothed in tall sorghum grass, and in the wetter hollows wild rice, *Oryza rufipogon*, grows. Goannas (*Varanus* spp.) and long-necked terrapins (*Chelonida rugosa*) live here, and after the waters recede they burrow into the clay to aestivate during the dry season and can be dug out then. Within the *kapal* terrain are swamps and former stream beds which constitute one of the prime foraging areas of the people. The old stream beds wind across the plain, and although their level is only about a metre or so below the surrounding land, they hold water in some cases right through the dry season. The dominant vegetation in them is the spike-rush, *Eleocharis dulcis*, a plant closely related to the Chinese water chestnut, whose sweet nutty corms are one of the chief foods of the Anbarra people. Called *kuleitj*, it is seen as the most important characteristic of these swampy depressions, so that people asking where someone has gone will reply *ana-kuleitj*—to the spike-rush [place]. Not only humans but also waterbirds, especially the magpie geese *Anseranas semipalmata*, congregate at these swamps to eat the rush corms, and in deep depressions there are both freshwater fish and estuarine fish trapped by the receding waters.

The flood plains afford wide open vistas which Anbarra people often comment upon favourably. The sense of space is accentuated by low ridges fringed by Pandanus trees which sometimes seem to cross the plains. These are the fossil sand dunes formed during the progradation of the plain in mid-Recent times, and they consist of sand upon which a soil has formed. They are referred to as *djaranga* or sand, but sometimes with the qualification *gun-gungundja* meaning dark or black, due to the soil formation, as opposed to the *djaranga gun-gungaltja*—light or white leached sand of the present coast (Jones & Meehan, 1978). These fossil sand dunes are well drained but with underground water bodies trapped at their interface with the surrounding clays, so they support in places a dense vegetation cover. The plants belong in general to what might be termed 'dry rain forest' or vine thicket, containing many trees with edible fruits such as *Sterculia* or native peanut, *Terminalia* or billy goat plum, *Brachychiton* or kurrajong, *Syzigium* or red love-apple, *Ficus* or figs and *Vitex*. A tangle of vines grow up during the wet season to die back as shrivelled tendrils during the dry. But some of these, especially the yams (*Dioscorea* sp.), are systematically sought by the Aborigines, and their tubers harvested. The linear thickets on the fossil dunes provide an excellent shelter for the agile wallaby which feeds on its edges and out on the plains during the night, but which at dawn and dusk can be seen hopping close to the edges of the trees. The bases of the dunes have sometimes blocked older drainage courses, so that bodies of water build up forming swamps, but even more importantly from the Aboriginal point of view, remain there underground to be tapped by wells dug into the soft sand. Without these wells called *rralila*, human life on these tropical coastal flood plains would be impossible during the late dry season, when almost all surface water has evaporated away.

Where underground water and suitable rich soils are in combination the vegetation can be dense, forming what the Anbarra call a *man-nga*, or what in Northern Territory English is referred to as a 'monsoon jungle'. These are thickets ranging in area from as small as a few square metres up to several square kilometres, and they contain a great diversity of plant species, many of them sensitive to fire. Dominating such thickets are often the banyan or fig trees (*Ficus virens*), the skin of whose roots provide much of the raw material for the cordage of Gidjingali technology. Botanically there are in these jungles many interesting species, which are also found in relict situations in protected localities on the edges of the Arnhem Land escarpment and which it has only recently been fully realised belong to a very ancient lineage in the evolution of the northern Australian plants. To the Aborigines, not only do these 'jungles' contain a wealth of yams and other vines on their edges, and trees useful for various purposes such as the hulls of canoes, but also within them trees often imbued with mythological significance, such as the tall slender palms *Ptychosperma elegans* and *Carpentaria acuminata*. The largest jungles are dark and mysterious, and they are seen by the Aborigines from a mythological point of view as being potentially dangerous. Some even are proscribed areas to be entered into by only the most ritually experienced old men and even then only under stringent conditions.

In this description of the Anbarra landscape, we are slowly moving towards the coast which, like so much of northern Australia, is as Dampier put it, 'low, but seemingly barricado'd with a long Chain of Sand-hills to the Sea' (1699:124). These dunes, and the beach which the Anbarra call *madjua*, contain a complex suite of vegetation, especially in the swales between sand ridges, where ephemeral swamps may form in the wet season containing water lilies (*Nymphaea* sp.) and other water plants. On the seaward edge of these dunes are hardy plants which survive all that salt and sun can batter them with: the hibiscus tree (*H. tiliaceus*) or *midjingalma-ngalma* whose inner bark can be stripped into fine and tough strands to make three-ply rope, and whose supple stems with pithy centres make excellent light shafts for composite three-pronged fish spears; *Morinda citrifolia* with its strange vomit-smelling fruit with the taste of apple and cloves and which is said by Aborigines to make your eyes go 'clear'; and by the shore, just above the sea wrack, the tall stately *Casuarina equisetifolia*, or *rula* trees, under whose shade people love to sit and gaze out across the shimmering sand flats exposed by a low tide. These extend outwards up to a kilometre and contain extensive beds of shell fish, especially the bivalve *Tapes hiantina* or *diyama*. As the tide comes in, so do schools of fish such as whiting which can be caught close to the water's edge with the use of hand nets or portable barriers woven out of stripped Pandanus leaves (plate 11.2). The best place for catching fish, however, is at the mouth of the Blyth River itself, and along its dense mangrove-fringed feeder channels. These mangroves called *guwurripa* provide nutrients and shelter for large populations of more than 40 species of fish exploited by the Aborigines. There is in the narrow channels a constant sound of plopping and splashes. Men in the prows of silently gliding dug-out canoes spear barramundi, mullet and threadfin. On the aerial roots of the mangroves themselves are thick encrustations of oysters, whereas up the trunks only subtle eyes can see the slight tell-tale movements of a white and black spotted mangrove-goanna adjusting its

Plate 11.2 *Gidjingali men fishing* **in an ephemeral swamp behind the camp site of Kopanga in the late wet season of 1973. They have laid out a barrier net, made partly from European materials, and are driving fish against it which will be speared and stored in Pandanus-frond baskets suspended from the neck**

position on the opposite side of the tree to the hunters below. Under the murky waters are sharks and in the deep muds, slides left by salt-water crocodiles splashing heavily into the water as a canoe comes into view.

The seasonal flux

I have so far given a static picture of the landscape. But the Aborigines do not see it like this, but rather as a cyclical process which through the passage of the seasons transforms each of these lands, and with them the availability of plants and animals, which in turn predicates the pattern of life of the people themselves.

The dominant event of the year is the slow build-up and eventual arrival of the north-west monsoon under the winds named *barra*. Great *barra* is the bringer of rain, sometimes accompanied by cyclones which periodically devastate the coastline and if accompanied with high tides can flood the plains with damage and danger to life. This is a time of fear, when people are careful to obey rules about how to hunt and which foods should (or should not) be eaten, and in which places. No woodland goannas, for example, may be cooked on the beach, lest the forces of the 'Dreaming' Rainbow Serpent take revenge at this transgression of the proper order of things, and drown out the land. In the four months between about December and April some 1000 mm of rain falls, being about 80 per cent of the annual rainfall, and this season is called *djambirr* by the Aborigines. The swamps and flood plain fill with water and people are forced to camp on higher ground. The Anbarra choose for their wet season camps the exposed spits at the mouth of the river, where the ground is dry and the winds tend to keep down the pest of mosquitoes. Because of the water and the chest-high grass, movement on the ground is difficult, and during this season people are relatively immobile and are confined to the coastal dunes. Women gather shellfish (plate 11.3), many of which are thrown up on the beach as debris from monsoonal storms. The men fish at the mouth of the river. Because of the heat and humidity, people tend to be lethargic during this period and social life is mostly at the domestic level. Occasionally there would be periods of food stress, when storms and flooding limited the amount of foraging that people could do, and of the plant foods, only *Morinda* yields its curious fruit.

Then with the winds beginning to swing around to the south east, the rains start to abate, and the flood waters to recede. People begin to fan out more and more from their wet season camps and exploit foods such as water lilies from the swamps. When the dry south-east trade winds or *djimarru* set in, the new season of *mirdawarr* approaches. The winds dry off, then blow down, the tall grasses. Movement is facilitated by burning off the old grass and people fan out from their old camps and set up new ones close to the inland swamps, where they can get water lilies and spike-rush corms. In the edges of the vine thickets are yams to be dug and many trees which bear edible fruits. As the waters recede, fish such as barramundi which have spent the wet season in the great swamps start to make their way back to the tidal estuaries and can be caught in wicker-work fish traps laid across their exit routes. This is the time of plenty in the Gidjingali year.

As the water starts to congregate in the deepest swamps and old stream beds, people also camp near them, sometimes on large earth mounds, formed by their ancestors having over countless times brought to the same spot piles of termite ant-bed with which to cook their game, so that the very level of the camp sites has been raised one or two metres in height, affording an especially dry spot from which the present generation can continue its exploitation of the same resources. These are primarily the *kuleitj* spike-rush

Plate 11.3 *Gidjingali women on the shell beds* **north of Lalarrgadjirripa.**

corms collected by women and magpie geese killed by men. Such a concentration of food resources means that there is enough to allow people to come together to carry out their ceremonial life, when up to 400 people may congregate for several weeks for their religious rituals.

Then slowly as the country starts to dry out, and the sand becomes so hot that it is hard to walk on it, the season called *barparanga* begins. On the brick-hard black-soil plains, women dig for long-necked terrapins. In the forests, cycads are collected and processed. Goannas are thin, and the yam tendrils having dried off, their tubers are hard to locate. Shallow wells start to fail and others become salty. People tend to split up into smaller groups and return to the river exploiting the dry landward side of the mangroves with its fish and shell fish. This was in the past the main period of stress and of famine.

Then once more, after the stifling doldrums when the sun above seems to bake the ground with a metallic sheen, clouds start to build up in the north west, and with the advent of humid air, great lightning storms stab the stone country to the south. Aborigines say that certain trees can smell the approaching *barra* and send out their fruit, first the *Vitex* with its tiny sweet black berries, then *Planchonia* the green 'custard apple', and finally *Syzigium* with its bright scarlet-skinned fruit and sweet crisp flesh tasting like an apple inside. The grass sprouts green again, wallabies can be hunted under cover of wind squalls and the Aborigines start to plan their wet season abodes.

Plate 11.4 *Frank Gurrmanamana explaining the order of appearance of vegetable foods* throughout the annual cycle. In front of him are two parallel rows of small hollows pressed into the sand, one representing the vegetable foods *gu-man-nga* (of the jungle i.e. fruits) and the other *gu-djel* (of the ground i.e. tubers). Each hollow referred to a named plant, and parallel ones were ready to eat at the same time of year. The order of appearance of the plants began at the outbreak of the wet season, continued through the dry season and ended with the oncoming wet of the following year. In that sense the design could be conceived of as a tube giving an endless procession of plant appearances throughout the seasons. In the background is Gurrmanamana's wife Nancy Bandeiyama

This strong cyclical passage of the seasons, with its effects on Aboriginal life, the foods they eat, the places where they locate their camps, and how they organise their social activities was vividly brought home to Betty Meehan and me one afternoon when our host in Anbarra society, Frank Gurrmanamana, tried to explain to us how the year ahead would unfold. He sat under our shade on the beach, and having cleaned off a layer of sand, carefully marked out two parallel sets of small holes (plate 11.4). One set, he said, were the vegetable foods which grew *gu-djel* (in the clay), namely roots and tubers. The other set were the vegetables *gu-man-nga* (in the jungle/vine thicket), namely fruits. These two sets were linked, a pair, one from each set, appearing together at the same time of year to be successively replaced by another pair, and so on. He then listed the names of both sets of plants in their predicted order of appearance in nature. They were likened according to Gurrmanamana to plants walking side by side through the seasons. At the end, the same pair would re-appear as the ones we had started with, and the whole process would begin once more.

Wells and clans

This cyclical concept of the environment in a secular sense is but part of a wider way in which the Gidjingali perceive their world. There is another more profound cyclical pattern, a religious one in which people and land are bound; one which involves the passage of a human being from birth through life and eventually via death back to the land itself.

The Gidjingali people did not believe that semen had any role in biological conception (Hiatt, 1965:23). They believed rather that women became pregnant by a spirit or essence of the land entering their bodies from a totemic well or waterhole as they were near it, for example when getting water. Women declared that they were pregnant only at about the fourth month of parturition, roughly at about the time when they first felt an infant inside themselves and when external physical changes started becoming noticeable. At this time they said that they dreamt the location and the occasion of their spiritual impregnation.

Thinking about or describing country in terms of named localities, rather than in ecological units, Aborigines conceive of it as a series of wells (plate 11.5), called in Gidjingali *rralila*, and depicted as concentric circles, which are often connected by lines which represent the tracks of totemic ancestors (plate 11.6). These ancestors in some ancient time before human beings existed—referred to as the 'Dreamtime'—strode across the land, formed its natural features, made the animals and named the wells. Each well is owned by a particular *baparu*, or patrilineal clan, and certain sets of animals and plants also belong to these. All of the world is divided into two halves or moieties, one Djowanga and the other Yirritjinga. Thus each patrilineal clan together with the wells and therefore the land, the people, the plants and animals associated with it, belongs to one moiety or the other. Within each moiety are four sub-sections or 'skins', and each patrilineal clan has a specific ascription within this system. Marriage rules are formally organised so that the preferred partner comes from a designated sub-section in the opposite moiety, and marriage is usually proscribed between people of the same moiety.

Plate 11.5 *A named well near Djunawunya*, **west of the Blyth River. In addition to having mythological significance, it is also used as a source of water for domestic purposes. The baler shell in the foreground is used as a tool to scoop out sand and also as a cup. Keeping such wells cleanly dug and free from rotting vegetation and silt is considered by the Gidjingali to be an important part of their curation of the countryside**

Plate 11.6 *Well system*. **Detail of a bark painting made in** *c.* **1960 by a Gidjingali man now deceased, whose country was situated near Inangandua (Cape Stewart) east of the Blyth River. It is a cryptic painting which may be thought of as a map depicting totemic wells connected by mythological tracks**

These relationships are cemented and celebrated in the great song cycles of Arnhem Land, where song, poetry and dance are integrated to delineate the various parts of the natural world as belonging to particular loci on the landscape. Totemic wells mark the places to be named on the land. Often these are real water holes (plate 11.5), but sometimes named localities will refer to other features of the landscape, in particular what might be called geomorphological 'anomalies'. Examples in Gidjingali territory are where some freak erosional event in the past has cut a gutter across the grain of a set of parallel sand dunes, or where some isolated outcrop of rock occurs in an otherwise flat clay plain. The way in which the Gidjingali saw these anomalies as needing some supernatural explanation is similar to that in which European folk culture ascribed glacial rock erratics or long forgotten prehistoric monuments to the work of giants or ghosts in some pre-Christian past. These wells or supernatural loci by which the land is defined, may be contrasted with the secular places where people live. Camp sites are referred to by the term *rrauwa*. This is the cleaned-off area with its fire hearths (*bol*) and its shade huts, and is seen as a domestic, humanised place surrounded

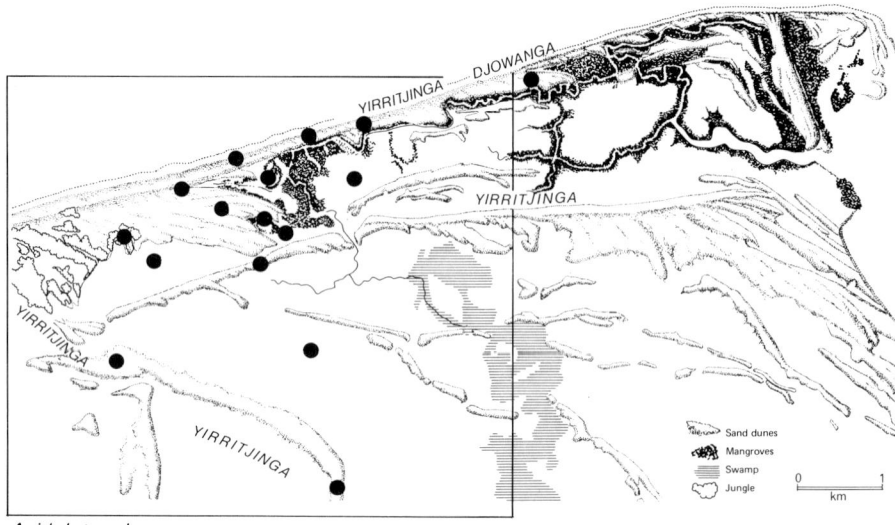

Aerial photograph

Figure 11.4 *Djunawunya named totemic wells, Blyth River mouth*. **The Djunawunya land owning group consists of two patrilineal clans of the Djowanga moiety. Surrounding it are the estates of the opposite Yirritjinga moiety. (Information after Hiatt 1982). The square encloses the area shown in figure 11.3**

often by a low mound of debris from this and previous occupations. Beyond this is the bush on the edge of illumination of the camp fires at night. But *rrauwa* can also be used in a more general sense to denote a place; thus a well can also be referred to as the *rrauwa* belonging to a particular spirit who is often said to 'sit down' within it.

The number of named wells in any particular part of country depends on how important it is ecologically. Thus in the deep *malpi* one may walk for many kilometres from one named locality to the next. On the other hand, on the rich coastal plains with their high population density and greater geomorphic diversity (figure 11.3), where there is the need to delineate and define social space more finely, different named totemic wells may occur every few hundred metres. For example, Les Hiatt has mapped no fewer than fifteen named totemic wells on the two square kilometres of dunes and swales of Djunawunya (figure 11.4), a major locality belonging to the Galamagondiya *baparu* or clan of the Anbarra community (Hiatt, 1965:19; 1982). This place is located about three or four kilometres west of the Blyth River mouth (Meehan, 1982:12).

A Gidjingali child is therefore literally seen as being fathered by the essence of the land itself, and this sense of belonging to a set of totemic wells is later reinforced at crucial life-crises of the individual, especially if it

Plate 11.7 *Burning off around Gidjingali coffin*. **A man, now deceased, extinguishing flames around an old hollow log coffin so that it is protected from damage during the burning of the dry grass. The grass is burnt so as to 'clean the country' as the Aborigines put it**

is a male. When a boy is circumcised at the age of about ten, his body is decorated with designs which belong exclusively to that set of clan wells, and songs associated with them are sung. The same songs eventually become his to perpetuate his links with a particular piece of land and the birds and animals that are seen conceptually to belong to it. At death, these same songs are sung, and the bones of the body are smashed up and covered with red ochre and then placed in a long, hollow-log coffin (plate 11.7) painted with the appropriate clan designs and set up close to the original well of the man's ancestors. Then as the ochres slowly peel off the weathered face of the coffin, so also the Aborigines say that the emanation of the dead person's soul is slowly receding back into the ground from whence he came. To sing the songs, to paint the designs and to carry out the dances is to look after the land, to curate its religious essence.

There is also another more secular way of curation. The beginning of the dry period when the first winds appear from the south east is the time when people start to burn off the tall sorghum grasses. The first fires are small since the vegetation is still wet, and the burnt areas start to form a mosaic pattern. Then as the grass and forest litter dry out, the main season of burning off occurs in late May to August. During this time, great plumes of black smoke can be seen all over Arnhem Land. The firing is done for a variety of reasons—to clear the ground to hunt, to drive game, to signal, for fun, but especially (in their own words) to 'clean the country'. Aborigines perceive an unburnt piece of ground with tall dry grass, with its skin-penetrating seeds and the lurking dangers of snakes, rather as we would a dirty untidy room. They set fire to it in order to curate it, to look after it. The firing is not indiscriminate but is usually done at times so that winds later in the day will blow against the flames and extinguish them, or directed against a break either natural or one already burnt. In this way, a mosaic of small burnt patches is set up. By the end of the dry season when potentially catastrophic hot fires could occur, much of the land has already been burnt and so such events are rare or are severely contained. After burning, the vegetation usually responds quickly by sending up new green shoots. These, the Aborigines say, attract game. There are other ways in which they 'look after' the country—they clean and curate the wells, and in an insouciant way distribute their fruit trees, by carrying and then eating the fruits and dropping them in their middens. These latter often contain shells and other rotting vegetable matter which decay to form a good soil conducive to plant growth. Discarding some *Syzigium* seeds on the edge of a shell midden one day at the end of the dry season of 1972, Frank Gurrmanamana, noticing my glance, said of them 'By and by they will grow—all the same gardeni'.

The chaos of Canberra

In 1978, Frank Gurrmanamana, having been elected a member of the Australian Institute of Aboriginal Studies, attended the Biennial Meeting of that institution in Canberra. This was his first visit outside the Top End of the Northern Territory and he was intensely interested in the new landscapes of what we call 'settled' Australia. Seeking to analyse elements within it, he constantly referred back to familiar entities in his own country by a process of analogy—much like that done in a reverse way when Europeans first saw the wombat 'badgers', the thylacine 'wolves', or the casuarina 'she oaks' of the new Australia. Thus for Gurrmanamana, the snow gums (*E. pauciflora*) with their smooth white bark were compared to the white-trunked *E. papuensis* of the north—'like *man-gowaka*, only a little bit different'. Similarly, the stately tall *Casuarina cunninghamii* trees in the gravels of the granite river bottoms of the Molonglo and Murrumbidgee rivers were seen as closely related to their more slender cousins, the *rula* of the white beaches of Arnhem Land. Eliciting considerable comment and interest were the pine plantations massed in their dark regiments on the lower flanks of the hills outside the city. These he said, belonged not to this country but to Balanda (white men). He thought that they might be somewhat similar to the *Callitris* 'cypress pines' of the north, but he doubted if they had any moieties—'don't ask me', he said, 'maybe you know'. The black ducks, the ibis and egrets floating in the shallows of Lake George were noticed with jocular relief that at least here was a familiar source of game in case of an emergency, whereas the sheep, bullocks and horses were familiar to a man who had spent some time of his youth in the buffalo shooting camps of the Alligator Rivers. Black swans were strange but could be coped with; snow was a novelty whose characteristics provided great amusement in camp-side story telling on tropical nights for years to come; and large boomer kangaroos seen as motor car kills on the side of the road to Bungendore were carefully and slightly warily inspected—obviously very similar to the *gandiyala* (*M. antilopinus*) of the eastern forests of the Matai, but having a different coloured pelt and with their great size, perhaps they were animals whose supernatural affiliations needed to be known a little more before tampering with them in ignorance. All of these aspects of the natural world Gurrmanamana was fascinated by, but also confident of being able to classify somehow within various categories of his own perception system.

The ordered streets and geometric vistas of the planned capital city of Australia (plate 11.8) left him totally uninterested. There was a calm acceptance of the various gadgets and machines of our technological world, which one might at first have assumed to be potentially rather intimidating or confusing to a man who hunts with a spear and spins string on the side of his thigh—the escalators, the jet planes, the revolving restaurants, all taken in as a matter of course. The questions that Gurrmanamana wanted to ask most were what was the moiety of the land on which we were staying and did the block next door have an opposite moiety, the boundary being marked by the fence-line? I said that they had none. He argued that they must have, and that if the land was mine, it would have the same moiety as that conferred on me through classificatory kinship with himself—it surely was Djowanga land and next door was probably Yirritjinga and so on—all of the world, he said, was divided off like that. But what if I sold the land, I replied and went to live elsewhere?—after all I had only been living here less than a decade. In our travels around town I had previously showed him houses and country blocks once owned and lived in by anthropologists, administrators and other people he had known in Arnhem Land but who

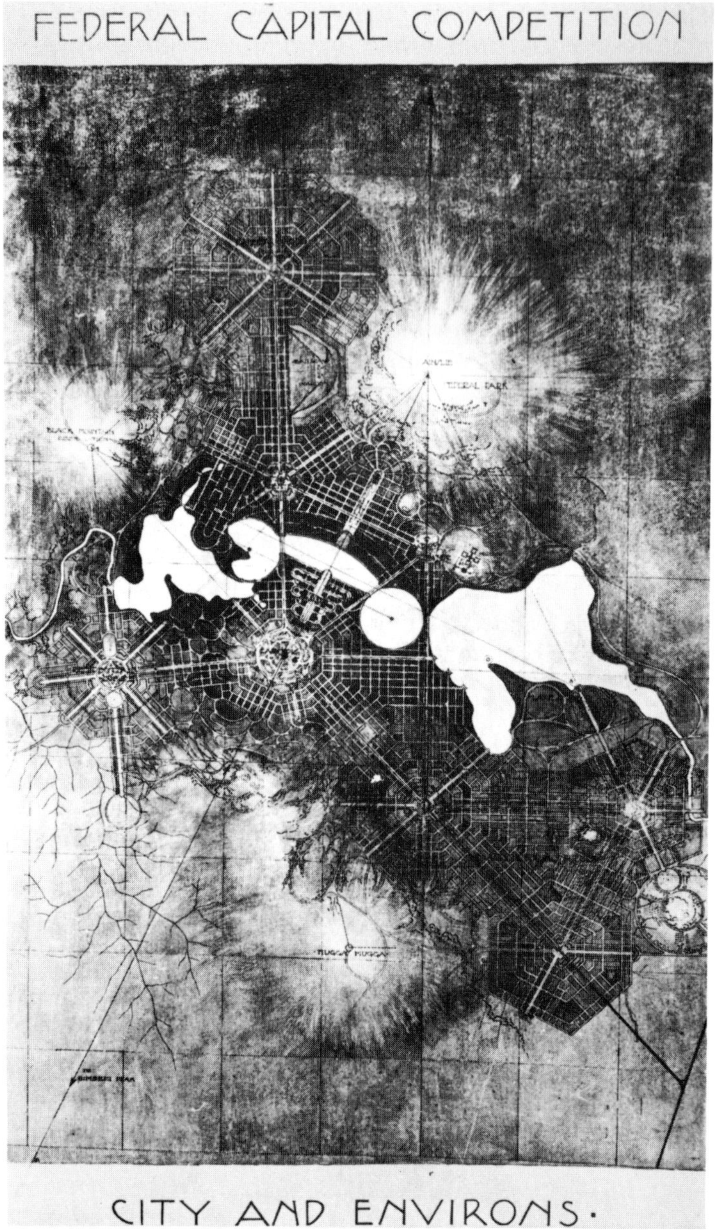

FEDERAL CAPITAL COMPETITION

CITY AND ENVIRONS·

Plate 11.8 *Plan for Australian Federal Capital Competition*: the architect W. Burley Griffin's successful design for Canberra. It shows an early 20th century concept of an 'ordered landscape' with nodal points connected by roads radiating out of them

now had sold off and gone to live elsewhere. The idea of buying and selling land like any other commodity and of attachment to the land only as a matter of transient convenience was totally alien to Gurrmanamana, and he regarded it with a mixture of suspended belief and with some mild revulsion, as if there was something deeply wrong in this state of affairs. Here was a land empty of religious affiliation; there were no wells, no names of the totemic ancestors, no immutable links between land, people and the rest of the natural and supernatural worlds. Here was just a vast *tabula rasa*, cauterised of meaning. Discussing the history of this place and being shown archaeological sites and nineteenth-century pictures of old Aborigines of the region, Gurrmanamana said that once long ago, Aborigines had lived here and that they would have known these attributes of the land which still existed somewhere, but that now, in his own words 'this country bin lose 'im Dreaming'. He was disturbed by this.

This sense of disorder was reinforced by the seeming lack of rules governing who married whom amongst his Canberra friends and acquaintances. People had no moieties and no subsection affiliations, so there were no permitted or proscribed categories of marriage partners. People were not related to each other but merely congregated together or went their own way as whim or circumstance directed. There were no correct relatives to bestow wives, no partners in religious ceremonies. The Balanda, said Gurrmanamana, mate as indiscriminately as camp dogs. This land and its people therefore were analogous to the state of all of the world once in some time before the Dreaming, before the great totemic Ancestral Beings strode across it, naming the places and giving it meaning. Viewed from this perspective, the Canberra of the geometric streets, and the paddocks of the six-wire fences were places not of domesticated order, but rather a wilderness of primordial chaos.

Acknowledgements

I owe a special thanks to Frank Gurrmanamana, who was not only my host in Gidjingali country but also my tutor in his own culture. The work upon which this essay is based was done jointly with Betty Meehan, whose knowledge of Gidjingali society I have drawn upon extensively. We carried out joint fieldwork over a period of 13 months in 1972 to 1973 and in several short seasons in subsequent years. Accounts of our ecological and archaeological researches are included in Jones, 1980 and Meehan, 1982. The social structure and kinship of the Gidjingali people have been described by Hiatt, 1965. The diagrams in this paper were drawn by Winifred Mumford.

Note

1 The spelling for Gidjingali words follows Hiatt 1965 for words which also occur there, with occasional exceptions. Between vowels *y* is used instead of Hiatt's *j*. A single *r* is to be pronounced as in American English, double *rr* as in Scottish, and *ng* as in 'sing'. A hyphen marks the boundary between a prefix and a root. For a preliminary phonemic analysis of Burarra (a cover-term for Gunadpa and Gidjingali) see Glasgow (1981). This is however based on work with Gunadpa speakers.

Bibliography

Aubrey, John (1656) Wiltshire Collections, Aubrey mss 3, folio 10 Oxford: Bodleian Library

Blackburn, J. (1971) *Milirrpum* v. *Nabalco Pty Ltd and The Commonwealth of Australia* 17 *Federal Law Reports* 141

Christian, C. S. and G. A. Stewart (1953) *General Report of the Katherine-Darwin Region* Australian Land Research Series No. 1 Canberra: CSIRO

Dampier, William (1729) *A Voyage to New Holland: The English Voyage of Discovery in the South Seas in 1699* London: J. and J. Knapton; 1981 facsimile edition, J. Spencer (ed.), Gloucester: Alan Sutton

Everingham, Paul (1982) *A Question of Balance: Address by the Chief Minister of The Northern Territory to the National Press Club, Canberra* Darwin: Government Printer of the Northern Territory

Fox, R. W., G. G. Kelleher and C. G. Kerr (1977) *Ranger Uranium Environmental Inquiry, Second Report* Canberra: Australian Government Publishing Service

Glasgow, K. (1981) 'Burarra Phonemes' pp. 63-89 in *Work Papers of SIL-AAB*, Series A Volume 5 *Australian Phonologies Collected Papers* Bruce Waters (ed.), Darwin: Summer Institute of Linguistics

Goldsmith, Oliver (1770) *The Deserted Village*, in Roger Lonsdale (ed.) *The Poems of Thomas Gray, William Collins, Oliver Goldsmith* London and Harlow: Longmans

Hiatt, L. R. (1965) *Kinship and Conflict* Canberra: ANU Press

Hiatt, L. R. (1982) 'Traditional Attitudes to Land Resources', in R. M. Berndt (ed.) *Aboriginal Sites, Rights and Resource Development* Perth: University of Western Australia Press for the Academy of the Social Sciences

Hookey, John (1972) 'The Gove Land Rights Case: A Judicial Dispensation for the Taking of Aboriginal Lands in Australia?' *Federal Law Review*, 5:85-114

Jones, Rhys (1980) 'Hunters in the Australian Coastal Savanna' in D. R. Harris (ed.) *Human Ecology in Savanna Environments* London: Academic Press

Jones, Rhys and Betty Meehan (1978) 'Anbarra Concept of Colour' in L. R. Hiatt (ed.) *Australian Aboriginal Concepts*, 20-39 Canberra: Australian Institute of Aboriginal Studies

Locke, John (1690) *Two Treatises of Government* London: Awnsham Churchill

Meehan, Betty   (1982) *Shell Bed to Shell Midden* Canberra: Australian Institute of Aboriginal Studies

Ovington, J. D.   (1980) Foreword *Kakadu National Park: Plan of Management* (first edition) Canberra: Australian National Parks and Wildlife Service, Commonwealth of Australia

Parry, Thomas   (1962) *The Oxford Book of Welsh Verse* Oxford: The Clarendon Press

Péron, M. F.   (1809) *A Voyage of Discovery to the Southern Hemisphere*, Translated from the French. London: Richard Phillips

Powell, Anthony   (ed.) (1949) *Brief Lives and other Selected Writings by John Aubrey* London: The Cresset Press

Robinson, M. M.   (1946) *Odes of Michael Massey Robinson, First Poet Laureate of Australia (1754-1826)* G. Mackaness (ed.) *Australian Historical Monographs*, No. 13. Dubbo: Review Publications

Scott, A. B. and F. X. Martin   (eds) (1978) *Expugnatio Hibernica: The Conquest of Ireland, by Giraldus Cambrensis* Dublin: Royal Irish Academy

Scott-James, Anne and Osbert Lancaster   (1977) *The Pleasure Garden* Harmondsworth: Penguin

Smith, Bernard   (1960) *European Vision and the South Pacific, 1768-1850* Oxford: The Clarendon Press

Stanner, W. E. H.   (1979) *White Man Got No Dreaming: Essays 1938-73* Canberra: ANU Press

INDEX